VIOLET AMERICA

THE NEW AMERICAN CANON

THE IOWA SERIES IN CONTEMPORARY LITERATURE AND CULTURE

Samuel Cohen, series editor

Violet America

Regional Cosmopolitanism in U.S. Fiction since the Great Depression

JASON ARTHUR

UNIVERSITY OF IOWA PRESS | IOWA CITY

University of Iowa Press, Iowa City 52242

www.uiowapress.org
Printed in the United States of America

Design by April Leidig

The University of Iowa Press is a member of Green Press Initiative and is committed to preserving natural resources.

Printed on acid-free paper

Library of Congress Cataloging-in-Publication Data
Arthur, Jason, 1976–
Violet America: regional cosmopolitanism in U.S. fiction since the Great Depression / by Jason Arthur.
p. cm. — (The new American canon: the Iowa series in contemporary literature and culture)
Includes bibliographical references and index.
ISBN-13: 978-1-60938-147-9, ISBN-10: 1-60938-147-5 (pbk.)
ISBN-13: 978-1-60938-148-6, ISBN-10: 1-60938-148-3 (ebook)
1. American fiction — 20th century — History and criticism.
2. Regionalism in literature. 3. Cosmopolitanism in literature.
I. Title.
PS374.R4A78 2013
813'.309382 — dc23 2012038179

For Joe Albert Rellihan

CONTENTS

ACKNOWLEDGMENTS

I would have never written this book had it not been for Andrew Hoberek's patient guidance and Jeffrey J. Williams's persistent belief in me.

Because of their insightful conversations and generous advice during the years I spent writing this book, I'm lucky to thank such brilliant people as Barry Chabot, Ann Charters, Wai Chee Dimock, Loren Glass, Oliver Harris, Yoon Sun Lee, Eric Lott, Sean McCann, Douglas Reichert Powell, and Tim Yu. John Evelev, Patt Okker, Tom Quirk, and Kristin Schwain helped me get the project off the ground.

Because they are friends and critical colleagues who have enriched my professional life (not to mention the evolution of this book), I want to thank Chris Breu, Tom Cerasulo, Jennifer Eimers, Dan Grausam, Jack Healy, Berkley Hudson, Crystal Lake, Steve Lovett, Gina Merys Mahaffey, Matthew Mahaffey, Andy Miller, Andrew Mulvania, John Porter, Jeremy Reed, Alison Shonkwiler, Annette Van, and Zak Watson.

I also need to thank my colleagues at Rockhurst University, especially Lou Oldani, my earliest mentor, Dan Martin and John Kerrigan, my latest friends and gracious-est readers of drafts, and Charlie Kovich and Patricia Miller, my eternal confidence boosters. Anne Austin Pearce, Joe Cirincione, Tim McDonald, Margot Stafford, and Margaret Wye, you are invaluable colleagues. And thanks to the staff of the Greenlease Library and to the committee that recommended I receive a Rockhurst Presidential Grant. That grant helped support the revisions of this book, and it gave a new faculty member the confidence he needed to finish up. And thanks to the students I imagine might read this book, students who, because I could imagine them reading it, helped me find this book's voice. Thanks especially to the students of my Spring 2012 Studies in the American Novel course, and to Amanda Hildebrand, who helped prepare the manuscript. Thanks also to the Harry Ransom Research Center at the University of Texas at Austin.

I'm lucky to have been able to work with Joe Parsons, who believed in the project back when it was twenty thousand words too long. And Samuel Cohen has been there every step of the way, mixing hardnosed critique and calming levity in a way that only Sam can. The editorial staff at Iowa — especially Elisabeth Chretien, Catherine Cocks, and Charlotte Wright — has been wonderful. And Rebecca Marsh is probably the best copyeditor in the blooming world.

And all you Arthurs and Rellihans and Niemackls and Cendóns and Calvins and Fernándezes, thank you for being my family. Mom, Dad, Jenée, Julie, and Jerrod, you raised me. Sara Fernández Cendón, you left your keys in the lock of the front door of Fifth Avenue Apartments and I found those keys and I wrote a note and you read that note and you came looking for me and you found me and it's been years and I still can't believe my luck.

This continent, an open palm spread frank before the sky against the bulk of the world. —James Agee, "The American Roadside"

INTRODUCTION

Regional Cosmopolitanism

Quite a bit of recent critical attention has been paid to American regional fiction.[1] This attention, however, hasn't changed the fact that regionalism is still considered the backwoods cousin of realism or that American literature survey courses still include only a micro-unit on "Local Color," in which short stories by Sarah Orne Jewett or Charles Chesnutt appear. Jewett and Chesnutt deserve their place in the canon, and they treat rural America in subtle, nuanced ways, but they are typically considered curators of provincial America.[2] Their stories get understood as textual artifacts of extinct places and people. Their settings are the lands just beyond the reach of industrial development, and their heroes, like Jewett's Sylvia or Chesnutt's Uncle Julius, are heroic in their attempts to stave off progress. Their attempts, alas, are always futile: Sylvia's pact with the white heron won't keep the armed ornithologist out of the forest forever, and Julius's conjure tale won't fool a single carpetbagger. Literary regionalism is a genre whose job it is to verify the imminent disappearance of its subject.

Against this assumption, *Violet America* will show that regional fiction is more cosmopolitan: it is more invested in articulating commonalities across cultures than it is in articulating differences. Regional fiction is alive and vital, and it is central to American fiction, not a tributary of nostalgia and quaintness. In fact, a spirit of *regional cosmopolitanism* persists in a good deal of American literary fiction since the Great Depression. This spirit reveals the interdependence and resemblance of otherwise disparate strands of American culture. It tends to resist such polarizing heuristics as the "red state / blue state" cultural geography of the twenty-first century.

Why is regionalism still considered and taught as a discrete, nostalgic literary period? The answer has something to do with how and where regional fiction became popular. Regional fiction first appeared in late nineteenth-century periodicals. Scholars give two reasons for its popularity: (1) it soothed urban, middle-class anxieties about the demographic and topographic shifts brought about by late nineteenth-century waves of immigration and industrialization, and (2) it consolidated the various regions of the U.S. while also underscoring the line between provincial zones and zones of high culture. As Stephanie Foote puts it, regional writing "represented various sections of the consolidating nation to an audience that was conscious of itself as a national elite" (4). By creating what Richard Brodhead calls a "mentally possessible version of a loved thing lost in reality," regional writing speeds up the process of pushing provincial people and places off social and political landscapes and onto a more strictly fictional landscape ("Regionalism," 155). Hence the idea of regional fiction as a curio cabinet — a literary genre wherein endangered folks and folkways get stuffed and displayed.

Yet as Tom Lutz argues in *Cosmopolitan Vistas* (2004), regional fiction is more than a container of weird, old America. It is the literary register in which occur important conversations about the concentricity of the local, the national, and the global.[3] Or, to use terms central to early twentieth-century intellectual debates, regionalism negotiates such polarities as "nativism" and "pluralism."

Part of the reason why we don't think of regionalism in these terms is because critics have assumed the frame of literary modernism. Literary scholarship on the early twentieth century focuses primarily on the role of modernism in shaping debates about nativism and pluralism. This tendency is evident in the subtitle of Walter Benn Michaels's *Our America:*

Nativism, Modernism, and Pluralism (1995). Susan Hegeman's *Patterns for America: Modernism and the Concept of Culture* (1999) echoes Michaels's point about modernism's centrality in framing the basic terms of most debates about culture in America. But Hegeman discusses regionalism's role, as well. According to Hegeman, "the culture concept is modernist precisely in the way that it enables alterity of a number of different kinds to be reconceived in spatial terms, as part of a complex social geography" (37). With this definition of "culture," Hegeman suggests that modernism is a kind of regionalism, that the shift of "the culture concept" from the Arnoldian sense of "the best that has been thought and said" to the social-scientific sense of "practices of everyday life" was navigated according to a fundamentally regional sense of "spatiality."[4] Hegeman's synthesis of regionalism and modernism has gained ground, as evidenced by the 2009 special edition of *Modern Fiction Studies* on regional modernism.[5]

The regional sensibility is committed to keeping open the question of what and where "culture" is. As Lutz puts it, regionalists have "maintained an ongoing conversation about the relation of part to whole, of center to periphery, about the interdependence . . . of the local and the global" ("Cather," 437).[6] This kind of conversation is the fundamental intellectual labor of cosmopolitanism. Then why does conventional wisdom still suggest that regionalism and cosmopolitanism are at odds? The answer lies in the way regional fiction gets institutionalized.

New York City, Iowa City

Regional fiction has been produced and promoted almost exclusively in the context of literary institutions. That is, it is not just an organic representation of the land but a genre of writing that has been promoted and maintained by two major infrastructures of American literature: (1) the "*Atlantic*-group" of periodicals and presses that originally popularized regional fiction and (2) the "Program Era" of university-based literary production that continues to validate regional fiction.

The nation's first regional fiction appeared in what Nancy Glazener calls "*Atlantic*-group" periodicals (for example, the *Atlantic Monthly*, *Harper's Monthly*, the *Nation*, *Scribner's*, etc.). These New York–based periodicals reinforced the legitimacy of New York–based conceptions of the business of American literary realism. They "shared contributors . . . , endorsed each other's cultural authority, and based that authority in similar understandings of class-inflected cultural trusteeship" (257).[7] The regional fiction that appeared in the pages of these periodicals supported the *Atlantic* group's claims to cultural superiority. It reminded readers, either directly or indirectly, where high culture in America was and where it most certainly was not.[8]

A testament to the success of this polarization is the fact that so many talented writers used their knowledge of provincial America to leverage entrance into official literary culture, particularly those writers of the generation following this first wave of periodical regionalism.[9] This generation — which Carl Van Doren dubbed the "village rebels"— offered unvarnished accounts of the cultural bankruptcy of the South and Midwest, and these accounts authorized membership into American literary culture. Anthony Hilfer acknowledges the paradox of these membership dues when he mentions that these writers "immersed" themselves into the "destructive element" of their provincial hometowns (254).[10] Hilfer implies that village rebels wrote about their provincial hometowns as a way of gaining entry into official literary culture in America.

As Mark McGurl has outlined, the overriding institution of the years following the Second World War has been the university writing program, and McGurl names the more recent period the "Program Era." In this period, homecoming-as-literary-enterprise has become pretty standard.[11] One of the key directives is "write what you know." Thus, many have offered their native knowledge up to the gods of first book contracts. Consider the logic of the "write-what-you-know" directive. The assumption is that native knowledge is something from which to demonstrate distance and mastery. "What you know" is a thing to represent; it is to be held at arm's length and reproduced as fiction. The "you" who writes this knowledge can't be a product of this knowledge. "You" must make this knowledge *your* product. I wonder if Faulkner could have written *Absalom, Absalom!* (1936) under such a directive. I also wonder if such an attempt to distance "you" from "what you know" wasn't what killed Quentin Compson.

In addition to this polarizing directive, which separates the writer from his home at the same time that it commands the writer to plunder home for content, the program era has yielded another familiar command: "Find your voice." The value of "voice" is virtually unquestioned these days; a distinct voice is a surefire way to generate legitimacy in a literary culture that knows how to value diversity. This unquestioned premium on "voice" has had an interesting impact on the regional sensibility of contemporary fiction. Joyce Carol Oates, a champion of the "find your voice" directive, alludes to the value of voice in her prose poem, "My Faith as a Writer":

> Through the local or regional, through our individual voices, we work to create art that will speak to others who know nothing of us. In our very obliqueness to one another, an unexpected intimacy is born.
>
> The individual voice is the communal voice.
>
> The regional voice is the universal voice. (1)[12]

Oates's explanation localizes voice, making "region" and "individual" into synonyms.[13] It also implies something profound about why we read and write fiction in the first place: not to find ourselves but to find someone very different from us, someone whose very difference from us produces an otherwise unavailable intimacy. This understanding of difference as an occasion for intimacy is ordinarily defined as "cosmopolitanism," a sensibility that promotes thoughtful consideration of the commonalities among dissimilar cultures. This consideration, for the cosmopolitan, is mediated by shared human qualities not shared local knowledge. To understand the value of individual voice — indeed the value of specificity itself — as a universal value is to be both cosmopolitan and regional: hence "regional cosmopolitanism."

Still, Jonathan Safran Foer, one of Oates's star students, suggests that there's something uniquely American — if not anticosmopolitan — about the command to cultivate a specific, individual "voice."[14] His first novel, *Everything Is Illuminated* (2002), can be read as a rebellion against the two central commands of the creative writing workshop. First, it is about a character's hunt for an almost unknowable family history. It is thus produced according to a "write what you *don't* know" directive. The novel is also reflexive about the "find your voice" directive. Many of its sections are written as letters from Alex, a Ukrainian man whose "voice" is filtered through a poor grasp of the English language. The novel's other narrator, a young would-be writer named Jonathan Safran Foer, can speak English perfectly well but confesses to Alex, "I'm looking for my voice." Alex's answer, "It is in your mouth," suggests that while the Ukrainian doesn't understand the craft of fiction, the American understands only the rules of craft (70). He does not understand what might motivate one to write fiction in the first place.

In other words, despite traces of cosmopolitanism — as demonstrated in Oates's understanding of the value of voice — program-era directives tend to be as polarizing as those issued by the *Atlantic* group. McGurl highlights the polarizing curriculum of the Iowa Writers' Workshop when he explains that "regionalism's celebration of the particularities of place was fundamental to the aesthetic sensibilities imparted at Iowa, and to the continuing power of the injunction to . . . 'write what you know'" (*Program Era*, 148–149). Yet the Iowa Writers' Workshop was founded to some degree as a reaction to New York–centrism. It exploited its proximity to the "heartland," giving it, in McGurl's words, a more "nationally representative status" than anything coming out of inauthentic Gotham. Indeed, Iowa was the first regionalist institution that "turned to face the imperial capital of U.S. cultural production head on" (149). And the weapon it used to assault this imperial capital was that credentialed misfit, Flannery O'Connor, B.A., M.F.A.[15]

The success of O'Connor's career, which began at Iowa, threatened the trusteeship of New York City. But O'Connor's regionalism is no less polarizing than New York's. It's more aggressive, and it set the agenda for a generation of fiction writers. McGurl discusses the "limitation theology" of O'Connor's approach to craft, seeing in her "embrace of the cognitive limitations of the 'regional perspective'" a prototype of the "ethnic perspective" of the later 1960s (*Program Era*, 155).[16] O'Connor's success created a legion of followers who understood commitment to the local not as a portal to cosmopolitan ideals but as a portal to deliverance. The problem with this theology is that it replaces Oates's cosmopolitan goal of finding the universal in the specific with a goal that is reducible to personal salvation (the life you save may, indeed, be your own and only your own). Another problem is that it understands local conditions as inescapable, sources of unrevisable marks onto the character of one reared among those conditions.

Regionalism, Cosmopolitanism

Cosmopolitanism is usually seen as the opposite of regionalism; it poses worldliness against provincialism. In "Patriotism and Cosmopolitanism" (1994), Martha Nussbaum defines cosmopolitanism as a sensibility through which local or national ties attain no "special salience in moral and political deliberation" (3). Cosmopolitanism in this sense is a mode of compassion that is similar to that suggested in Oates's definition of regionalism. When it first appeared, Nussbaum's argument stirred up quite a backlash.[17] Detractors as progressive as Kwame Anthony Appiah and as conservative as Gertrude Himmelfarb argued that Nussbaum's call to abandon local affiliations was irresponsible and unfeasible. Indeed, not since Charles Pasqua and Laurent Fabius joined forces to oppose the European constitution have proponents of right-wing and left-wing extremes so unanimously opposed a proposal. In one way or another, all of Nussbaum's critics exploit a shortcoming that she herself concedes, that cosmopolitanism "seems to have a hard time gripping the imagination" (15). Nussbaum is proud that her approach is passionless, as it is precisely passion for the local that subtracts compassion from the landscape of political possibility. Richard Rorty's essay, "The Unpatriotic Academy," which also appeared in 1994, only added to the infighting about cosmopolitanism.

The soon-to-be poet laureate of the U.S., Robert Pinsky, found a compromise between the bloodless cosmopolitanism of Nussbaum and the power chords of Rorty's patriotism. In his response to Nussbaum, Pinsky articulates a form of *regional* cosmopolitanism, which views the geographical coordinates of affection as important precisely because these coordinates are the epicenters of global citizenship. Pinsky argues against Nussbaum's claim that local attachments only muck up the process of developing a sense of global compassion; rather, it is only through immersion in specific conditions that one develops the means to make meaningful, worldly connections. Pinsky locates the birthplace of his own cosmopolitan "spirit" (Pinsky's word) in mid-1940s Brooklyn. This borough was young Pinsky's microcosm of the world: it was "historic and raw, vulgar and urbane, many-tongued and idiosyncratic, . . . provincial enough to have its own newspaper yet worldly beyond measure" ("Eros," 90). Pinsky's Brooklyn was thus both a small regional town and a cosmopolitan zone.

Pinsky doesn't present Brooklyn as an exceptional zone. In fact, he focuses on the Dodgers, the team that had expressed so much of Brooklyn's character. For Pinsky, the Dodgers' abandonment of Brooklyn for Los Angeles is a portal to cosmopolitanism, a reminder that cultural value is determined by forces indifferent to local affiliation. Only the cosmopolitan sees that "culture," in the context of late capitalism, is always "going, going, gone" ("Eros," 90). Only the regional cosmopolitan artist can represent the consequences of these abandonments, can resist the impulse to wax nostalgic about Ebbets Field (thus creating a "mentally possessible version of a loved thing lost in reality"), and can instead clock the wrecking ball and count the casualties (Brodhead, "Regionalism," 1994, 155).

This kind of regional sensibility — the kind that redeems provincial America without being nostalgic about it — rarely makes it onto literature-survey reading lists. It's also the kind of sensibility that makes America *violet*, instead of red or blue. It expresses deep local affiliations without falling prey to the fallacy of thinking of one American place as more or less "American" than another; it also engages global, ethical issues as they are lived in specific places and does so in a way that reveals interregional similarities that might otherwise go unnoticed. From Pinsky's point of view, Brooklyn is one link in "thousands of Broadways" that stretch across the U.S.[18] This conception presents a reconciliatory regional sensibility rather than a polarizing one, and it is particularly a post-Depression phenomenon.

Two works from the major American critic, Van Wyck Brooks, both published in 1941, explore this reconciliatory regional sensibility in the immediate aftermath of the Great Depression: *Opinions of Oliver Allston*, a quirky work of literary criticism wherein Brooks reads the journals of his titular alter ego, and *On Literature Today*, a speech Brooks gave at Hunter College. Gordon Hutner refers to these titles as "two documents that were once central to the nation's literary conversation but that now need to be retrieved from obscurity" (203). It's not immediately clear to Hutner why these titles (indeed, why all of Brooks's titles) have dropped into obscurity, though their ambivalence about New York City cultural trusteeship might have something to do with this drop. Perhaps another reason is Brooks's unabashed championing of something called the "regional feeling."

On its face, a celebration of the "regional feeling" sounds pretty worthy of being dropped into obscurity.[19] But the regional feeling Brooks is after is "quite different from the 'local colour' movement that had swept the country in the days of Howells" (Brooks, *Opinions*, 260). The regionalism of the periodicals that Howells edited and influenced was too easily mistaken for quaint celebrations of difference. In Brooks's words, this fiction "was concerned with pointing out the 'differences' of local life, the elements of oddity and quaintness in the local scene." The regional feeling Brooks celebrates, on the other hand, is "not concerned with local differences." It's the kind of sensibility that "sprang from a self-identification with the local group to which one belonged" but that does more than call attention to the unique roots of that group. Roots matter, though. Brooks endorses commitment to the "group in which one's roots were most firmly embedded" so that one might "best achieve the universal" (*Opinions*, 260). Hilfer's "village rebels" and the program era's "write what you knowers" did something similar. The difference is that Brooks's regionalists immerse themselves into a specific place not to gain entry into a literary culture that is indifferent to the life of that place but to create a center of culture that might radiate outward and affect literary culture at large.

Brooks is wary of New York: its literary institutions showcase regionally inflected fiction in order to ensure that New York remains the uninflected center of American culture (as Glazener points out). Brooks reacts against New York by championing writers from the hinterlands who do not sell out the hinterlands. He even fantasizes about artists reacting against the mandate of establishing tenuous residence in the Village, about a Greenwich Village that is emptied of its exiles, with writers "streaming homeward" from New York, "settling in the remotest regions, determined to find them interesting or make them so" (*Opinions*, 263). His ideal fiction writer is a "village reformer," neither a "village rebel" nor a writer who merely lives in "the Village." Brooks uses the example of Mary Austin, who, when she left New York and returned to her home in the West, "expanded and blossomed" (264). He also, ominously, alludes to the creation of the Iowa Writers' Workshop when he remarks that those who would have lived in the Village were busy "founding schools in Iowa City" (*On Literature*, 29).

Favoring literature produced beyond the imprimatur of New York City is not solely reactionary, Brooks promises. Such a literature might actually prepare America for a postnational era better than any New York–centric literature could. Though it may be a microcosm of the world, New York does nothing to prepare America for a "time when all the national sovereignties would yield before a planetary political system" (*Opinions*, 256). New York can be a cultural dictatorship, standing in for the world, whereas the regional sensibility that thrives in American letters does so only from beyond the reach of New York. The regional sensibility *should* thrive because deep local commitment is the first step to a tangible global citizenship, and such a sensibility would support American fiction on a global stage.

Brooks might have been right. It might be that American fiction's lack of regional sensibility has led to its drought of Nobel Prizes for Literature.

Indeed, in 2008, Horace Engdahl, the Nobel Academy's permanent secretary, accused American writers of being "too isolated, too insular" (quoted in Simpson). According to Engdahl, this trend of insularity begins with the expatriate generation of American writers (namely, Hemingway and Fitzgerald), who reacted to America's civic failures by abandoning America, and extends to the fiction of Philip Roth and John Updike. What Roth and Updike have in common with Hemingway and Fitzgerald is that they "don't really participate in the big dialogue of literature"—a bold claim that only one with the words "permanent secretary" in his job title might venture to make (quoted in Simpson). Despite how unsupported such dispatches from Stockholm may be, they do suggest that conventional wisdom may be wrong. Regionalism may be quite relevant.

IN *VIOLET AMERICA*, I will demonstrate that "regional cosmopolitanism" didn't go extinct in the 1940s. I will explore the ways in which American literature has developed along regional lines, as well as the tensions of that development. As Lutz reminds us, the value of regionalism lies in its capacity to keep alive conversations about interdependence. Whether it is James Agee's documentary prose that refuses to hide the interaction between documentarian and subject or Jack Kerouac's spontaneous prose that refuses to hide the false starts of a journey in the making, the texts I study represent the simultaneous presence of both rooted subjectivity and detached observation. The point of this simultaneity is to make vivid the interdependence of each to the other.

My generation of scholars, I feel, is particularly attuned to this business of conversation maintenance. I was introduced to academic work by overhearing seemingly unrelated conversations: one in my American literature seminars about the confluence of literary "-isms" (the real/natural/regional/modern/postmodern-isms) and the other in Friday afternoon colloquia as my mentors discussed the relevance, or irrelevance, of critical theory. Having been introduced to the profession in this mixed-message context, my generation survived by trying to make these conversations seem interdependent, as indeed they were an interdependent part of our daily lives. What separates my generation from the one more comfortable with theory is that we saw theory-born rhetorical conventions as insincere, routinized ways of thinking. We were a post-against-theory generation, barely out of adolescence and already steeped in a glut of arguments about "Theory," arguments that were happening in curious proximity to the grunt work of literary scholarship that we were expected to produce, if we ever wanted a job.

My history with Walter Benn Michaels's work exemplifies the peculiar way in which I was socialized into the profession. While he was still making arguments against theory and subsequently against multiculturalism, I was reading his *The Gold Standard and the Logic of Naturalism* (1987) and loving it.[20] I saw little overlap between Michaels's "against-theory" work and his literary-historical work, although Fredric Jameson's response in *Postmodernism* helped change my mind.[21] The former was polemic and the latter was a rigorous literary history. To use Jameson's language, *The Gold Standard* performed "the more neutral work of the establishment of homologies" and fitting these homologies onto a specific literary and cultural history (200). I wanted to be fluent in the agonism of the argument culture that was going on in the lecture halls on Friday afternoons, but I wanted to write *The Gold Standard*.[22] I wanted to do the kind of "neutral work" that wound up making a surprising contribution to the more pressing issues of my field, a contribution that may not sort out the cacophony or replace the ritualized agonism with a more sincere approach to the field but that may be less polarizing than such debates.

And, I'll admit it, I wanted to be a cultural poet. The Stephen Greenblatt–edited series in which *The Gold Standard* appeared was titled "Studies in Cultural Poetics." That's part of why I call this "*Violet America*," to suggest a left-leaning reconciliation of the gridlock of red and blue states (violet is bluer than purple). I also hope that "violet" places a flower in the barrels of the agonists. The goal is to rescue the idea that literary fiction has a civic purpose, that novel reading is a way of engaging the world, not of escaping it. More specifically, I hope to suggest that the "regional cosmopolitan" books I examine here actually have the power to "depolarize" American culture, to make the interdependence of poverty and privilege, margin and mainstream, minority and majority, vivid and consequential—the consequence being a more explicitly compassionate populace.

I think that regional cosmopolitanism has value, especially for literary criticism in the twenty-first century. It is valuable because it calls us to reflect on the interrelationship between center and periphery, global and local. When we avoid such reflexivity, we assume that location is destiny in American life. We thus perpetuate a cultural geography that asserts the very twentieth-century idea that America's cultural landscape consists of a series of inland cultural deserts and very few fixed centers of culture. This kind of thinking, as I will argue in chapter 1, becomes naturalized by the reductive regional imagination that accompanied the New Deal dream of social welfare. And, as I will explain in subsequent chapters, this reductive regional imagination has since plagued many a literary fiction writer.

Violet America also reflects a desire to add an intellectual dimension to the experience of being a first-generation college student from the Midwest who enrolled in a liberal arts college in the mid-1990s and couldn't articulate his interest in literary fiction without also bumping against the stigma of regionalism. It's not a compliment when people define you as provincial. The regional cosmopolitans I examine in this book articulate the consequences of such stigmas. They show there is an American fiction that redeems provincial America without also being nostalgic about it. The writers I study — James Agee, Jack Kerouac, Maxine Hong Kingston, Russell Banks, and Jonathan Franzen — oscillate from deep affiliation with local conditions to liberating detachment from them. This oscillation mixes cultural polarities: it *violets* the Americas they imagine.

Each text I examine also balances rootedness and detachment. Chapter 1 is about how Agee's deep engagement with the specific soil of poverty is also a commentary on the literary genres through which poverty is represented. Chapter 2 examines Kerouac's oscillation between specific sites of America and the sightline of highway travel. Chapter 3 returns to pointedly engaged writing, looking at the way Kingston reclaims the multicultural realities of San Francisco from a generation that loved but misread Kerouac. Chapter 4 examines the global resonance of contemporary regional fiction by Russell Banks and others. The epilogue considers the possibility that the polarized debates that have sprung up around Jonathan Franzen are the kinds of debates that regional cosmopolitanism works to keep alive.[23]

Chapter Summaries

In chapter 1, "Specific Soil," I look at Agee's response to the reductive regional imagination of documentary art. I examine Agee's meditation on the role of documentary art in inaugurating the "limitation theology" that gets perfected in the fiction of Flannery O'Connor and other program-era

Southern writers. In *Let Us Now Praise Famous Men* (1941), Agee concerns himself exclusively with the limitations of documentary writing. He focuses to an uncomfortable degree on the charged environment produced by the presence of a detached documentarian at the site of rural poverty. He denies himself the invisibility normally affected by documentarians. Agee's reflexive approach to "documenting" rural poverty foils the reader's ability to commit to an emotional response to poverty and forces the reader to acknowledge his position in the production of knowledge about poverty.

In chapter 2, "Pavement," I discuss Kerouac's wide (as opposed to Agee's deep) engagement of the ethically charged conversations about poverty and privilege in America. Simulating the unanchored experience of highway travel, Kerouac's road novels enact a form of national belonging that engages multiple American regions at once. I call this engagement "delocalization." The value of delocalization lies in its capacity to produce the disorienting, depolarizing experience of belonging to an entire continent rather than a specific zone within it. Kerouac's narrators are magnetized by regional difference, but they never settle anywhere. Kerouac's novels are thus divining rods for "the real America" that go haywire. Of course, this inability to find America adds up to its own form of essentialism, best represented in Kerouac's career-defining, cringeworthy pronouncement that "everything belongs to me because I am poor."[24]

Chapter 3, "The Chinatown and the City," is about how Kingston taught me how to read Kerouac. Kingston's fiction both rescues the liberatory potential of Kerouac's prose and accounts for the damage done by a generation that misread delocalization as a bohemian form of Manifest Destiny. Specifically, Kingston reveals how the 1960s mass migration to San Francisco contradicts the spirit of delocalization that Kerouac imagined in his road novels. Her novel, *Tripmaster Monkey: His Fake Book* (1989), exposes 1960s bohemianism as a form of provincialism. She satirizes the tendency to migrate west and settle in urban, multicultural zones only to ignore the material realities of those zones.

Chapter 4, "The Deflowering of New England," is about Banks's career-long engagement with the tradition of literary regionalism. Banks begins his career in the late 1970s, writing metafictional accounts of what it's like to be from rural New England. By midcareer, he "finds his voice" and writes straight-ahead, first-person narratives about surviving rural New England. His New England novels keep alive conversations about the continued relevance of the onetime epicenter of American literary culture. In his expertly wrought first-person narrative voices, Banks expresses the trauma of the "remnant people" of rural New England. In his internationally set novels (*Continental Drift*, *Book of Jamaica*, *The Darling*), Banks takes this localized narrative sensibility on the road, demonstrating what the local traumas of rural America and those of the so-called Third World have in common.

My epilogue, "Jonathan Franzen and the Unity of Discord," addresses a type of fiction whose indifference to regional cosmopolitanism still ironically produces the kinds of conversations that carry on the fundamental business of regional cosmopolitanism. Franzen, a writer on record as having little tolerance for regionalism, counters the popularity of regionalism with novels that actively resist Oates's contention that the "regional voice is the universal voice." Franzen refuses regional inflection to such an absurd degree that he doesn't bother to distinguish between the voice of the omniscient narrator of his novel *Freedom* (2010) and the voice of Patty Berglund, the character whose "memoir" takes up nearly two hundred pages of *Freedom*.[25] This refusal to value diversity draws various readerships into meaningful contact with one another. The love-hate relationship that readers have with Franzen creates the conditions for a violet public sphere, a culture of conversation about literature that might finally ensure a civic life for literature in the twenty-first century.

VIOLET AMERICA

Rather than ask, "What is the *attitude* of a work to the relations of production of its time?" I should like to ask, "What is its *position* in them?"
— Walter Benjamin, "The Author as Producer"

Even the composition conceived in the head and, therefore, physically private, is public in its significant content, since it is conceived with reference to execution in a product that is perceptible and hence belongs to the common world.
— John Dewey, *Art as Experience*

If I could do it, I'd do no writing at all here. It would be photographs; the rest would be fragments of cloth, bits of cotton, lumps of earth, records of speech, pieces of wood and iron, phials of odors, plates of food and of excrement. . . . A piece of the body torn out by the roots might be more to the point.
— James Agee, *Let Us Now Praise Famous Men*

ONE

Specific Soil

James Agee and the Poverty of Documentary Work

James Agee played a crucial role in carrying regional cosmopolitanism from the Depression era to the Civil Rights era. Specifically, his documentary book, *Let Us Now Praise Famous Men*, kept alive a conversation about the legacy of rural poverty in America. Such conversations went out of style in America in the 1940s. During that decade, the nation awoke from the New Deal dream of social welfare and found itself in the polarizing atmosphere of the Cold War. Arthur Schlesinger Jr. expresses the effect that this shift had on intellectual life in America. In the introduction to *The Vital Center* (1949), Schlesinger claims that the "fundamental enterprise" of the New Deal was "re-examination and self-criticism" and that the logical next step was to carry the insight gained from reflection and self-criticism — specifically the insight that democracy *can* check the excesses of capitalism without also falling to national socialism — into an anticommunist form of liberalism (vii). Hence, the New Deal got old quickly.

Let Us Now Praise Famous Men (*Praise*) arrived on bookshelves about two years after Congress defunded all New Deal arts projects and four years before half of Europe disappeared behind an iron curtain. The book went unread in the 1940s (barely selling six hundred copies); it became a favorite of Civil Rights activists when it was republished in 1960. This shift in reception reflects a general cultural shift in the country. In the early 1940s, the country was still recovering from the Great Depression and needed the stability of the comforting facts that *Praise* refused to offer its reader. In 1960, a significant portion of the reading public was gearing up for a new era of efficacy and sought instruction from a text such as *Praise*, which taught its reader what it felt like to commit oneself to the sites of injustice. To the reader in the 1940s, *Praise* was an admonishment for not doing enough. To the 1960s reader, it provided a model for how to "feel what wretches feel" (to quote one of the book's epigraphs). To any reader, the book is a warning about the ethical ambiguities of art about poverty. Such art could become counterproductive. It could reinforce cultural stereotypes or, worse, assert a geography of economic disparity that might, in turn, be hard to redraw.

This interpretation is impossible, however, if Agee gets attached to the Cold War generation. Once Agee is brought into such a fold, *Praise* loses its status as a corrective to the reductive regional imagination of documentary art. But why is such an erasure troubling? What gets lost when we read *Praise* as characteristic of the generation of liberals that follows the Depression, a generation too sobered by the Hitler-Stalin pact of 1939 to give credence to the New Deal dream of social welfare? The answer is that we lose sight of the fact that Agee is doing exactly what the best American literature about poverty does: avoiding what Gavin Jones calls "easy recourse to sentimental or melodramatic neutralization of the poor" that has long plagued political and social discourse on poverty in the U.S. ("Poverty," 780).[1]

Agee began worrying about this potential byproduct of art about poverty in 1933 when he wrote a profile of the Tennessee Valley Authority for *Fortune* magazine. His fears were not allayed when, in 1936, he was asked by the same magazine to spend the summer in Hale County, Alabama, living with three sharecropper families. The result of this fieldwork was an unpublishable treatise on the unholy invasion of privacy that *Fortune* had commissioned.[2] It's an understatement to say that Agee's experience in Hale County changed his outlook on poverty. It instilled in him, a poet disguised as a journalist, a regional cosmopolitan sensibility that would motivate the journalism, fiction, and screenwriting that he would produce until he died, young, in 1958. Agee's insight in *Praise* is that art that is unreflexively sentimental about poverty iconizes poverty, fixes it in the public imagination as evidence that "we shall always have the poor with us."[3] Such art justifies civic inaction; it allows the ineffectual commitments that readers make to their own emotional responses to poverty to pass for an actual commitment to justice.

Agee stages his Cassandra-like warning by doing something unprecedented in the genre of documentary art; he draws attention to himself—a lot of attention. He also implicates the reader as an accessory to his unethical task of producing knowledge about poverty. In other words, he exposes the operations that make possible an epistemology of poverty. Much of *Praise* is a meditation on the awkward, uncanny experience of invading privacy, of fingering and prodding the meager materiality of a specific site of poverty. Agee forces his reader to watch these acts, to understand the preproduction phase in the production of knowledge about poverty. He denies himself the invisibility normally allotted to documentarians, an invisibility that Donna Haraway refers to (in a slightly different context) as the "conquering gaze from nowhere" (188).[4] This reflexivity, this insistence on acknowledging his own and his reader's position in the production of knowledge about poverty is the heart of the book's regional cosmopolitanism. It is also precisely what readers either love or hate about *Praise*. It puts documentary art in the service of what Tom Lutz calls "the fundamental business of the literary," which is to "engag[e] the broadest, the most global ethical issues" ("Cather," 442). In what follows, I will examine Agee's uniquely reflexive brand of regional cosmopolitanism, his insistence on demonstrating the connections between poverty and those who consume knowledge about poverty. In the context of that fraught moment of American history wherein the New Deal model of art production suddenly ceased, Agee's attempt to show that "commerce" between privilege and poverty in America is an attempt to keep the dream of social welfare from devolving into the nightmare of a politically and socially polarized nation.

I

In September of 1939, Congress defunded all New Deal arts projects, effectively putting an end to that period wherein America's emerging literary talents (for example, Conrad Aiken, Nelson Algren, Saul Bellow, Arna Bontemps, John Cheever, Ralph Ellison, Zora Neale Hurston, Claude McKay, Tillie Olsen, Kenneth Rexroth, and Richard Wright) worked for the federal government.[5] What Congress did not do, what it could not do, was revoke the vast multimedia archive of documentary photos, caseworker studies, muckraking exposés, informant narratives, and state guide books that had been produced by the various arts agencies of the New Deal. This archive thus outlived the mission under which it was produced. It continued to evoke pity and fear from its beholders. Being untethered from its mission, this archive became not a visual and verbal appendage to social welfare; it became an end in itself: a source of knowledge about poverty during the Depression.

For instance, the thousands of photographs produced by the Historical Section Project of the Farm Service Agency (FSA) had been commissioned to serve as what Naomi Rosenblum calls a "visual analogue" to the New Deal's social welfare agenda (379). This analog was important. Without it, the Depression may have been, according to William Stott, "easy for the casual eye to miss" (68).[6] Without documentary art, the Depression would have been noticeable primarily in scenes of negation — an absence of smoke coming from chimneys or delivery trucks on Main Street. In short, the point of most documentary art was, as Michael Szalay puts it, to "sell to the nation the severity of the hardship the New Deal intended to redress" (63). FSA photography was a key piece of evidence about this severity. When these photos lost their mission, they stopped being evidence for a need to redress poverty and became evidence about what poverty was. These photos thus transformed from being a call to action to being an object of viewing.

Agee tries to thwart this transformation. He places a slate of Walker Evans's photos in the front of *Praise* and follows these photos with a 400-page meditation on the network of interrelationships that link poverty and privilege in America. Agee's insistence on exposing this network seems, at times, self-indulgent. But the effect is a work of art that exposes its own position in the production of knowledge about what poverty is and is not, and *where* poverty is and is not, in America. Unfortunately, the work never got to its intended audience. *Fortune* passed. The first word of Agee's project that did reach print did so in a very different forum: in James Laughlin's annual anthology of experimental writing. The first audience of *Praise* was thus not the middle-class reader who felt compelled to be informed about social injustice but a self-grouped contingent of literary experimentation advocates. The cultural moment into which *Praise* first intervenes is thus not a moment of crisis about social welfare but a moment of opportunity for the engineers of the avant-garde in America.

A brief section from *Praise*, a digressive aside titled "Colon," appeared in the 1940 edition of *New Directions in Prose & Poetry*. It appeared in a section Laughlin made exclusively for the 1940 edition, titled "American Scene." One other title appears in "American Scene," Wright Morris's photo-text, "Inhabitants." Laughlin prefaces this special section with a note that announces these two texts as examples of the cutting edge of a verbal-visual aesthetic that Archibald MacLeish had, two years earlier, heralded in a *New Directions* essay as "The Soundtrack-&-Picture Form: A New Direction."[7] In his note, Laughlin highlights the experimental nature of the two photo-texts.[8] He ignores altogether Agee's brooding about the ethical dilemmas of documentary art. By highlighting only the avant-garde resonance of "Colon," Laughlin enters Agee's reflexive documentary style into the record of American letters under false pretenses. He likewise removes Agee from the very conversation into which he so painstakingly tries to enter.

This hijacking of Agee's intentions doesn't stop with Laughlin's appropriation of the text. In a gesture that signals the persistence of New York literary institutions' interest in maintaining cultural trusteeship, Laughlin also appropriates Agee and Morris (a Southerner and a Midwesterner, respectively) as East Coast writers. The contributor note on Agee (born and raised in Tennessee) insists that "James Agee is in New York City when he is not on his farm in New Jersey. He has worked for *Time* and for *Fortune* and is the author of . . . a book of poems published by the Yale University Press" (ix). Morris's note likewise begins with a biographically inaccurate claim and ends on an East Coast tangent: "Wright Morris is properly a New Englander. . . . There is to be an exhibition of [his work] at the Kamin Bookshop in New York City in the near future" (xi).[9] This effort to make Agee and Morris seem like East Coast natives is an effort to filter the influence of provincial America out of their biographies and thus to imply that it is New York and nowhere else that is responsible for the "new directions" Laughlin anthologizes.

Laughlin's decision to highlight only the avant-garde nature of Agee's piece and only the East Coast affiliations of Agee's biography has the same macro effect as Congress's defunding of New Deal arts programs. It amounts to a mishandling of the transition of documentary art from an era of social welfare to whatever would replace that era. In a broader context, when, for example, the FSA photo archive gets separated from its social welfare mission, what emerges is a reception logic wherein, according to Susan Sontag, "middle-class people who needed to be convinced that the poor were really poor, and that the poor were dignified" get exactly what they need (*On Photography*, 62). In such a context, the poor get no help other than dignification. So dignified, such icons of Depression-era poverty as Dorothea Lange's "Migrant Mother" and John Steinbeck's Joad family become models of self-sufficiency. As I have argued elsewhere, self-sufficiency itself has become the virtue du jour of neoconservative revisions of the Depression.[10]

Agee first became wary of the dignification of poor people when *Fortune* assigned him to write a profile on the Tennessee Valley Authority (TVA). During his research, Agee noticed that the TVA was supplementing its very effective "social-industrial-agrarian scheme" with a patronizing regional imagination ("Tennessee," 644). Specifically, the TVA had created a sentimentalized icon of the Tennessee River Valley: the so-called mountaineer. The TVA's regional imagination motivated Agee to be wary of popular, even populist, representations of rural poverty. Such representations never tell the whole story, and they always sever the ties that bind privilege to poverty. In short, *Praise* was born out of an attempt to add a regional cosmopolitan sensibility to the regional imagination through which the New Deal tried to sell the public on its social welfare mission.[11]

The standard literary-historical narrative about the book, however, neglects this prehistory of *Praise*. The book is commonly understood as a work of Cold War liberal introspection. In the following section, I will suggest that Agee is wrongly associated with the Cold War and that it is more accurate to call *Praise* a reappraisal of the New Deal than to call it an inroad to the so-called liberal imagination. To classify *Praise* as a prototype of liberal introspection and retreat from the sphere of social justice is to misunderstand Agee's reflexivity as a type of liberal guilt and not a work of regional cosmopolitanism. Before I make my case for dissociating Agee from the Cold War, I will discuss the emergence of Agee's regional cosmopolitan sensibility. This sensibility begins the moment Agee recoils from the personification of the Tennessee mountaineer. It reaches maturity when Agee grounds his bourgeois anguish in the specific soil of the New Deal's orphans.

II

Agee first identifies the danger of representations of poverty in 1933, when he writes a profile of what turned out to be the most effective social welfare initiative in the nation's history. The TVA began with an implausible mission: to modernize the infrastructure of a seven-state region of the American South, to manage the river erosion of the virtually untamable Tennessee River Valley, and to develop an almost nonexistent electrification system into a functioning grid. Funding for such a mission was to come from the region's own untapped resources: its aluminum ore, asphalt rock, coal, copper, iron ore, lead, limestone, manganese, marble, phosphate rock, and zinc. The region's forests would also be converted into roughly "7,000,000,000 board feet" a year, yielding $38.5 million in lumber sales in Tennessee alone. Before the TVA, the "natural resources which should have sustained local industries indefinitely [had] been shipped away in crude form and exhausted," and as a result, "whole communities have been and are being pauperized, abandoned" (Agee, "Tennessee," 633). What's worse, many of the resources were literally flushed downriver by a wily Mississippi. Wilson Dam had been one attempt to tame the river, but that had cost the federal government $150 million (in 1918). The only way to raise the region from poverty and dependence was to build communities that would refine their own materials, convert their resources into capital on their own.

It's the TVA's manner of selling this idea of social-industrial-agrarian self-sufficiency that worries Agee. Before it can properly "fashion a civilization" that is a self-sustaining region, the TVA must first excavate and refine the region's main human resource: "the mountaineer." The purpose of this preliminary step in the TVA's scheme is to forge a regional identity that will empower citizens. The mountaineer was to personify the "strong backbone of the Valley," project the Tennessee Valley population as a pure product of America, a human resource made of "that incomparably pure

American stock which produced such men as Lincoln and Chief Justice Marshall and, for that matter, Cordell Hull" ("Tennessee," 634, 635).[12] By beginning its aid scheme with such a personification, the TVA could convince locals that it was something other than an indifferent agent of industrial progress (such agents traditionally have bad reputations in rural America).[13] But by shining a mirror onto the region and by encouraging its inhabitants to recognize in their reflection an image of self-sufficiency, the TVA becomes more of a consultant than an engineer of regional uplift. At worst, the TVA's "deep but realistic respect for what it calls the native culture of the valley" was a somewhat pandering incubator of pride (635). Even through Agee's reportorial tone, his skepticism is apparent.

Agee, a Tennessee native, predicts that the TVA's "great experiment" (which had begun only in the year of Agee's reporting) will succeed. By focusing on rhetoric about the mountaineer, this success is to be predicated on the creation of a personification of the Tennessee Valley. What's wrong with this personification, Agee implies in his *Fortune* profile and expounds upon in *Praise*, is that such personifications become permanent: they outlive their usefulness as preliminary steps in social welfare initiatives. Once the mountaineer becomes a surrogate for the region, he enters the popular imagination for good.

Such regional personification became standardized during the 1930s. Just as the mountaineer comes to personify "the people" of Tennessee Valley, the sharecropper comes to personify the same stock along the Cotton Belt, and the migrant farmer personifies the West. This pattern of regional personification determines the kinds of documentary projects that get produced for decades to come. For instance, Robert Coles's 1973 Pulitzer Prize–winning installment of his *Children of Crisis* series is titled *Migrants, Sharecroppers, Mountaineers*.[14] By recognizing this pattern at its moment of formation, Agee tracks a flaw in the production of knowledge about poverty from its inception to its peak. From the TVA's mountaineer to Margaret Bourke-White's photos in *You Have Seen Their Faces* (1937), Depression-era representations of rural poverty tend to simultaneously dignify the poor and "wheedle the viewer into emotion by making it seem that what he looked at was fresh . . . and not what it was: a sentimental cliché" (Stott, 270).[15] This system of representing and receiving poverty outlasts the wounds of the Depression. Ironically, it solidifies in the popular imagination the very kind of poverty that social welfare schemes like the TVA were trying to eradicate.

This is how documentary art unwittingly places poverty — specifically the iron-rations level of rural poverty experienced by the Southern sharecropper — beyond the reach of civic support. Though it seems counterintuitive, it is arguable that the New Deal never directly helped sharecroppers. It created huge numbers of industrial jobs, which produced thousands of miles of roads, airports, dams, hospitals, libraries, parks, playgrounds, power flumes, schools, and sewers. But with this improvement in infrastructure came stiff farming regulations. The Agricultural Adjustment Administration (AAA) initiated sweeping production controls that reduced production quotas. Thus, sharecroppers were forced to produce fewer crops. The AAA even paid landowners subsidies for the land left idle. Since they owned no land, sharecroppers received no aid. What's worse, these antideflationary crop reductions led to large-scale crop and livestock destruction at a time when many sharecropper families were starving.[16]

In such a context, spectral dignity is small consolation for a segment of the population whose role in the production of social welfare is that of pity stimulation. To counteract this pathos-centric model of representing poverty, Agee represents poverty in a way that inspires a palpable sense of shared social space, a sense of the nearness of poverty to privilege in America. In *Praise*, he highlights the spirit of cooperation that he finds embedded in the TVA model of social welfare and eradicates the personification of regional identity. Like the TVA profile, the project that became *Praise* began as a *Fortune* assignment. Unlike the TVA profile, *Fortune* rejected Agee's work, on the grounds that it was not journalism. It also wasn't anything else. Indeed, it is no surprise that David Shields in *Reality Hunger* (2010) follows his bold claim that "all great works of literature either dissolve a genre or create one" with a brief list of books that begins with *Let Us Now Praise Famous Men*.

Indeed, *Praise* is a document that is in a constant, deliberate state of generic in-between-ness. Agee refuses to commit to any convention of documentary prose, and his refusal is a result of his having witnessed the shortsighted regional sensibility of the TVA. Agee's regional cosmopolitanism is thus a correction to the oversights of the New Deal model of social welfare, oversights that, especially after the New Deal mission gets defunded, threaten to establish a fixed geography of economic disparity in America. The product of this regional cosmopolitanism is a book that never seems to finally become a "work." It's as if Agee wants to keep raw his experience in Hale County, if only to ensure that that experience might never become a consumable piece of knowledge about what poverty is.

In *Art as Experience* (1934), John Dewey claims that it is "no linguistic accident" that "work" is the name we give to both the process and the product of labor: "Without the meaning of the verb that of the noun remains blank" (58). In *The Body in Pain* (1985), Elaine Scarry further explores the double valence of "work." According to Scarry, to work is to make private pain public. "Work" is what we call

> the phenomena of pain and the imagination as they begin to move from being a self-contained loop within the body to becoming the equivalent loop now projected into the external world. It is through this movement out into the world that the extreme privacy of the occurrence (both pain and imagining are invisible to anyone outside the boundaries of the person's body) begins to be sharable, that sentience becomes social. (170)

Agee wants *Praise* to be such a "work." He wants it to project into the world of his reader that "extreme privacy" of pain and imagining. He wants to make this pain and imagining "sharable" and "social." The best way he knows how to do this is to keep reminding his reader that the very act of reading about poverty is part of the production of knowledge about poverty.

These reminders start early. The book literally opens onto sixty-two photographs by Walker Evans, whom Agee jokes is "on loan from the federal government" in order to take pictures of the book's "nominal subject."[17] The photos, which precede the copyright pages of *Praise*, contrast quite sharply with standard Depression-era photos of rural poverty. Most notably, they register the presence of the photographer on the very faces of his subject, possibly even in the pupils of Annie Mae Gudger.[18] Evans's photos thus do something documentary photos usually, as a matter of form, avoid: they confirm the unnatural presence of the photographer and his shutter snap. A quick comparison of Dorothea Lange's "Migrant Mother," the most recognized FSA photo, and Evans's photo of Annie Mae Gudger, a photo that W. J. T. Mitchell calls the "Mona Lisa of the Depression," makes clear Evans's unconventional aesthetic (*Picture*, 294).[19]

Lange captures a mother in a moment of privacy and contemplation.

Evans captures Gudger in an awkward face-to-face interaction with a stranger. She is unaffiliated; no connotative procedures locate her in relation to a family. She could just as easily be a daughter or a sister as a mother. Whoever she is, her most notable relationship is to the photographer, for whom she has agreed to stand still and have her picture taken. She gazes mutely at the lens, squinting slightly in the sunlight behind him, straining the muscles in her neck. With her eyes pointed right at the lens and her expression full of attention, she is very much calling attention to the fact that she's being photographed.

Next to Lange's "Migrant Mother," Evans's photo seems like a yearbook headshot. Lange's photo has none of the awkward nearness of Evans's. Lange's "mother" is literally surrounded by evidence of her status as a mother. Two exhausted children rest weary heads on either shoulder. She is undeniably maternal. Her hair is not, like Gudger's, pulled behind her ear in preparation for the photo. She has not been alerted to the imminent shutter snap. Though her clothing is more pitiful than Gudger's, with a sweater sleeve missing at the elbow and a bundle of fabric that serves as both her leg covering and the wrappings of a third, sleeping child, almost imperceptibly lying in her lap, this mother transcends poverty through her very dignified embodiment of its markings.

Lange's mother's face is contemplative, not of the children at her ears and lap but of something distant. The lines stretched across her forehead and the fingertips lightly touching her chin indicate that the mother is caught in a moment of introspection. Her thoughts are remote and complex, and they are hers alone. She is intensely focused on the question of what to do with this sad lot, which is likewise hers alone. She can't be bothered by some pesky, government photographer. Photography is no concern. It is through this photo that Lange perfects the message that poor people are dignified to such a degree that they do not need us. The fact that "Migrant Mother" is so ubiquitous suggests that we have accepted the proposition that the poor will always be with us, if not also the proposition that they will always not need us.

Rather than being caught in such moments of introspection, Evans's sharecroppers actively participate in the production of their images. All of Evans's portraits show traces of a prearranged agreement between photographer and subject. They get ready for the camera and this labor of production is visible in the portraits: Mr. Woods covers his shoulder lesions with a bandana, and the Ricketts children wipe their eyes and tie their hair behind their heads. Such premeditated portraits seem to accomplish much less than do Lange's images. While Lange's poor confront with courage and honor the general condition of poverty, Evans's only confront a stranger facing them with expensive camera equipment.

What makes Evans's photos more respectful than Lange's is the fact that his subjects are coworkers in the production of their images. They participate in the various adjustments that occur at the point of contact between documentarian and subject. Thus they participate in the process of preparing this private pain for public consumption. In this way, Evans's photos set the theme of cooperation in *Praise*. They make the invisible bond between poverty and privilege palpable. Following these photos, Agee's self-consciousness and introspection seem indulgent, incredibly disrespectful of the very subjects Evans had taken such pains to respect. However, Agee's insistence on announcing his subject position and explaining his methods of examination is in some way symptomatic of all great literary imaginings of poverty.

Gavin Jones points out that American literature about poverty—specifically such pinnacles of the realist tradition as Dreiser's *Sister Carrie* (1900) and Wharton's *House of Mirth* (1905)—"explore poverty . . . as a haze of shifting socioeconomic relations" ("Poverty," 781). This method of representing poverty refuses the idea that poverty is a stable category. The representation of poverty that such literary narratives produce is incomplete, applied to the narrative in a way that reveals the oscillating relations that cause poverty. In other words, literary representations of poverty operate according to a regional cosmopolitan cultural logic. This logic, Jones argues, counteracts social-scientific efforts to understand poverty, efforts whose factual conceits "moved issues of exploitation and inequality into the realms of identity, morality, and race" (769). Unlike sociological and journalistic accounts of poverty, literary accounts refuse to offer stable, quantitative portraits of poverty or simple answers to difficult questions. Agee's refusal is a sign that *Praise* belongs alongside Depression-era representations of poverty, if only as a corrective.

Nevertheless, Susan Hegeman reads *Praise* as an exercise in introspection—that pastime so common to left-leaning artists and intellectuals of the Cold War era. Hegeman describes *Praise* as an "exploration of the interior spaces of the liberal intellectual" (191). From this vantage on *Praise*, Agee appears representative of what Lionel Trilling calls the "liberal imagination"; he appears introspective and not retrospective, and his relationship to the legacy of the New Deal dream of social welfare becomes the stance of one who is, at best, ambivalent about the role of political commitment in literature. This reading of *Praise* overlooks the fact that Agee's exploration of "the interior spaces of the liberal intellectual" is occasioned by encounter with the private sites of rural poverty in America. It's this simultaneity of bourgeois mental anguish and the specific soil of poverty that makes *Praise* so powerful. It "grounds" introspection, giving the process of exploring one's consciousness something resembling a civic purpose. Its also exposes the interrelationship between poverty and those who produce and consume knowledge about poverty.

By embodying all the shortcomings and ethical ambiguities of documentary art, Agee localizes the source of the problem that Cold War liberals had with New Deal idealism. Hegeman's claim that Agee retreats into an ether of introspection is thus partly true. His introspection is a response to his realization that the New Deal mission was either doomed or doomed to be abandoned. His commitment to embodying the shortcomings of documentary work is its own, albeit convoluted, type of commitment to social welfare. This commitment exposes the class prejudice of documentary art. Though such an exposure might lead a reader to retreat from political commitment, it should not itself be considered a retreat. Thus, we should not include *Praise* in the canon of Cold War liberal works.

Yet this small literary-historical misstep is easy to make: *Praise* does not play well with the rest of the books on the shelf of late Depression-era narratives about poverty. When it was first published, *Praise* appeared alongside titles that melodramatically, sentimentally represented poor people. Dwight Macdonald describes the context in which *Praise* appears like this: "novels about 'plain people' that are garnished with humanitarian rhetoric and a condescending little-man-what-now? pathos, as in *The Grapes of Wrath* and such exercises in liberal right-mindedness" (143). In such a context, reader compassion is guided by a reassuring pathos that never undermines the reader's commitment to an emotional response. *Praise*, on the other hand, raises sympathies only to subvert them. Even its epigraphs send a mixed message. The first epigraph is a line from *King Lear*: "Expose thyself to feel what wretches feel" (3.4.34), and the second is the last line of the *Communist Manifesto*.[20] The first is literary and the second is political, forcing the reader to ask if this is a work of art or a work of propaganda. Should the reader's emotional response be that of pity or outrage?

In true regional cosmopolitan form, Agee keeps such questions unanswered. He also, in the spirit of regional cosmopolitanism, disobeys the unwritten "don't-ask-don't-tell" rule of documentary art with regard to privacy invasion. Agee is explicit, even lewd, in his representation of the undignified postures he must assume as he rummages through poor people's personal belongings. What's worse, he enlists the reader as a secondary voyeur, one whose interest encourages Agee's rummagings but who refuses to venture into the world in which such activity occurs. Agee describes his reader as "all those who have a soft place in their hearts for the laughter and tears inherent in poverty viewed at a distance, and especially for those who can afford the retail price" (*Praise*, 11). By evoking their consumer dollars up front, Agee forces readers to acknowledge that they have helped finance an ethically unstable work. He also forces them to consider the "distance" they enjoy from poverty, the fact that documentary art about poverty confirms this distance.

Agee announces this game of evoking then ridiculing emotional responses in his preface, wherein he calls the book "a swindle, an insult, and a corrective" (*Praise*, xi). It's a "swindle" because it subverts expectations about what a documentary book about poverty should do (that is, produce a clear sympathy toward poor people). It's an "insult" because it makes the reader feel dirty for wanting what readers of documentary books about poverty are supposed to want. It's a "corrective" because it refuses to confirm the distance between poverty and its reader. In his study of poverty, *Poor People* (2007), William T. Vollmann describes the experience of reading *Praise* as the experience of being "slapped" in the face for wanting to read it (xiii).

Such a commitment to upending reader expectations was not welcome in the early 1940s. During this era, the nation was still licking its wounds. Readers of nonfiction wanted simplicity. They wanted, in Gordon Hutner's words, "facts over truth"— facts that would make the world understandable, make readers feel like something was being done about recovery, even if that "something" was only assuring readers that their sympathies and their raised awareness about poverty were somehow useful (207). Agee's big affront to the documentary genre is that he reveals just how little raised awareness is worth, how useless such awareness is if not the preliminary step in a painful commitment to experiencing the interrelationship between poverty and the middle class — a commitment to "feel what wretches feel."

Despite its initial failure, *Praise* became a best seller. In 1960, it became "legendary," "a book that young college students took south with them during the Freedom Summer of 1961" (Hegeman 178). This shift in reception reflects a standard cultural history of the U.S. in the 1960s. The summer after the first Freedom Rides was precisely the cultural moment for which *Praise* was written. It was a cultural moment wherein a critical mass of middle-class youth wanted to make injustice its business not by reading about injustice but by putting its bodies into the very spaces of injustice, the public buses and lunch counters of the American South. *Praise* taught the Civil Rights generation what it means to commit oneself to a site of injustice.[21] In short, it revealed *not* the attitude that one should have about poverty but the position that one ought to occupy within the production of knowledge about poverty. In the following section, I will demonstrate how Agee's uniquely politicized form of modernism produces a regional cosmopolitan sensibility that makes palpable the network of affiliations linking poverty and privilege in America.

III

Most literary histories of the 1930s dodge the topic of literary modernism. Even Michael Szalay's *New Deal Modernism* (2000), whose very title combines the literary category with the historical period, "sidesteps traditional debates about modernism" (Entin 138). Rather than discussing the "modernism" of the literary figures who worked for the Federal Writers' Project (FWP), Szalay focuses on the "modernism" of FWP itself. For Szalay, "modernism" describes an attitude toward production, not a type of product. The FWP is "modernist" to the extent that it conceives of authorship as a category of production that is ultimately not answerable to a market. Being salaried, New Deal writers had the freedom to produce art for social welfare's sake, which is the same thing as producing for art's sake insofar as it allows artists to be indifferent to the needs and expectations of an audience.[22]

Audience indifference is the only characteristic of modernism that Szalay takes seriously. In fact, he argues that "modernism" is a self-consuming category:

> Depending on the critic, modernism is historically explosive, containing within itself all the chaotic energies of the new, or an evasion, a project of autonomy struggling to awake from the nightmare of history; given to the streamlined and the technocratic, or to myth and the archaic; the subversion of the semiotic codes of bourgeois society or a sequence of master narratives that are the very embodiment of hegemony; awash in a stream of middle-class consciousness or a shaft into the primal imagination of the primitive unconscious; committed to the transcendent powers of the lone genius, or impersonal, steeped in the objectifying mechanisms of modern science and sociology; acutely self-conscious and metadiscursive or the very dream of a self-identical logos; pure and sanitized of generic confusion or the polyglot vanguard of multimedia society. (4–5)

It's hard, after such a litany of contradictory claims, to fault Szalay for sidestepping debates about modernism and defining the category in an "unabashedly general sense" (5). It's even possible that such a nonfinicky approach to defining "literary modernism" might allow literary critics the freedom to make the kinds of contributions about the relationship between avant-garde and documentary aesthetics that film and art historians have been making for quite a while.[23] Indeed, that's exactly what *New Deal Modernism* does so well. Szalay's very broad definition of modernism liberates him from deeply entrenched arguments of definition.

This broad definition of modernism proves useful when thinking about *Praise*. Because it was dropped by *Fortune*, *Praise* shares the central freedom of the salaried art of the New Deal: freedom from deadline. Agee was definitely interested in such freedom. In a letter dated 1937, he asks Archibald MacLeish, his former boss at *Fortune*, about working conditions at *Life*, the magazine to which MacLeish had moved after Henry Luce repurposed *Life* into a photojournalistic weekly. Agee asks MacLeish if *Life* might accommodate a writer whose work would be produced under "immunity" from the forty-hour workweek (Agee, Letter, 2). According to Agee, writers and photographers alike should consider ideas "from the ground up [and] submit a given piece of work not according to [a] deadline but when we considered it finished." The editorial policies at *Fortune* were stifling. In Agee's words, the "detailed and repeated modification of an idea to the reactions of an editor can seriously damage not only the given idea but the faculty for getting and developing ideas" (2). This is the erudite slacker logic of the brilliant young writer whom Macdonald once claimed had "the worst set of work habits in Greenwich Village" (152). It is also evidence that Agee is among a group of "radical writers . . . who responded to the rise of salaried patronage by theorizing the relation between the specific modes of support used to enable writing and the aesthetic criteria used to justify that support" (Szalay, 28).

The freedom Agee experienced writing *Praise* was thus not freedom from caring about his audience but freedom to consider the relationship between "patronage" and product. Ironically, what Agee produces is a book that relies for its vitality on the very thing that Szalay claims New Deal modernists had transcended: "the public's response to what that labor did in fact produce" (68).

Throughout *Praise*, Agee foils the documentary reader's tendency to commit to sentimental responses to representations of poverty. Much of the book catalogs the "wealth" of the sharecropper families he documents, specifically that of the Gudger family. Agee devotes fifty pages to detailing the Gudger house (*Praise*, 119–169). This section of the book recounts everything from major structural spaces (hallway, bedrooms, kitchen, storeroom) to domestic fixtures (furniture, fireplace, mantel, closet, beds, table, lamp). It also includes indices of odors and the "bareness and space" that exist in between the possessions recounted (109). In fact, Agee describes bareness according to a design principle of "exact symmetries" (137). He describes their home as though the Gudgers were posh minimalists whose discrete spacing "gives each object a full strength" (137).

In the midst of this upending of expectations about the genre, wherein the reader is most alert to Agee's unorthodox perspective on poverty, Agee becomes very descriptive about his privacy invasion. He dissects the Gudgers' "altar" (a partition wall with a fireplace) and "tabernacle" (the house's one table's one drawer). As he searches this tabernacle, he finds a collection of baby toys, cloths, scraps of newspaper that have been used for wrapping. He transcribes a scrap of newsprint that appears on one such wrapping:

GHAM NEWS
hursday afternoon, March 5, 1936
Price: 3 cents
in G
(else

Thousa
are on d
througho
cording its

for the Birm (146)

In addition to this scrap piece of newsprint, Agee finds photos of labor strikes. These shreds of newspaper are saved not for their content. They are not used for their value as "news" but for their value as wrapping paper. The transcribed piece of newsprint had been used to wrap a swan figurine. In Agee's hands, these scraps become objets trouvés, found art curated in Agee's text around a principle of juxtaposition. By aestheticizing the things he finds in the tabernacle, Agee puts the technique of defamiliarization in the service of reappraising the private spaces of poverty. Readers react to the sacrilege of Agee's behavior—the liberties he takes in penetrating the Gudger tabernacle—and this reaction calls attention to the otherwise invisible ethical ambiguities of documentary work.

As he enters these "sacred" objects into the public record, Agee insists that the family whose privacy he is invading "love me, and I, how dearly, them" (165). This acknowledgement of an intimacy at the very moment that the trust that makes intimacy possible is broken forces the reader to react, to be repelled, pushed away from the documentarian and toward the family whose privacy Agee is violating. It's the reader, not Agee, who aligns with the sharecroppers. The reader gets defensive; he forgets pity and commits to an emotional response more akin to outrage.

This is Agee's way of desentimentalizing poverty. His inventory of the Gudgers' "wealth" never explicitly announces the awful economic situation that the Gudgers are in. The reader is thus denied the easy recourse of pity. This denial is most pronounced in the moments that combine literary language and documentary precision. A good example of this combination is the passage that describes the pair of overalls that George Gudger wears in the photo that serves as the cover of *Praise*. The passage is both thickly descriptive and overtly literary. Agee spins a self-conscious metaphor out of the overalls, referring to them as a "map of a working man," a "badge and proclamation of his peasantry" (235, 234). In aestheticizing the overalls, Agee exposes the process of transforming something that is poor into something that is beloved. The central passage reads as follows:

> The texture and the color [of the overalls] change in union, by sweat, sun, laundering, between the steady pressures of its use and age . . . into a region and scale of blues, subtle, delicious, and deft beyond what I have ever seen elsewhere approached except in rare skies . . . and some of the blues of Cézanne . . . a fabric as intricate and fragile, and as deeply in honor of the reigning sun, as the feather mantle of a Toltec prince. (236–237)

Such passages catch the light of hagiography that one might expect to find in a book with the phrase "*Praise Famous Men*" in the title. They also graze the high-stakes satire on social-scientific seriousness that W. E. B. Du Bois engages when he, in both *The Souls of Black Folk* (1903) and *The Negro* (1915), refers to black sharecroppers using the French word "*métayers*."[24]

In contrast to Du Bois's satirically high-toned language, Agee warns his reader against taking interpretive liberties with the picture of poverty that they are witnessing. He preemptively corrects a mispronunciation that the urbane reader is likely to make. The word "overalls," Agee explains, is "pronounced overhauls" (234). This preemptive correction allows Agee to make an important pun. Agee makes the "badge" of rural poverty (its "overalls") into something that is homonymous with a process of revising expectations about rural poverty ("to overhaul"). The play on words here summarizes Agee's contract with his reader. The job of *Praise* is to "overhaul" the system by which knowledge about poverty gets produced, to build into the documentary genre a cosmopolitan sensibility that acknowledges the interrelationship of the laboring and the leisure classes and that, more specifically, understands leisure as an important kind of "labor" in the production of knowledge about poverty.

Elsewhere in *Praise*, Agee describes the division of labor like this: the documentarian's job is "to make a number of physical entities as plain and vivid as possible, and to make a few guesses, a few conjectures; and to leave to you much of the burden of realizing in each of them what I have wanted to make clear of them as a whole: how each is itself; and how each is a shapener" (97).[25] By making a noun out of the past participle of the verb "to shape," Agee calls attention to the cocreation that *Praise* is supposed to be, to the fact that everybody works. By making this statement of purpose nearly one hundred pages into his book, Agee calls attention to the fraught connection between "work" (the verb) and "work" (the noun).

The "work" of *Praise* is a composite of the interaction between the reader, the prose printed on the pages of *Praise*, and the photographs that precede these pages. As Agee suggests early on, prose is an insufficient medium through which to "document" poverty:

> If I could do it, I'd do no writing at all here. It would be photographs . . . fragments of cloth, bits of cotton, lumps of earth, records of speech, pieces of wood and iron, phials of odors, plates of food and of excrement. Booksellers would consider it quite a novelty; critics would murmur, yes, but is it art; and I could trust a majority of you to use it as you would a parlor game. (10).

The problem with a "work" of prose is that it too easily gets classified. It gets labeled as "'scientific' or 'political' or 'revolutionary' . . . 'literature' or 'religion' or 'mysticism' or 'art,' and under one such name or another might in time achieve the emasculation of acceptance" (11). Agee does not want *Praise* to become a "work" that gets "accepted." Once a work gets accepted, it *becomes* a "work of ______" and stops *doing* any work. It enters a state of being understood so completely as one kind of thing or another that its every utterance signifies not a unique experience but a symptom of the kind of label the book has received.

The process of handing private space over to the public is problematic, and Agee does not shy away from this fact. By dedicating the Gudger house to public property, he desacralizes the house's private "tabernacles." The secret drawers of the house become virtual zones of privacy built into an otherwise publicly owned space (not unlike a public restroom in a national park). Agee underscores this implication when he assumes the role of a depraved cruiser:

> I took off all my clothes . . . planted my obscenities in the cold hearts of every mirror . . . : I permitted nothing to escape the fingering of my senses nor the insulting of the cold reptilian fury of the terror of lone desire which was upon me. (120–121)

Though this vision of privacy invasion seems obscene, it lacks "open sexual desire" (121). He carries out his invasion with "no restiveness, nor despair: but the quietly triumphant vigilance of the extended senses before an intricate task of surgery . . . not for shame of the people, but in fear and in honor of the house itself, *a knowledge of being at work*" (121, my italics). His invasion is comparable to that of a surgeon's. It is intimate and necessary. And Agee respects his patient's welfare, though he deliberately cuts into the patient. No matter how sensual and unbefitting a gentleman his "desecration" of the tabernacle becomes, he is "at work." He retains all the skill and professionalism of one whose job it is to invade privacy.

This version of privacy invasion is hard to bear. Readers flinch instinctively. The result is an irreversible *impression* of poverty, a mark that is likely to live with readers. They are the recipients of that outward radiation of private pain that Scarry describes, inheritors of the "loop" that Agee's prose projects into the world. Sentience has indeed become social.

With this newly acquired inheritance freshly impressed upon his readers, Agee continues his sober cataloging of the Gudger house. He includes even the debris that has fallen through the cracks of the house:

> bent nails, withered and knobbed with rust; a bone button, its two eyes torn to one; the pierced back of an alarm clock, greasy to the touch; a torn fragment of pictured print; an emptied and flattened twenty-gauge shotgun shell, its metal green, lettering still visible; the white tin eyelet of a summer shoe; and thinly scattered, the desiccated and the still soft excrement of hens. (130)

Agee discovers these fragments in the spirit of "the earliest and profoundest absorptions of a very young child" (132). By equating the act of documenting every square inch of a poor family's home with the "absorptions" of a child, Agee suggests that the ground of rural poverty is enchanted. Much like a curious child exploring a new hiding place, Agee remarks on every nook and cranny of the underside of the Gudger house. But these fragments are not simply the curios of a young child, nor are they simply the aestheticized fragments of a modernist's assertively fractured worldview. They are items on a list of things that Agee and his reader have *inherited*. The infrastructural decay of the Gudgers' house may be fun to rummage through, but it is a decay that will eventually have to be redressed.

In a cultural context that includes such sentimentalized representations of the dignity and strength of poor people as this line from *The Grapes of Wrath*—"We're the people! We go on!" (280)—Agee's ethically ambiguous, co-owned representation of poverty is remarkably bleak. But Agee closes *Praise* with a hopeful gesture, a scene that suggests the benefits of the rare, complex type of interrelationship that results from a regional cosmopolitan representation of rural poverty. In the final section of *Praise*, titled "On the Porch 3," Agee writes about how he and an unnamed companion hear a curious sound in the darkness beyond the porch. The porch, a shared, communal space of leisure, has been something of an extended metaphor for Agee. It's been a place of horizontal kinship between Agee and the sharecroppers.

This sound enlists them in a pact of "mutual listening" (409). Like Evans's photos, this final section of *Praise* follows the book's "Notes and Appendices" section. The mysterious sound seems right at home here, in a space beyond the boundaries of the "work." Indeed, this final section is yet another reminder of how unbound the work of *Praise* is. It's a reminder of the outward radiation of the pain that Agee has made public. Agee and his unnamed companion listen together:[26]

> All the darkness in near range . . . as far as we were able to hear was strung with noises that were all one noise, and to this we had become so accustomed that this new sound came out of silence, and left an even more powerful silence behind it, so that with each return it, and the ensuing silence, gave each other more and more value, like the exchanges of two mirrors laid face to face. (409)

This description of the white noise to which both parties have grown desensitized is a reminder of the world beyond the documentary frame. Agee and companion become "one hollowed and listening ear" jointly absorbing this noise of the world as it finally invades their leisure space (409). This final section puts documentary work into a larger regional context. It amplifies the fact that rural poverty exists in the same national space as the reader.

The sound is "so entirely itself, without regard for us" that it makes palpable "our near perspective of kinship" (411). Acknowledging the world beyond the porch both places poverty on the shared space of the national and relieves Agee of the painstaking work of making poverty public. He and his companion can relax into the "frightening joy of hearing the world talk to itself" (414). The two "lay thinking, analyzing, remembering... until at length we too fell asleep" (416). These are the last words of *Praise.*

By ending his book with an ode to intersubjectivity, Agee punctuates the fact that he intends his work to never harden into a static "work." Agee explicitly intends *Praise* to be publicly useful. Unlike the floating liberal thinkers of the Cold War, Agee is not finally untethered from civic responsibility. If anything, it is civic responsibility that is untethered from the representations of poverty that, unlike Agee's, do become popular in the immediate aftermath of the Great Depression. In the final section, I will contrast Agee's method of representing poverty against Steinbeck's method in *The Grapes of Wrath* as a way to further sharpen the distinction between Agee's regional cosmopolitanism and other, more polarizing ways of representing rural poverty. Rather than focusing on the interrelationship between poverty and privilege, Steinbeck represents poor people as a special category of American, one that is too self-sufficient to need civic aid and too dignified to suffer fussy, effeminate privacy invaders like Agee.

VI

The Grapes of Wrath (*Grapes*) is a pretty polarizing novel. On the one hand, writers like Vollmann see it as unambiguously valuable, "one of the best books about poor people I have ever read" (xii). On the other hand, critics like Michael Szalay see the novel as incredibly counterproductive, a "high-water mark in twentieth-century American sentimentalism" (167). Michael Denning synthesizes these polarized perspectives. According to Denning, the value of the novel lies less in its status as either a good book or a problematic book than in its status as a novel that founded a narrative template for representing poverty in America: "the best-known Popular Front genre is probably the 'grapes of wrath,' the narrative of the migrant agricultural workers in California" (259). Such a genre proved useful as a pattern for both literary and social-scientific discourse on poverty, serving as inspiration for such divergent texts as T. C. Boyle's novel *The Tortilla Curtain* (1995) and Vollmann's journalistic tome on global poverty, *Poor People.*[27]

Vollmann devotes a section of his introduction to the question of why *Grapes* is a better model than *Praise.* The short answer Vollmann gives is that *Praise* is an "elitist expression of egalitarian longings" and that *Grapes* is a more overtly "populist" book (by which Vollmann means that it is a book that the people it's written about are likely to read and feel that it was written both *about* and *for* them). *Praise* is not written for poor people: "James Agee sought to know *them*, to experience, however modestly, what they did; his heart went out to them, and he fought with all his crafty, hopelessly unrequitable passion to make *our* hearts do the same" (xii, my italics). The book is for "us," readers who are not poor. This intended audience is obvious even during the passages wherein Agee apologizes directly to the sharecropper families. Even Agee's method of apology is of "an abstruse gorgeousness of abasement that only the rich will have time to understand" (xiii).

In addition to having this elite audience, *Praise* contrasts with *Grapes* in more obvious ways: (a) it's about static, as opposed to migratory, poverty, and (b) it never portrays its subject in public. Readers never see a sharecropper in a context wherein they might actually encounter a sharecropper in real life (that is, in cotton fields). Steinbeck's Joads, on the other hand, are almost always in public, often viewed from an indifferently public perspective. This contrast between private and public representations has something to do with the contrasting conditions of encounter that Agee and Steinbeck experienced. Both writers spent the summer of 1936 doing the fieldwork. Agee lived in three different sharecropper quarters in Hale County, Alabama. Steinbeck spent the same months touring Hoovervilles and "Little Oklahomas" in rural California. Steinbeck was researching a series on migrant farmers for the *San Francisco News*, whereas Agee was writing a profile for *Fortune* magazine. Steinbeck's work was published in a quick succession of seven articles beginning the first week of October, 1936, whereas the fruits of Agee's labor were not published until five years later. Steinbeck's research yielded a longtime friendship (and silent partner) in Tom Collins, whereas Agee's research was profoundly isolating. Looking for favorable publicity, Collins, a manager of a California migrant farmer camp, drove Steinbeck through California's agricultural valleys, detailing for him the lay of the land. Seeing poverty from this managerial vantage point, Steinbeck's perspective lacks the unmediated contact upon which Agee's text is founded.

Steinbeck scholars suggest that this partnership with Collins may have directed the racial politics of *Grapes*, which are subtly supremacist and surprisingly eugenicist.[28] Whereas Steinbeck chooses to focus on white migrant workers, Agee has no choice. As he describes in the preface of *Praise*, the assignment was "to prepare, for a New York magazine, an article on cotton tenantry in the United States, in the form of a photographic and verbal record of the daily living and environment of an average white family of tenant farmers" (ix). Agee's mention of the whiteness of his subject is not unlike his mention of the "retail price" of *Praise* (11). It draws attention to the racial and economic gears of the production of knowledge about poverty. The whiteness of Agee's subject is something the reader simply has to live with. Agee does not justify this condition, nor does he make value judgments about it. The reader is left alone to consider the consequences of the odd racial bias. However, despite the suggestive absence of reflexivity about the racial limitations of *Praise*, Agee does indicate its conspicuousness when he places, between the preamble and part 1 of *Praise*, three vignettes ("Late Sunday Morning," "At the Forks," and "Near a Church") about awkward encounters between Agee (sometimes Evans) and groups of black people in rural Alabama.

Steinbeck meditates on race quite a bit in his article series, later collected as *The Harvest Gypsies*, which includes all seven articles and an eighth chapter titled "Their Blood Is Strong." Under Collins's influence, Steinbeck produces a heroic journalistic defense of the white migrant laborer's purloined right to property. Throughout both *The Harvest Gypsies* and *Grapes*, Steinbeck asserts that it is the loss of property that is the primary affront to white migrant farmers. According to Charles Wollenberg's introduction to *The Harvest Gypsies*, Steinbeck "mined [Collins's reports] for material for *The Grapes of Wrath*" (ix). This access to Resettlement Administration reports compels Steinbeck to align with Collins's conviction that white migrant workers are "displaced Jeffersonian yeomen who needed and deserved their own small plots of land" (Wollenberg, "John Steinbeck," 140). The white farmer, according to Collins, is a unique kind of poor person, the kind that doesn't deserve to be poor. This special category of cosmically unjust poverty is the result of the fact that the commercial protocols established during the Gold Rush discouraged small-farm ownership in California. As far as Collins was concerned, it is the job of New Dealers to promote the removal of these protocols, especially when they are applied to white Americans.

By the 1930s, California agricultural employers no longer imported foreigners but relied on "white labor . . . American labor [that] will insist on a standard of living much higher than that which was accorded the foreign 'cheap labor'" (Steinbeck, *Harvest*, 56). The supremacist overtone of this proclamation that white Americans won't accept the same low standard as foreign labor is obvious. Indeed, according to Wollenberg, Steinbeck's message is that only "white Americans could successfully resist conditions that had regularly been imposed on nonwhites and immigrants" ("John Steinbeck," 141). But this message is both racist and a matter of legal fact. Since the completion of the transcontinental railroad, California had imported and exported a steady stream of foreign labor from China, Japan, Mexico, and finally the Philippines. This pre–white labor force was afforded no constitutional safeguards against exploitation and therefore had little leverage through which to resist bad conditions and poor treatment.

Counter to Collins's-cum-Steinbeck's assurance about the resolve of white labor, Wollenberg assures readers that Oklahoma migrants were "less willing to organize and join unions than the Mexicans and Filipinos" had been ("John Steinbeck," 141). In addition to miscalculating the pride of white laborers, Steinbeck fetishizes their racial distinctions. In the first installment of *The Harvest Gypsies*, he claims this of his subject: "their blood is strong. They are descendants of men who crossed into the middle west, who won their lands by fighting. They are gypsies by force of circumstances" (22). It might be expected that racializing a group of white Americans would have the effect of "lowering" the group to a level normally occupied by foreign labor. However, Steinbeck's racialization of white men is a way of asserting that the denial of both landownership and the vote results in a specifically American form of racial marking. It is private property, the yeoman's distinguishing characteristic, that whitens Americans. In other words, though we may always have the poor with us, these poor needn't always be white.

Where the visual icons of the Depression, such as Lange's "Migrant Mother," place poor people in a world beyond the boundaries of civic duty, Steinbeck's novel suggests the inevitable ascendancy of the migrant farmer. This suggestion has the same effect of relieving the reader of responsibility to do anything, save acknowledge the dignity of the Joads. Rather than stewing in private zones of poverty, the reader follows them onto the open road, into a state of permanent, self-sufficient homelessness. The reader's role is simple: root for the Joads as they carve out a better life for themselves, and wait for Tom Joad to reappear as the revolutionary hero he'd promised to return as. Consider Tom's famous last words to Ma:

> I'll be all aroun' in the dark. I'll be ever'where. . . . Wherever they's a fight so hungry people can eat, I'll be there. Wherever they's a cop beatin' up a guy, I'll be there. . . . I'll be in the way guys yell when they're mad an'— I'll be in the way kids laugh when they're hungry an' they know supper's ready. An' when our folks eat the stuff they raise an' live in the houses they build — why, I'll be there. (419)

We needn't worry; Tom Joad has all the sites of injustice covered. He will "be there" at all public and private cases of class struggle. Next to such reassurance, Agee's regional cosmopolitan reflexivity seems indecisive. It makes poor people seem doomed, and it ties their fates in with the reader's own. In comparison to Steinbeck's omnisciently reassuring narrative control, Agee's manic reflexivity looks downright fatalistic. Where Steinbeck moves his Joads toward a definite solution, Agee moves his reader only closer and closer to a sharply focused, private scene of poverty.

For these reasons, *Grapes* succeeds New Deal paradigms for representing poverty. As a result, the market indifference of New Deal practitioners is replaced by a contract model of narrative fiction wherein the reader exchanges his sense of civic duty for a sense of solidarity with an ultimately ineffectual ideal of justice. In this sense, *Grapes* both abandons civic duty and valorizes this abandonment. Like the novel's intercalary chapters, or even like the fact that Steinbeck's lived experience with migration occurred primarily in the passenger seat of Tom Collins's bakery truck, this new narrative abandons the weight and solidity of rural poverty.

Additionally, *Grapes* represents migration as a form of self-inflicted disenfranchisement. The Joads relocate without the aid of social welfare. In fact, the only sign of government sponsorship in *Grapes* is Weedpatch camp, an environment that is "sanitary" to the point of registering in the world of the novel as a utopic setting — a nonplace from which to criticize the world that does exist. The narrative logic of *Grapes*, regardless of whether or not it resembles the actual migration and desolation brought about by the Dust Bowl and Depression, undermines the New Deal model of interactive social welfare. It implies that the poor are superhuman.

As I will bear out in the following chapter, Kerouac develops a similar attitude toward poverty and mobility. Much like the way Steinbeck represents the movement of the Joad family down Route 66, Kerouac represents the children of the Depression as a generation that must move, no matter the cost. When Kerouac's characters attempt to establish roots, they go crazy or get tagged as vagrants and are nudged back on the road. In short, Kerouac seems to be the beneficiary of Steinbeck's narrative template. However, he also inherits Agee's reflexivity about sites of economic trauma in America. This reflexivity reveals the network of interrelationship between poverty and privilege that Agee exposes. In the next chapter, I will examine the virtues and limitations of Kerouac's transformation of this network into a series of highways that set the stage for a reimagining of the American continent.

Time is the essence of the undertaking, time to live into the land and absorb it; still more time to cure the reading public of its preference for something less than the proverbial bird's-eye view of the American scene, what you might call an automobile eye view, something slithering and blurred, nothing so sharply discriminated that it arrests the speed-numbed mind to understand, characters like garish gas stations picked out with electric lights. The one chance of persuading the young reader to make these distinctions for himself would be to whet his appreciation on the best regional literature of our past so that he may not miss the emerging instance of his own times. — Mary Austin, "Regionalism in American Fiction"

Trying, let us say, to represent, to reproduce, a certain city street, under the conviction that nothing is as important, as sublime, as truly poetic about that street in its flotation upon time and space as the street itself. . . . Try to give the street *in its own terms*. — James Agee, *Let Us Now Praise Famous Men*

Yes, zoom! — Jack Kerouac, *On the Road*

TWO

Pavement

Jack Kerouac and the Delocalization of America

In "Regionalism in American Fiction" (1932), Mary Austin predicts that, as American culture starts to speed up, the American reading public will start to settle for "less than" the careful localization of regional fiction. In effect, the sharp, inclusive geography of the "American scene" will give way to the "automobile eye view," a point of view that corresponds to the "speed-numbed mind" of modern society. Fiction of the nature Austin predicts is normally considered symptomatic of the midcentury. However, Austin sees this fast fiction coming from a distance. Likewise, Agee foresees a state of distraction about to permanently befall the American reader. His advice to young writers: "give the street *in its own terms*" (*Praise*, 208). Treat the terrain of speed and mobility, the pavement itself, not as a source of distraction but a source of the sublime interconnection that, from the poet's point of view, every street symbolizes.

This agreement between Austin and Agee about the coming seismic shift in culture and literature echoes the fundamental resemblance of regionalists and modernists, a resemblance that boils down to William Carlos Williams's dictum: "No ideas but in things." It also implies that what undoes the popularity of regional and modernist aesthetics alike is the fact that concepts of time and time's relation to experiential reality change thanks to the 650,000 new miles of pavement laid down by New Deal works projects. Where "time is the essence" for writers such as Austin and Agee, both of whom are from a generation whose literary influences draw them close to the documentary impulse of the 1930s, time is essentially a nonissue for a writer like Jack Kerouac. After trying and failing to imitate his homeward-looking idol, Thomas Wolfe, Kerouac counteracts what John Tytell calls the "embalming insecurities" of the 1950s with a narrative dynamism of highway mimesis (12).

Kerouac's fiction, as well as the offerings of most of the Beat Generation, sustains Agee's iconoclastic vigor during an era whose icons are the "Molochs" of postwar global capital.[1] Kerouac, like Agee, has a bone to pick with the tendency to mark boundaries between poverty and privilege in America. As I will demonstrate below, Kerouac has a similar regional cosmopolitan sensibility to that of Agee. In his road novels, Kerouac blends the detachment of an affectionate invader of privacy and the regional pride of a rooted subject into a single narrative sensibility. He writes fiction that inhabits a cosmopolitan perspective based on what W. T. Lhamon terms the principle of "deliberate speed." Lhamon applies this phrase to a slate of artists who rebelled against the dualisms that Schlesinger describes in *The Vital Center.* Deliberate speeders are "always telling and denying a story, always catching and freeing a connection, encouraging and discouraging an interpretation" (*Deliberate,* 128). In this sense, they are similar to Agee, whose documentary prose is marked by attempts to subvert the reader's impulse to commit to an emotional response. The objective of both Agee and the speeder is to create a sense of space that resists a fixed set of relations. This resistance comes vis-à-vis what I'll call "delocalization," an approach to representing American terrain that sustains a sense of disorientation that actually blurs the boundaries of a continent otherwise racked by social and political attempts to polarize it.

Kerouac's narrators admire most Americans who represent multiple intersecting local affiliations: hobos with names like "Mississippi Gene," who have been "crossing and recrossing the country every year, . . . only because he had no place he could stay in without getting tired of it and because there was nowhere to go but everywhere, keep rolling under the stars, generally the Western stars" (*On the Road*, 26). Such "citizens" are attractive because they are incapable of shortsighted provincialism, incapable of mistaking a local condition for an essential condition. And it's this instability that the narrators of Kerouac's road novels take to the road to find. Sal Paradise, for instance, covets Mississippi Gene's transcontinental sensibility, because it is both patriotic and cosmopolitan. It is both an inventory of American places and a denial of the expectation that one be affiliated solely with one part of the country. Such is Kerouac's version of American freedom — a freedom from roots. Kerouac's solution to cultural polarity is thus to combine community building and flight into a single gesture — to engage in something like the mutual listening that Agee and his companion find in the back pages of *Praise* and light out for the territories at the same time.

The Beats are always popular, but Kerouac's style specifically has received a renaissance of interest in the past decade. Some of this interest has to do with the fiftieth anniversary of the publication of *On the Road* (1957), which occasioned such major critical works as John Leland's *Why Kerouac Matters* (2007) and such major publishing coups as the publication of *The Original Scroll* version of the novel's manuscript. In a more scholarly context, Kerouac's prose style is being taken seriously in ways that Kerouac himself, a great theorizer of his own prose style, may not have imagined. Kerouac's bilingualism and Canadian sensibility have become the subjects of serious study. Also, Kerouac's prose has been applied to certain fashionable Continental aesthetic theories.

For instance, Marco Abel's article, "Speeding across the Rhizome: Deleuze Meets Kerouac on the Road" (2002), compares Kerouac's sentences, his "lines of flight," to the aesthetic theory of Gilles Deleuze. According to Abel, *On the Road* "demarcates a new form of writing: not the slow, deliberate sentence of the dominant modernist tradition, but the speedy, visceral, combinatory, over-exuberant conjunction of words that form sentences radically different from their predecessors" (232). Such sentences indicate that Kerouac's technique of delocalization and Deleuze's concept of "minoritarian" politics share a goal: "to relate to other social assemblages not based on knowledge but [on] desire" (240). I agree with Abel's claim that Kerouac envisions a mode of connecting various tributaries of American culture through something other than suspect "knowledge" of these "minor" cultures. Ignorance is a virtue for Kerouac. It clears the way for visceral forms of contact. But rather than continue to point up the parallels between Kerouac's sensibility and Deleuze's "rhizomatic" ideal, I find it more productive to examine how Kerouac decouples local affiliations from identity and, in the process, reveals provincialism and cosmopolitanism to be kindred sensibilities.

In chapter 1, I examined Agee's method of exposing the dubious ethics through which documentary art elicits pity about poor people. Here, I will demonstrate how Kerouac replaces pity with admiration as the intuitive emotional response to such characters as shiftless hobos and migrant workers. Because Kerouac wants to represent the interconnectedness to the American continent, hobos and migrants are the natural heroes of his fiction. This elevation of downtrodden figures has led to much discussion of Kerouac's naïve essentialism, his slumming aesthetics, and his interest in "the road" as a source of idealized poverty. Consider Kerouac's career-long mantra: "Everything belongs to me because I am poor."[2] A generous reading of this mantra indicates that Kerouac sees cosmopolitan credentials as the reward for having abandoned local ties. This assumption that there is a wealthy kind of poverty—a poverty based on the freedom from local ties—has become one of the most enduring ethical problems critics have with *On the Road*. The novel's white narrator envies homeless orphans and likens himself to "an old Negro cotton-picker" and "a Mexican" in a span of three paragraphs (97–98). He also wires home for more money whenever he starts to actually suffer the systemic, ambient pain of such marginalized figures. The novel is thus dismissible. It fails to analyze itself as ethically problematic, fails to contribute anything but the most self-satisfied gesture in the direction of diversity.

However, by including naïve middle-class affections for the "less fortunate," Kerouac externalizes the very impulse to consume knowledge about poverty that Agee confronted. He makes this impulse something that is vulnerable to critique. Until recently, critique is all this impulse has received. Critics like Abel argue that we can do better as readers: "we need to ask questions different in kind from the ones that have been asked thus far. Instead of asking, 'How has Kerouac represented gender or race relations in his fiction?' we need to ask 'What kind of gender, race, or class relationships has he invented?'" (246). The short answer is that Kerouac has invented a narrative form for what Elaine Scarry refers to as the "weightless" subject position ("Difficulty," 105). Sal Paradise — whose name alone suggests a dematerialized space — achieves weightlessness through highway travel. This weightlessness allows an "alternative strategy [for achieving] equality between self and other." This strategy also knocks down the inequalities of identity not by "trying to make one's knowledge of others *as weighty as* one's self-knowledge, but by making one ignorant about oneself, and therefore *as weightless as* all others" (Scarry, "Difficulty," 105). The contrast between Kerouac's narrator's self-ignorance and Agee's weighty self-awareness sets up an aesthetic continuum in which regional cosmopolitanism registers in literary culture today.[3]

Below, I will examine the broader significance of Kerouac's calculated naïveté. In short, Kerouac's narrator's lack of "official" knowledge about impoverished and minority groups produces an inclusive form of cosmopolitanism. His narrators' ignorance is what allows Kerouac's vision of equal access continental citizenship to develop. Kerouac, who, according to Beat lore, was himself a bad driver, constructs a road novel whose narrator is a road-trip novice. In Sal's own words: "I'm not much of a driver" (13). Sal miscalculates at the navigational level. He misunderstands the granular dilemmas that accompany highway travel, dilemmas similar to those encountered by the Joad family. One of the consequences of Sal's navigational miscalculations is that *On the Road* represents movement west as indistinguishable from movement east. This directional confusion seems inconsequential. However, Sal's inability to know what direction he's heading in is a key component to the type of delocalization that Kerouac accomplishes. In subsequent sections, I will analyze "the road" as a key corresponding symbol to delocalization, arguing that Kerouac develops the road trope as a way of revealing the counterintuitive provincialism of expatriate modernism. Ultimately, Kerouac tries to reveal the contour lines that link the continent together. In the process, he both exposes the false polarity between provincial and cosmopolitan sensibilities in America and showcases what by today's standards is a naïvely liberatory politics of identity.

I

The setting of *On the Road* is no less than the entire North American continent. Kerouac directs the reader to "the immensity" of America (307).

Kerouac's expansiveness of setting allows him to test the elasticity of the network of interconnectedness between poverty and privilege in America. Thus Kerouac avoids the fixation on difference that usually motivates a writer to represent multiple cultural locations. Through sustained interest in the immensity and immediacy of American diversity, rather than a sustained interest in difference per se, Kerouac invents new relations among economic classes and racial groups, relations that amplify the resemblance among all things American.

In literary-historical terms, Kerouac's fiction dramatizes the decline of documentary protocols. Indeed, the Beat generation at large inhabits the inscrutable margins that encroach on Agee and his companion in the final pages of *Praise*. Kerouac peeks onto stable settings as infrequently and with as much diffidence as Agee attends to what's beyond the porch of his subject. For instance, at one point in *On the Road*, Sal sneaks into a "four-room shack" reminiscent of the Gudger house in *Praise*. Sal makes this slapdash observation: "There were no screens, just like in the song, 'The window she is broken and the rain she is coming in'" (99). He thus treats the shack, occupied by a family of migrant farmers in the San Joaquin valley, as a reference point for a popular song that traffics heavily in ethnic stereotypes: "Mañana" (1947) by Peggy Lee.[4] Doing this, Sal answers Agee's earnest encounter with rural poverty with the shallow, referential thinking of a mass-media-infused youth culture. Sal's comparison of the shack to the pop-song indicates his position as a middle-class white kid having his first real encounter with poverty. The irony is that Sal's reductivism is as earnest as Agee's complexity, perhaps more so, as Kerouac doesn't shy away from dramatizing the ubiquity of the dichotomizing cultural logic that Agee's prose tries so hard to dissolve.

In a nutshell, Kerouac's fiction is about getting away from the very complex zones of private pain that Agee obsessively inhabits. This agenda can be seen even in Kerouac's "Essentials of Spontaneous Prose," wherein Kerouac explains that the "image-object" used to "set up" the conditions for spontaneous prose should never take precedence over the thousand words of "sketching" that such images and objects inspire (72). Where Agee wants "the street *in its own terms*," Kerouac relishes the displacement offered by such paved means of flight. The difference between Agee's placement and Kerouac's displacement, then, is that the first affirms the material conditions of (or "localizes") material reality and the second sets itself in motion and never reestablishes an anchor to (or "delocalizes") a specific place.

No one place is permanently inhabitable for a narrator whose last name is "Paradise," a narrator who makes believe that he circulates freely above cultural divisions, never to be snagged by the details that spell the differences between people. This means that Sal's perspective often allows ignorance of cultural divisions, as in the scene of the migrant shack, ignorance of any civic duty he may have to repair such divisions. No corresponding economic need propels Sal to cross and recross the continent. His goal is simply to flee the cramped spaces, to liberate readers from the "either/or" approaches to poverty and privilege, even if this liberation leads to a blurred perspective on the material conditions of poverty.

For instance, the final paragraph of *On the Road*, one long sentence, demonstrates Kerouac's delocalizing narrative perspective and reasserts his argument that the goal is to by God keep moving:

> So in America when the sun goes down and I sit on the old broken-down river pier watching the long, long skies over New Jersey and sense all that raw land that rolls in one unbelievable huge bulge over to the West Coast, and all that road going, all the people dreaming in the immensity of it, and in Iowa I know by now the children must be crying in the land where they let the children cry, and tonight the stars'll be out, and don't you know that God is Pooh Bear? the evening star must be drooping and shedding her sparkler dims on the prairie, which is just before the coming of complete night that blesses the earth, darkens all rivers, cups the peaks and folds the final shore in, and nobody, nobody knows what's going to happen to anybody besides the forlorn rags of growing old, I think of Dean Moriarty, I even think of Old Dean Moriarty the father we never found, I think of Dean Moriarty. (307)

Here, Sal reflects on the melancholy experience of multiple transcontinental road trips. Beginning with the trite, ambitious introductory phrases, "So in America when the sun goes down," Kerouac shows Sal's enduring naïveté. The first half of the sentence is an accretion of prepositional phrases that indicates that Sal's seen much and absorbed little: "*in* America . . . *on* the old broken-down river pier . . . *over* New Jersey . . . *in* one unbelievable huge bulge *over* to the West Coast . . . *in* the immensity of it . . .

in Iowa . . . *in* the land where they let the children cry" (307, my italics). Taking this twilight inventory, Sal recaps the tension among being "in," "on," and "over" various geographical and topographical particularities, the tension that has driven the novel's forward action. The sentence speeds the imagination from the East Coast where Sal is to the West Coast where he has been, peeking down at the inland prairie regions, remarking with an air of wisdom that it is "the land where they let the children cry." In addition to being one of the least intuitive ways to finish the sentence "Iowa is the land where ______," this piece of acquired local knowledge evokes the image of children in mock pain, the pain of not going to bed early rather than the pain of going to bed hungry.

On the Road indulges such insatiable, childish pain. The knowledge of the country that this indulgence yields includes the fact that there are giant roadblocks (the size of Iowa) that shackle Sal and his friends to harsh, unpleasant responsibilities. Sal recoils from this standard moral, blurting out a half-formed, very nonstandard, rhetorical question: "don't you know that God is Pooh Bear?" This question, likely a ventriloquial consolation to the crying children of Iowa, stands in the place of the earnest discovery that Sal's travels were supposed to have yielded. Walter Kirn calls the Pooh Bear reference "as ugly a pimple on the ass as can be found in a famous American book." The fact that the Pooh reference was premeditated, not the involuntary blemish that one expects from spontaneity, means that Kerouac had a reason for planting the Pooh pimple.[5] He is speaking to America as though it were a child. "Complete night" arrives and "cups the peaks and folds the final shore in," covering the land the way one who is bidding a child goodnight might cover and tuck in a child's bed. This is the consolation (or punishment) for having traded one's roots for a delocalized sense of unity.

This particular paradigm for knowing America leads to Kerouac's interest in writing about surfaces, in representing the boundaries that separate one object from another. Kerouac's delocalized landscape is all surface; it changes shape and refracts different dimensions at the liberty of a beholder in motion. In short, to abandon local affiliations is not to abandon locale but to imagine the democratic availability of the surfaces that make up all places in America.

The novel's very title presupposes the road to be a kind of stabilizing surface, positioning (or "*pre*positioning") the reader to be "on" it. The road itself becomes a locative surface for Kerouac, as well as for many other midcentury American writers.[6] It is a kind of transcendent soil that makes the rest of America seem like a fluctuating mess. Only from the road is one properly placed to have any vision of America en masse. The road, then, as I discuss at length in section 3, is to post-Depression writers like Kerouac what the river is to post–Civil War writers like Mark Twain: a place from which to criticize the stagnant social mores of provincial America.

Whenever Sal momentarily drifts from the road, he gets profoundly disoriented. For instance, after waking up on the third day of his first journey west, Sal experiences an intense defamiliarization amid a commonplace motel setting. Sal describes this "one distinct time in my life" as follows:

> I didn't know who I was—I was far away from home, haunted and tired with travel, in a cheap hotel room I'd never seen, hearing the hiss of steam outside, and the creak of the old wood of the hotel, and footsteps upstairs, and all the sad sounds, and I looked at the cracked high ceiling and really didn't know who I was for about fifteen strange seconds. I wasn't scared; I was just somebody else . . . halfway across America, at the dividing line between the East of my youth and the West of my future. (15)

The silent panic of being alone among silence and privacy, the very private spaces Agee exposes to his reader, is precisely the kind of experience Sal systemically avoids. This moment of estrangement from himself is thematically similar to other midcentury models of alienation, the most influential of which being Jean Paul Sartre's *Nausea*.[7] As opposed to the heady estrangement of Sartre's narrator, Roquentin, Sal's estrangement comes from the simple fact that he's stopped moving. He attempts to retreat from this estrangement and reconnect with the delocalized identity that the road allows, the identity of the hitchhiker. In short, Kerouac begins his masterpiece with a pronounced flight from the uncanny self-realizations that come from sustained contact with a rooted affiliation.

This doesn't mean that Kerouac doesn't share Agee's regional cosmopolitan objective. As is evident even from the above passage, Kerouac explicitly confronts "dividing lines" head-on. The difference is that he chooses to think in spatial rather than interpersonal terms. He answers Agee's weighty meditation on dividing lines by flying weightlessly over them. In the following section, I will discuss the regional cosmopolitan sensibility through which Kerouac confronts the "dividing line." What makes

Kerouac's regional cosmopolitan sensibility distinct is its systemic denial of the authority of traditional urban centers.

II

As an episodic narrative whose significant episodes are set in both established urban centers (New York, Denver, and San Francisco) and Old West boomtowns (Central City and Cheyenne), *On the Road* enacts an equal-opportunity cosmopolitanism that refuses to recognize the hierarchy of American places. In fact, Kerouac's narrator is contemptuous of the urban East Coast, whose pretensions draw lines even between fellow New Yorkers. Sal gets belittled often by his "intellectual friends." Thus he is compelled to be in the shadows of such life forces as Dean Moriarty, whose massive appetite trumps big intellects. In short, Sal prefers instinct-driven frontier types to urban sophisticates. However, no matter how radiant his anti-urban prejudices become, Kerouac's hostility toward sophistication does not imply indifference toward the provincialism and moral hypocrisy of the commercial West. On the contrary, Kerouac criticizes all forms of shortsightedness and hypocrisy — and his own is so vulnerably presented as to be itself a source of criticism.

Sal's primary reason for leaving "the East of my youth" for "the West of my future" is to escape the cold and pervading culture of sophistication in New York (15). In the opening pages of the novel, Sal evokes a stark contrast between Dean, the embodiment of the West, and Sal's New York friends:

> All my other current friends were "intellectuals"— Chad the Nietzschean anthropologist, Carlo Marx and his nutty surrealist low-voiced serious staring talk, Old Bull Lee and his critical anti-everything drawl — or else they were slinking criminals like Elmer Hassel, with that hip sneer; Jane Lee the same, sprawled on the Oriental cover of her couch, sniffing at the *New Yorker*. But Dean's intelligence was every bit as formal and shining and complete, without the tedious intellectualness. And his "criminality" was not something that sulked and sneered. (7)

It is this "intellectualness" that Kerouac's narrative most resists, preferring instead an "intelligence" whose objective is comprehension rather than critique. Dean's covetousness of intellectualism reveals intellectualism as a sham, an insincere pose that can be learned and honed. Dean thus desires not a legitimate cosmopolitan sensibility but a set of tricks. What makes Dean different from Sal's New York friends is his lack of interest in winning arguments, or in even acknowledging disagreement. He is "the west wind" (7) both because he has no localized home — Dean "actually was born on the road"— and because he has no firm cultural ground to defend (1).

Dean understands that the moves of intellectualism can have a street value. He is enamored of sophistication —"a young jailkid all hung-up on the wonderful possibilities of becoming a real intellectual" (3–4). Dean thus easily learns to "talk in the tone and us[e] the words . . . that he had heard from 'real intellectuals,'" revealing mechanisms that legitimate the cultural authority of East Coast intellectuals. Because the onus is not on his ability to negotiate the interrelations among various incongruent sensibilities but on his ability to sound a certain way, Dean uses intellectual moves as though he were operating an automobile. Through Dean, Kerouac reveals New York cultural trusteeship as a form of provincialism, an affectation that needs "oriental covers" and *New Yorker* magazines in order to function properly. Dean is never indoctrinated as an East Coast intellectual; he merely adds its "terms and jargon" to the pastiche of gestures that passes for his personality (4). His initial allure is thus his ability to put the scavenged trappings of intellectualism to work. Devoid of self-reflection and beyond humiliation, Dean is a desirable alternative to Sal's New York friends. A road-wary trickster is especially desirable to a narrator who, as I will discuss in the following section, is ill prepared for the frequent snags of road travel.

By pointing up the provincial sensibility of traditional intellectualism, Kerouac attracts obvious criticism. His first, and most vehement, critic was Norman Podhoretz, who renounced Kerouac's fiction as an affront to New York intellectualism. In the essay "The Know-Nothing Bohemians" (1958), Podhoretz lambastes Kerouac and the rest of the Beats as philistines who are "hostile to civilization" and amenable only to "primitivism, instinct, energy, 'blood'" (307–308). As pushovers for "mystical doctrines, irrational philosophies, and left-wing Reichianism," the Beats have none of the discerning, intellectual rigor of either Podhoretz's cohort or previous generations of American bohemians (308). Podhoretz contrasts the Beats with the expatriate bohemians of the 1920s (who include Sherwood Anderson and Ernest Hemingway). The latter group is characterized by its "repudiation of the provinciality, philistinism, and moral hypocrisy of

American life" (307). Where the "typical literary figure of the 1920s was a Midwesterner . . . who had fled from his hometown to New York or Paris in search of a freer, more expansive, more enlightened way of life," the Beat bohemian does not have the least interest in running away from home (307).

I agree with Podhoretz that the Beats do not follow the standard trajectory of moving from provincial zones to cosmopolitan zones. However, the Beats are not anti-intellectual. Or, more accurately, what looks like anti-intellectualism is, in Kerouac's fiction at least, a valid exposure of the provincial allegiances traditionally known as the realm of disinterested intellectual culture. Kerouac avoids New York intellectualism by avoiding both New York and the smug postures that accompany its intellectual crowd. In so doing, he avoids the fallacy that cosmopolitanism has a home. As I will discuss in chapter 3, the bohemian generation that follows Kerouac does not avoid this fallacy.

As opposed to exclusive urban-centered cosmopolitanism, the cosmopolitanism Kerouac seeks is conversant with styles and spheres of interest that exist outside the city. Urban-centered cosmopolitanism consists of what Amanda Anderson calls "Arnoldian disinterestedness," a system of evaluative means that signify cultivation. This system stifles the "reciprocal intersubjective dimension" of cosmopolitan exchange. Such disinterestedness is cosmopolitan insofar as it allows for "transcendence of situatedness *tout court*." However, it is also "a highly particularized practice of taking one's distance from a specific set of conditions . . . through a cultivated posture of contemplation, calm, or aloofness." Aloofness is exactly what Sal hates about his New York friends. Aloofness is a symptom of exclusive cosmopolitanism, which involves "a neutral thinning out of affiliation." Inclusive cosmopolitanism, on the other hand, "embraces multiple affiliation, dialogue, and intercultural experience" (110). Kerouac's fiction promotes the latter. The exclusive cosmopolitanism does not interest Sal, because it leaves him incapable of intersubjectivity — the ability to experience a nearness to and the pain of another's interior state. The inclusive cosmopolitanism, on the other hand, allows Sal to feel at home anywhere within the diverse body politic of the American continent.

And Sal is very inclusive. He is excited to be around "mad" people, the very type of people that his New York friends dismiss as uncultured. His motivation is voyeuristic. Sal's observation of others encourages the behavior of "people who interest" him, as he has always "shambled after" them (5). He follows Dean Moriarty and Carlo Marx as they "danced down the streets like dingledodies," remarking that "the only people for me are the mad ones, the ones who are mad to live, mad to talk, mad to be saved, desirous of everything at the same time, the ones who never yawn or say a commonplace thing" (5–6). This naïve hero worship glorifies the very "madness" that eventually betrays Sal. But, considering that Sal mentions in the opening pages of the novel that Dean eventually "put[s] me down . . . on starving sidewalks and sickbeds," the hero worship takes a cautionary tone (8).

By the logic of Sal's cosmopolitanism, the goal is not to be "mad" but to be in the presence of madness. Ann Douglas argues that this brand of voyeurism is Kerouac's career-long goal. Kerouac wants "to record rather than precipitate, to watch the fabulous, divinely inexplicable doings of a world he never made" (*Dharma*, xi). His novels do function as a kind of documentary record, what Kerouac himself referred to as a "contemporary history record" (viii). But this record differs from documentary records in that Kerouac's subjects are uncommon. They neither "say a commonplace thing" nor care too much about the common places they inhabit. Due to this interest in uncommon subjects, Kerouac's relationship to locale might be considered an afterthought, especially since the manic living and omnivorous desire Kerouac admires exists in the city as well as on the frontier. But, as I will discuss in the following section, Kerouac is interested in locale to the extent that the road itself can be considered a locale.

III

In the first two sections, I examined the regional cosmopolitanism of Kerouac's narrative sensibility, a sensibility that affords Kerouac a rarefied view of the relationship of racial and economic difference to white privilege. In this section, I will examine the key symbol through which Kerouac connects the disparate pockets of American culture. In the opening sentences of the novel, the reader learns that Sal has "split up" with a wife he never again mentions. The reader also learns that Sal has "just gotten over a serious illness that . . . had something to do with the miserably weary split-up." This experience of being "split" is behind him. It is not part of the story Sal wants to tell. Sal intends to ignore that part of his story and tell "the part of my life you could call my life on the road" (1). This postbreakup road-trip format has become common in contemporary road narratives. William Least Heat-Moon's memoir *Blue Highways* (1983) comes to mind. But, where Least Heat-Moon uses a prenarrative split as an occasion to sample the scenic byways of America, Sal chooses the biggest, straightest thoroughfare on the preinterstate highway map (Least Heat-Moon 1).[8] He is not seeking solitude, but the shortest path to another identity.

Sal's expectations are a veritable index of the idealized conception of frontier mobility that he reads about in explorer tales and that he dreams of when he pores over maps of America. Sal plans to hitchhike west in a barrage of virile gusto. His plans get foiled the minute he makes contact with the "red line" of Route 6. The standard masculine mythos of the "open road" is thus nowhere to be found in the opening pages of *On the Road*. Instead, we find "the street *in its own terms*" (Agee, *Praise* 208). Route 6 is no mystic line; it is indifferent pavement. And Sal, who cannot weather the letdown, ends up on a bus with a delegation of schoolteachers. Sal thus begins his process of "discovering" the West by discovering that the West he had learned about in books does not exist. As I will examine in section 4, the actual midcentury West is shallowly and self-referentially nostalgic. This actual West threatens Sal's fantasy of himself and his gang as the inheritors of the "outcast" group identity made popular in nineteenth-century local color writing about the West.[9]

The other kind of nostalgia that Sal discovers in the West, which contrasts starkly with local color nostalgia, is a nostalgia for cosmopolitan masculinity à la Ernest Hemingway, the original "most interesting man in the world." Kerouac's critique of both frontier and modernist masculinity suggests that the goal of delocalization is to occupy neither type. Indeed, the goal is to never arrive at any stable identity. This goal is dramatized in Sal's frequent, random narrative reframings from specific sites and social situations to the immense omnipresence of a continent so vast as to blot out the drama of even the stickiest predicament. Sal's affection for the horizon, that locale that is always visible and never inhabitable, and his impersonations of flight — seen in such frantic non sequiturs as "Yes, zoom!" — are the effects of Kerouac's unique brand of regional cosmopolitanism (181).

Kerouac's objective is revealed through his narrator's initial misunderstanding of the road as an artery of effortless conveyance. Much like the Mississippi River in *Adventures of Huckleberry Finn*, the road in *On the*

Road becomes a terrain upon which the novel's narrator is allowed to experience the world unmediated by social codes.[10] It is a multifaceted terrain: a symbol of postwar America's freedom to circulate independent of agenda, a democratic thoroughfare that privileges private conveyance and public transportation alike (though the former more so than the latter), and the basic path of late 1940s intercontinental regional migration. It is also, as the successor of Huck's river, a symbol of infinity *and* propinquity, conceptually threading the disparate regions of the continent into some form of contact with one another. The road is a means of escape, a source of cultural literacy, a producer of community, and the approximate locale of the new New World sublime. Though Sal's road never becomes a utopic space, as Huck and Jim's river becomes, it facilitates Sal's learning experience, becoming the center of his burgeoning awareness of an America wherein local affiliations are disappearing.

But Kerouac does not simply replace the river with the road as the emblematic thoroughfare of escape. Sal's ignorance and idealization of the road contrasts with Huck's granular literacy of the river. Huck can "read" the river — predict its behavior and its capacity to facilitate clean escape. Sal has no such familiarity with the road. The opening pages of the novel demonstrate a disconnection between the abstractions of travel that Sal has gleaned from his cartographic research and his exposure to frontier lore and the actual pavement that he must carry himself across.

After "poring over maps of the United States" and "reading books about the pioneers," Sal falls in love with a "long red line called Route 6" (10). He decides he will hitchhike the entire length of the U.S. on this one road. But in order to get to Route 6 from his aunt's apartment in Paterson, New Jersey, Sal has to hitchhike north up the entire length of the Hudson Valley to the Peekskill Mountains. When he reaches Route 6, Sal finds it black, deserted, and awaiting a thunderstorm to come down Bear Mountain. A driver sees Sal standing dumbly on the side of the road and belches: "there's no traffic passes through 6" (11). This gruff bit of local knowledge punctuates Sal's colossal navigational error and his naïve romanticization of the "long red line." What he thought was a main artery of America is actually vacant blacktop whose origin in the East offers none of the brassy send-off he'd fantasized would score his departure. Defeated, Sal rides the bus back to New York. To add insult to injury, Kerouac puts him with "a delegation of schoolteachers" whose "chatter" makes him feel like a besieged schoolboy (11). This discomfiting initial experience with the road demotes it from being a *symbol.* It instead becomes a setting, the location of Sal's learning process.

Sal knows maps well and his love for the West is born of this knowledge. In Kerouac's hands, this type of knowledge of the American West is not a sign that Sal needs experience, nor an indication of the kind of experience that Sal will have. It is an indication of the kind of comprehension Sal prefers to glean from texts. Sal is a bad navigator not because he doesn't read atlases, but because he reads atlases for emotional and not semantic content. Like the great historian of American nomenclature, George R. Stewart, Sal is enamored of the names on the land.[11] For instance, when reading his maps and pioneer books in his aunt's apartment, Sal does not retain the information and explanations he finds in them. Instead, he commits to "savoring names like Platte and Cimarron" (10). Sal prepares himself for travel by learning the names of rivers, treating these names as though they have topographic contours.

This type of learning, which seems to miss the whole point of westward travel, creates the conditions for a regional-cosmopolitan form of patriotic sentiment. Sal's sentiment is tested when Roland Major, the novel's surrogate expatriate, invites Sal to savor Continental vistas: "Ah, Sal, if you could sit with me high in the Basque country with a cool bottle of Poignon Dix-neuf, then you'd know there are other things besides boxcars." Sal responds naïvely: "It's just that I love boxcars and I love to read the names on them like Missouri Pacific, Great Northern, Rock Island Line" (40–41). This declaration of love for the rail-line names stenciled onto boxcars, like the "savoring" of river names, bypasses the masculine ethos of traditional patriotism. He counteracts the territorializing efforts of the virile pioneers who moved West and erected a nation. Such efforts culminate for Sal not in specific places into which to sink unwavering commitments to local pride. Instead, the naming of the land culminates in an unprecedented poetic language.

Boxcars feature a delocalized type of place naming. The emotional resonance of the words on boxcars is derived not from pride in the place named but from the impulse of recognition that Sal experiences upon reading them. Sal passes much of America in a blur of highway travel. Boxcar language recounts and verifies the material reality of these blurs. The very scale of boxcar language, the size of its letters, likewise excites Sal. The largeness of the language presupposes a very broad readership. All of America is the intended audience of the phrases "Missouri Pacific, Great Northern, Rock Island Line." Boxcar language transforms the names of states into an unruly, shuffling index of words on an America-sized page. In this way, Sal answers the betrayal of the apartment roadmap by finding the living cartography of America, where the signifiers of place know no borders. Whereas the indifferent pavement at the foot of Bear Mountain was ominous and threatening, in the world of boxcars it is playful and inviting.

It also, somewhat absurdly, connotes a reader who is running parallel to the boxcars at equal speed. It calls to mind the childish impulse to put your arm out of a car window and imagine yourself released from inertia. Indeed, Sal and Dean share similar fantasies of their own childhood. Sal recounts the conversation, which takes place in the back of a moving car, as though it were a watershed moment in his friendship with Dean:

> Then I began talking; I never talked so much in all my life. I told Dean that when I was a kid and rode in cars I used to imagine I held a big scythe in my hand and cut down all the trees and posts and even sliced every hill that zoomed past the window. (208)

Dean describes a similar childhood fantasy. Indeed, this mutual experience is Dean's invitation to wax poetic about the abject poverty of his childhood, about "the time my father and I and a pisspoor bum from Larimer Street took a trip to Nebraska in the middle of the Depression to sell flyswatters." According to Dean, "my old man in those days was always singing 'Hallelujah, I'm a bum, bum again'" (208). These horrifying stories of Dean's impoverished childhood are reinterpreted in the backseat of the speeding car. In the same way that boxcar language liberates place names from their cartographic destiny, Dean's stories (horrifying as they are) liberate Depression-era poverty from its status as source of middle-class pity. Dean's childhood seems almost enviable.

Kerouac's inclusion of "Rock Island Line" in the list of boxcar names offers him a kind of symbolic continuity between the road and the rover. Earlier in the novel, when Sal first sees the Mississippi River, he is crossing from Rock Island, Illinois, to Davenport, Iowa. Sal notes, "for the first time in my life I saw my beloved Mississippi River, dry in the summer haze . . . with its big rank smell that smells like the raw body of America" (13). Sal assumes an automatic ownership of the river. He calls the river "my beloved." Kerouac here is expressing an ownership that indicates that Mississippi lore is necessary to the development of his new narrative form of "lighting out."[12] As the location of well-seasoned narratives of American freedom, the river represents that manifestation of liberty that, when applied to the road, dupes Sal from the start. Noticing its "big rank smell that smells like the raw body of America," Sal indicates that the river has become a memento mori (13). It is to be acknowledged and passed over. Thus Kerouac demonstrates a literary-historical perspective on the American landscape. In the following section, I will discuss how Kerouac represents his generation's feeling of having been betrayed by the way commercialized versions of New Deal–era public works ironize the grandeur of the West.

IV

In *On the Road*, Kerouac displays a frontier economy that has privatized the New Deal social and economic programs into free-market "revitalization" efforts. These efforts amount to unsavory consumer spectacles of repackaged frontier lore supplied by corporate-sponsored chambers of commerce.[13] This is not the rugged alternative to East Coast sophistication that Sal hoped he'd find in the West. As is always the case in Kerouac's world, the destination is less savory than the journey. Sal described his introduction to the West as "the greatest ride in my life," an all-night ride across the prairies of Nebraska on flatbed truck, under a tarpaulin with a band of fellow hitchhikers (22). The truck is driven by two fun-loving brothers whose job it is to annually transport farm machinery from Los Angeles to Minnesota. On their trips back, they habitually "picked up everybody on the road" (24). Everybody includes "farm boys" from Montana and North Dakota following the harvest and "city boys" from Ohio hitchhiking to L.A. for fun. Finally, there is Mississippi Gene, who is traveling with a silent blonde boy who "seemed to be running away from something" (23). Sal loves Gene, partially because he helps the boy run away from his trouble and partially because Gene is happily delocalized.

By "crossing and recrossing the country every year," Gene exemplifies Sal's ideal relationship to the American continent (26). Having "nowhere" and thus "everywhere" to be, Gene embodies Sal's desired local affiliation. As with the "Everything belongs to me because I am poor" mantra, Gene's condition of being everywhere because he has nowhere to be once again allows Kerouac to assert the wealth of the disenfranchised. This assertion is different from an assertion that makes Gene's poverty an ingrained part of who he is.

However, Sal does attach racial tags to Gene and thereby suggests that his status as a hobo is akin to the citizenship status of a disenfranchised racial minority. With no shortage of problematic connotations, Sal announces that there is "something of the wise and tired old Negro in him" (26). But this announcement is less a of a conflation of race and class than it looks. Considering the negation of place ("no place" and "nowhere") in Sal's description of Mississippi Gene's character, Sal's racialized description of Gene contributes to the delocalization of his identity. The "Mississippi" in Gene's name, like the "Negro" in Sal's description of his demeanor, is an empty signifier. It presumes to "locate" the distinguishing characteristic of one who has literally been in motion for years on end. More than any self-conscious region or self-conscious racial identity, Gene represents the ideally "wild," evasive figure that Sal hopes to find in the West. He finds him, instead, in the liminal space between the East and the West, on a flatbed that is simultaneously nowhere and everywhere.

Accordingly, Sal disapproves of what he finds in Cheyenne, a city that he arrives at during "Wild West Week":

> As the truck reached the outskirts of Cheyenne, we saw the high red lights of the local radio station, and suddenly we were bucking through a great crowd of people that poured along both sidewalks. . . . Big crowds of businessmen, fat businessmen in boots and ten-gallon hats, with their hefty wives in cowgirl attire, bustled and whoopeed on the wooden sidewalks of old Cheyenne; farther down were the long stringy boulevard lights of new downtown Cheyenne, but the celebration was focusing on Oldtown. Blank guns went off. The saloons were crowded to the sidewalk. (30)

Sal immediately recognizes "to what absurd devices [the West] had fallen to keep its proud tradition" (30).[14] The localizing devices are blatantly capitalist, contrasting with the federal programs of a decade earlier (à la the WPA State Guide series), whose localization techniques were designed to produce a living record of the region and thus to revitalize that portion of the body politic. The legions of FWP writers and artists who scoured the West in the 1930s have, by the time Sal reaches Cheyenne, disappeared and along with them the dream of social welfare. What replaces these writers and artists are "fat businessmen in boots and ten-gallon hats." In addition to their obviously vast political differences, the key difference between New Deal and free-market versions of revitalization lies in the audience's position in the production of regional identity. In theory, the audience and producer of WPA work are the same, since all WPA labor (that of the artist and of the bridge-builder alike) is the compensated procedural labor of autonomous community-building; everyone pays for revitalization and everyone is paid.[15]

The audience of Wild West Week, on the other hand, is a consumer. The irony is that these consumers constitute an autonomous community reproducing itself. Businessmen pool together into raucous crowds of money-spenders siphoning beer from Oldtown saloons. Their boots, ten-gallon hats, and wives in cowgirl attire produce the signs of the "Wild West." But they are not producers in the same sense that New Deal citizens are producers. They are barely even citizens, since their relation to the region (and by extension the nation) is mediated strictly by capital. They are in the West only insofar as they can purchase that fact. Local affiliations unmediated by capital are things of the past. In the present of the early 1940s, there are only the performances of prior models of affiliations. Being in the Wild West is a matter of participating in a special weeklong occasion, rather than of inhabiting a special place. Even the location of Wild West Week, in "Oldtown" rather than in the actual city center of 1940s Cheyenne, projects the city's "Western" identity into a spectral past. The businessmen like the saloons and the boots and the rest of it because they can afford to like these things, not because these things have any bearing on their identities as Cheyenneans.

The "Wild" of "Wild West Week" is thus sarcastic. When Sal remarks that the "fat burpers" are "wild as ever," he does not mean they are feral or uncultivated, but that they are temporarily unrestrained from their middle-class behavioral proprieties. Even Sal goes a little "wild," spending five of his remaining seven dollars to buy drinks for himself and Montana Slim. One is "wild" in Cheyenne to the degree that one can afford beer, just as one is "Western" to the degree that he can dress appropriately. Every condition is reduced from an expression of regional affiliation to a consumer transaction. For instance, when Slim hands Sal a postcard he's written to his "Paw," he makes the "strange request" that Sal "find a mailbox and put it in." It is clear from this strange request that, during Wild West Week, even intimate familial communication threatens to join the ranks of impersonal economic exchange. Sal finds Slim's handwritten note "tenderly polite" (33). When juxtaposed against the histrionic gestures that make up Wild West Week, this note acquires an aura of authenticity, the kind of honesty that is missing from the commercial West. Of course, this rare authenticity is found only on a type of surface (in this case a postcard) that is designed to travel cross-country. As with boxcar language, writing is once again represented as ambulatory, the one site of authentic expression in the West.

In short, the Wild West exists for Sal not in the West but on the flatbed truck that heads west over the prairie. In motion, "farm boys" and "city boys" alike yell back and forth stories of their misadventures in rural and urban America. Doing this storytelling while speeding west, these boys dramatize a frontier freedom that no longer exists. In setting their voices to the sound of highway travel, Kerouac delocalizes the personal narratives that make up the colorful characters that an easterner traditionally expects to find in the West. In the same way that place names on boxcars delocalize the boundaries that separate states, the place-based reminiscences of the hitchhikers delocalize the boundaries that separate the personal experiences that add up to an individual identity.

Unlike the businessmen in the geographical West, the flatbed boys have rich pasts and futures. Their stories are varied and are of a piece with Bret Harte's "outcasts of Poker Flat" and Willa Cather's Otto Fuchs. They are rough-and-tumble hired men with big scars and bigger hearts. They are the very Western types whom the fat businessmen ape in Cheyenne. But, in Kerouac's world, they are no longer anchored to their eponymous regions.

The West itself is no longer a recognizable region. It has been lost to private revitalization programs that sell frontier local color. Frontier fraternity and liberty, as exemplified by Mississippi Gene, have fled "the West." Even the stable signifiers of "Westernness" differ radically from Sal's preconception of the West. Chad King (a.k.a. Hal Chase) is described as *the* Western visage—"the beauty and grace of a Western hotshot who's danced in roadhouses and played a little football." Chad is also an anthropologist specializing in "Plains Indians" (36).[16] This ironic professionalization of the "Western hotshot" into one who studies, rather than violently subdues, Native Americans further exemplifies the disappearance of traditional local affiliations in the American West.

Even when Sal finally reaches his Denver cohort, it is thoroughly anti-rugged and stratified by a "war with social overtones" (37). The war is a petty status feud between those, like King and Major, who are gainfully employed and those "underground monsters" (that is, Dean and Carlo) who have nowhere to be (38). In the end, then, the idea that the West is still "wild" is replaced by the realization that the same petty polarities from which Sal fled exist also in Denver. This omnipresence of what is undesirable, as I will discuss in the following section, leads Kerouac to interrogate the forms of cosmopolitanism available to midcentury writers who want to expatriate themselves from modern capitalism. Kerouac provides his protagonist with two choices: bohemianism or Eurocentric modernism. In the following section, I will look closely at how Kerouac evokes the contrast between these two lines of flight from commercial realities. Ultimately, Kerouac demonstrates that the effort to parse the virtues and limitations of each alternative actually produces a new method of negotiating the ethnic and class divisions still haunting the American West (divisions that are obscured by a prevailing logic that designates the urban East as cosmopolitan and the frontier West as provincial).

V

Sal wants to be affiliated with bohemians because they are neither conspicuously attached to a place (that is, provincial), nor are they pretentiously worldly (that is, cosmopolitan). The problem is that his economic status establishes his affiliation within the "professional" stratum of the Denver gang. His first and most important interaction with another writer occurs within this stratum, with Roland Major, a pretentious Europhile. A naysayer of naïve bohemianism, Major embodies the exclusivity that Kerouac's narrative agenda so aggressively counteracts. A "Hemingwayan short story" writer trying to live a Parisian literary life in the coldwater flats of Denver, Major is a caricature of the wrong kind of cosmopolitanism. He refuses to allow unwashed Beats into his "swank apartment," preferring instead to savor old wine in the company of his own fictional creations (40). Sal's unflinching naïveté in his response to Major does not (nor is it designed to) convince the high-art aficionado to love boxcar language. Beat narratives never argue with a competing cultural sensibility. They only flail their tender illogic without blushing. This innocence, which in the presence of sophistication looks a lot like sophomoric amateurism, originates in Sal's defense against (rather than reaction to) sophistication. Major's brief but meaningful presence in the novel brings to the surface the mode of smug cosmopolitanism that Kerouac and the Beat movement at large all but eradicates from American letters.

Major's Eurocentrism allows him to make believe that he transcends situatedness. But situated in the American West, Major has to defend his cosmopolitan credentials against the fact that he looks pretty stupid trying to flaunt his discerning palate among hungry bohemians. He dons hyper-particularized postures of cultivation, calmness, and aloofness that deliberately disassociate him from the American West. As an expatriate marooned in Denver, writing stories about expatriates marooned in Denver, Major is simultaneously worldly and provincial in the attitudes through which he can express worldliness. He is the means through which Kerouac demonstrates how foolish cosmopolitan sensibilities look within contexts of actual community building.

Through Major, cosmopolitanism equals isolationism. He never lends a hand to the Denver group's attempts to produce a desirable world, preferring instead his bubble of fantasy. On a weekend trek to the mountains, Sal and the gang spend an evening with rich tourists watching Beethoven's opera *Fidelio* in a newly renovated opera house in Central City, Colorado. Central City is a former mining town turned ghost town that, like Oldtown in Cheyenne, the "Chamber of Commerce types of the new West [have] decided to revive." Walking to the opera house, Major lights up. He declares to Sal, "just look at this old town. Think how it was a hundred ... eighty, sixty years ago; they had opera!" (51) Major doesn't see the renewal efforts that have gone into producing opera in Central City. Sal, on the other hand, knows corporate revitalization when he sees it and has learned how to see contemporary America without pining for the past.

Kerouac dramatizes the cultural agency of the Beat generation in direct contrast to Major's stationary connoisseurship. After the opera, Sal gets busy transforming a "miner's shack" into a suitable party locale (52):

> I took off my duds and joined the boys in the cleaning. It was an enormous job. Roland Major sat in the middle of the front room that had already been cleaned and refused to help. On a little table in front of him he had his bottle of beer and his glass. As we rushed around with buck-

ets of water and brooms he reminisced. "Ah, if you could just come with me sometime and drink Cinzano and hear the musicians of Bandol, then you'd be living. Then there's Normandy in the summers, the sabots, the fine old Calvados. Come on, Sam," he said to his invisible pal. "Take the wine out of the water and let's see if it got cold enough while we fished." Straight out of Hemingway, it was. (52–53)

This scene exposes Major's inflexibility alongside bohemian adaptability. Major's sophistication is finally shown to be parasitic, a snobbish posturing that is reducible to childish petulance. His vision of the past is composed in the very space cleared by the labor of those whom Major discredits as cultural know-nothings. Stationary amid hurrying buckets and brooms, Major muses about "Cinzano," "sabots," and "Calvados." His proclivity for these European liquors (Cinzano is a brand of Italian vermouth, and Calvados is an apple brandy from the French region of the same name) is represented here as a nuisance in the work of actual community building. Eurocentric local knowledge thus becomes impractical bric-a-brac at the dawn of the Beat generation.

Even the footwear to which Major alludes is impractical. Sabots are wooden shoes worn over other footwear for the purpose of navigating sodden ground. This reference calls to mind the shoe choice Sal makes when he first goes on the road: cloth huaraches, which Sal admits were "not fit for the rainy night of America and the raw road night" (11). Both Sal and Major have conspicuous affinity for the footwear of cultures not their own, a shared interest in transcending their respective affiliations via physical points of contact: their feet. But Major's European shoes contrast with Sal's Mexican shoes. Where sabots would be strictly ornamental in the paved world of *On the Road*, would in fact prohibit foot travel or hitchhiking, huaraches are designed for foot travel. Both Major and Sal acculturate based on tenuous affection for cultures they exoticize. However, Sal's relationship with his Mexican shoes does not proceed without levity. When lampooned by his flatbed brethren, Sal concurs that "they were the silliest shoes in America." But at least Sal has a utilitarian excuse for his otherwise exoticist interest in Mexican footwear: "I didn't want my feet to sweat in the hot road" (27). Sal's acculturation is always in the service of movement. Major's affection for Europe, on the other hand, is strictly nostalgic and static: "Straight out of Hemingway, it was," Sal says of Major's one-man show of companionship (53).

Major's efforts to imagine himself as a deracinated Hemingway seem to have more of a demonstrable conclusion than does the Central City party. However, the party does have a cultural function. Because it is not governed by the principles of Major's retrogressive musings and because it is not aimed at any preconceived forms of socialization, the party renders the principles that govern "partying" indistinguishable from the particularities of the experience that lets one know he is at a "party." For instance, Sal observes that "there was no music, just dancing. The place filled up. People began to bring bottles" (53). By dancing without music, the partiers initiate an action normally considered to be re-action to some external stimulation, some music. Though it sounds like I'm making too much of a seemingly throwaway observation, dancing without music is actually a dramatization of the delocalized identity Sal craves. The dancers are a group that inhabits makeshift spaces of its own creation. The group *wills* action into being before there is any legislating form to regulate the gestural limits of the action.

Like the novel itself, the party divorces itself from cultural precedents. In contrast to Major's reminiscences, which feature "musicians of Bandol" and specific kinds of alcohol, Sal's party has no musical forms to regulate its dancers' moves. It is also freed of other specifics; Kerouac obscures the nature of the libations and the attendants into "bottles" and "people." Even the miner's shack itself disappears as a localizing force — it is the "night" that gets "more and more frantic," not any specific place (53–54).

But all parties have their problems. Though the miner's shack party delocalizes its members and expels nostalgic cultural postures from the novel, it also eclipses the labor of its own creation. As everything drifts into the abstract (anonymous "people," "bottles" of nonspecific alcohol, undetermined dancing, the "night"), Sal gets seized by the same crippling failure of perception that set upon him during his disastrous first encounter with the abstract "red line" of Route 6. As a space of pure celebration, the mining shack is disorienting. In much the same mood as the realization that Route 6 is made up of crude materials that don't correspond to his excitement about it, Sal realizes that the party is "a great big fraternity-type party . . . with banging of beerbottles and roars." In other words, what started as sublime has become ridiculous. Teenage opera-house ushers showed up and "just grabbed girls and kissed them without proper come-ons." The life of Central City itself gets anthropomorphized in a bawdy epicurean with an ironically localized name: Denver D. Doll. He greets everyone with the same well wishes, "Merry Christmas" and "Happy New Year, m'boy" (though it is summer) (54). These greetings conflate all types of celebration into one cosmic holiday party. Though it seems like Sal should welcome the delocalization of the concept of partying, Denver D. Doll and the ushers rope Sal back from the ideal. They reassert a central theme of the novel, that the labor of production, or the journey to the goal, is more valuable than the product. Once the party gets made, it offers no pleasure.

Kerouac's reason for subverting Sal's good time in the West is clear here in a way that it isn't in the Bear Mountain episode. The party fouls of Denver D. Doll and the ushers remind Sal to never take root. The Central City party amounts to little more than a reminder that Sal is an ambivalent member of a privileged class, a class that inhabits impoverished shacks for fun. This reminder is more troubling than the previous reality check. At the foot of Bear Mountain, Sal at least looks like a child of crisis, despite the fact that he can afford to (and does) take a bus to Chicago when things get too tough. In Cheyenne, Sal is an indignant observer of a touristic spectacle. As a reaction, Sal tries to adopt the perspective of the "Indians," on the side streets of Oldtown, "who watched everything with their stony eyes" (33). But in Central City, Sal can't help but see himself as one of the fat businessmen. Having rejected Major's cosmopolitan blinders, Kerouac's narrator has nowhere to retreat to when an unwanted reminder of his class privilege appears. Just as Sal's metonymic self-alignment with his favorite children of crisis — the migrant Mexicans whose shoes he wears and the stoic Native Americans whose eyes he shares — is an appropriation, the "heroic" transformation of the miner's shack is another capitalist renovation. It only serves those who are entitled to circulate to and from America's sites of poverty. In other words, Kerouac recognizes the complicity between post–New Deal capitalist revitalizations and his own self-interested document of vast America.

This recognition is obviously disconcerting, as it means that social justice is to some degree impossible. Regional cosmopolitanism here, at the witching hour in Central City, seems to be an unrealizable fantasy. Indeed, in the same year that *On the Road* is published, Kenneth Rexroth issues an argument that the only way to transcend cultural polarization in the U.S. is not to delocalize but to "disaffiliate." Rexroth's article, "Disengagement: The Art of the Beat Generation," defines disaffiliation as a process of "divorce" from U.S. civic life (35). As exemplified by Rexroth, an elder Beat who had actually worked for the Federal Writers' Project, the disaffiliated artist is not delocalized but relocalized. His identity is the result of a deep provincialization of the Bay Area. (I discuss Rexroth's provincialism at length in chapter 3.)

When Sal finally finds the West in the closing pages of part 1, 365 miles from his aunt's home in Paterson, New Jersey, he meets "the Ghost of the Susquehanna." An eccentric old white man walking west along the Susquehanna river, the ghost of the Susquehanna insists that he is walking east and that he is "headed for 'Canady'" (104). The ghost is "a semi-respectable walking hobo," a demystified old man (104). In this sense, he stands in stark contrast to the mystical old men — the Beat versions of Beethoven's Florestan — whom Sal imagines in Central City.[17] He is not demonstrating some mystic truth by walking in the opposite direction of his proposed destination. He is simply confused about which direction he is traveling, and his remarks enter into the story not as wisdom but as miscalculation. Sal names him "ghost" because the man haunts "the entire Eastern Wilderness on foot" (104). Sal and his traveling companion try to explain to the "ghost" that he is heading the wrong way. But the old man's confusion is never corrected. Instead, the ghost corrects Sal's misconception that "all the wilderness of America was in the West" (105):

> No, there is a wilderness in the East; it's the same wilderness Ben Franklin plodded in the oxcart days when he was postmaster, the same as it was when George Washington was a wildbuck Indian-fighter, when Daniel Boone told stories by Pennsylvania lamps and promised to find the Gap, when Bradford built his road and men whooped her up in log cabins. (105)

What his dealings with the Ghost of the Susquehanna bring into focus is the fact that there is as much American wilderness in Sal's own backyard as there is in the West, maybe more. The differences Kerouac draws between the East and West at the beginning of the novel thus disappear by the end of part 1. On the flatbed to Cheyenne, Sal learns that Western freedom is no longer a feature of the West but of movement west. Here Sal learns that historical richness and wilderness is a feature of the East.

The basic lesson of Sal's misunderstanding of the West still holds significance. The West still functions as an almost prelinguistic terrain, or space whose scale of signification (that is, whose boxcar-sized letters) corresponds to an in-progress mythology rather than to a bound volume of history. The East, on the other hand, is storied to capacity, crowded with the great names of America's founding. Unlike the monumental, serious names and place names of the East, the West is made up of nouns that — like the place names on the sides of boxcars — move like verbs.

The point of closing the first part of *On the Road* with the Ghost of the Susquehanna is to reaffirm the central lessons of delocalization: (1) rote memory must give way to lived experience, and (2) local knowledge must come from interaction with locales rather than from official knowledge about them. When one gets out of a car and walks around, the elemental differences between "East" and "West" start to disappear. Even historical narratives change. The cast of heroes remains the same, but Washington and Franklin live in a wilderness far from the locations of their historical feats. Thusly dislocated, these founding fathers become virile youths. In short, Kerouac closes the first part of *On the Road* with an appeal to a patrilineal mythopoesis, or the cast of old-boy American mythmakers (Franklin, Washington, Boone) as young men. No matter how much progress Kerouac makes in the direction of delocalizing American identity, indeed how much his style predicates such a new imagination, his achievements at the level of style are always undone by the very localizing assumption that he, the youthful male writer, is always already at the center of America.

Regardless of how effective any argument about Kerouac's blunted multicultural message might be, Kerouac will never be read under the rubric of "multicultural fiction." For some reason, and that reason is the subject of chapter 3, Kerouac's idealism regarding delocalization is so naïve that we can't look past its failures to be smarter about race and gender. We can't see Sal's declaration that "I'm a Mexican" as carrying any significance beyond that of fetishism and appropriation. We can't believe that a white male writer so interested in seizing the compass points of America might have helped imagine nonformulaic models for representing multicultural experience. At least not until Maxine Hong Kingston teaches us how to, in 1989.

Both the content of Kerouac's personal politics and the content of his fiction have a lot of irresolvable problems. But one masculinist problem that Kerouac does not have is the enterprising use of place for "richness" and stability, place as a setting through which to pilot a "soul search." Because the Kerouac who wrote *On the Road* preferred bohemian collectivity to individuality, all local knowledge is filtered through a desire for what Deleuze calls a "collective assemblage of enunciation"— a howl from a flatbed truck full of boys stripped of their stable identities and speeding across the Great Plains at night (*Kafka*, 18). As a metaphor of Kerouac's very style of writing, the moving community symbolizes a weightless syntax, free from the inertia of local decisions and revisions. Just as the flatbed howlers transgress the boundaries between counties and states, the words on the page of *On the Road* seem governed by a law of grammar that has been modified by the aesthetic of deliberate speed. Its utterance along lines of flight vibrates with a disobedience that transcends the boundaries among identity categories. In the final section, I will examine the way in which Kerouac's regional cosmopolitanism is foiled by his naïve identity politics.

VI

It goes without saying that the communal dynamic in *On the Road* is homosocial. Indeed, much of the production of Beat literature is done in (or in hopes of) an all-male community. The Beats seek a version of literary bohemia that protects its members from the polarizing heteronormativity of the Cold War. The Beat version of literary bohemia is thus a paradox: it is both progressive and all male. The "progress" that the Beats seek, at the expense of an equal distribution of gender representation, is an alternative to New York City literary trusteeship. The motivation for homosocial bohemianism is to get away from what Michael Davidson calls the "pressures of East Coast sophistication and privilege" more than it is to get away from women (*Guys*, 86). The Beat literary movement is inspired primarily by an interest in fleeing the main infrastructure of cultural polarity in American letters. This interest highlights the gender exclusivity notable in Kerouac. The homosocial component of Beat literature explains a lot about the methods through which a midcentury literary movement disassociates from the legitimating forces of its literary engines. Much as Agee had to abandon the confines of *Fortune* before he could develop his regional cosmopolitan sensibility, Kerouac and the Beats needed to enact the masculine master-narrative of fleeing "sivilization" (that is, New York) before they could produce a communal form of depolarization.

However, Beat bohemia leads to infighting. Bohemianism operates according to a group dynamic that replaces individuality with togetherness. Kerouac, who often lived an isolated and somewhat monastic life, eventually rejects this doctrine of togetherness.[18] David Savran claims that the togetherness doctrine creates a "bifurcated evolution of the white hipster" (4). The typical Beat persona is a "divided self" (41). He "is at once a victim of the repressive and conformist society of which he is a part and a potentially violent, if directionless, opponent of that society" (49). This divided self, Savran claims, is "godfather" to both 1960s revolutionaries and current reactionary partisans of the so-called Patriot movement (4). Lee Siegel clumsily attempts to make a similar point in his article "The Beat Generation and the Tea Party" (2010).

Normal Mailer's essay, "The White Negro" (1957), attests to the accuracy of Savran's perspective. According to Mailer, the Beat-inflected hipster is best characterized as "equally a candidate for the most reactionary and most radical of movements." Mailer's prediction proves true; in the 1960s, Kerouac becomes a reactionary creep and Ginsberg a flower child. In this sense, it seems that the process of detaching from the polarizing force of New York literary institutions creates its own form of polarization. Indeed, as Kingston will demonstrate, the Beat project of creating a bohemian social group is doomed to reinforce a cosmopolitan/provincial polarity through which naïve relations to ethnic and class difference continue to plague both ends.

As the frenetic counterpart to the "organization man," the Beat bohemian joins up with other like minds, loses individuality, and increases mobility. Like the organization man, the bohemian has the kinds of relationships and does the kinds of work that are essentially "interchangeable." He is part of the emerging subjectivity that most confounds Jane Jacobs in her opus, *The Death and Life of Great American Cities* (1961):

> There are people who seemingly can behave like interchangeable statistics and take up in a different place exactly where they left off, but they must belong to one of our fairly homogeneous and ingrown nomad

> societies, like Beatniks, or Regular Army officers and their families, or the peripatetic junior executive families of suburbia. (178)

Being free from local affiliations, Beatniks circulate to whatever locale accommodates their "work." But, as I'll discuss in the next chapter, homosocial bohemianism requires an urban base—and the base becomes San Francisco. In other words, the West Coast manifestation of the Beat movement translates Kerouac's combined denial of aloof sophistication and embrace of group identity into a bohemianism that overcomes New York provincialism by asserting a competing form of provincialism.

It was the fantastic drowse and drum hum of lum mum afternoon nathin' to do, ole Frisco with end of land sadness — the people — the alley full of trucks and cars of businesses nearabouts and nobody knew or far from cared who I was all my life three thousand five hundred miles from birth-O opened up and at last belonged to me in Great America.
— Jack Kerouac, "The Railroad Earth"

San Francisco has become an Asian city. To speak, therefore, of San Francisco as land's end is to betray parochialism.
— Richard Rodriguez, "Late Victorians"

THREE

The Chinatown and the City

Maxine Hong Kingston and the Relocalization of San Francisco

Maxine Hong Kingston is widely considered to be a pivotal figure in what Yunte Huang calls the "multicultural recanonization" of American literature (142). Her memoirs, *The Woman Warrior* (1976) and *China Men* (1980), are regularly read both in and out of academic settings. They have received scores of scholarly articles and major national awards.[1] Less attention and fewer accolades have been paid to Kingston's fiction. Part of the reason is that Kingston has written only one novel, *Tripmaster Monkey: His Fake Book*.[2] Another part of the reason is that this novel seems to be too radical a departure from the subject and sensibility of her memoirs for readers to place its significance among Kingston's other work. However, Kingston's novel explicitly dramatizes the interaction between canonical and multicultural literature.

Kingston claims to have written *Tripmaster Monkey* in order to explore this question: "what use is a liberal arts education?" (quoted in Skenazy, "Kingston," 140). This question seems to differ from the questions she explores in her memoirs, questions about the role of Chinese cultural knowledge in the production of American history. Whereas Kingston's memoirs uncover the Chinese immigrant's role in the production of American history, her novel explores the role of canonical literary knowledge in the production of art that gets labeled "Chinese American." To some readers, *Tripmaster Monkey* kowtows to highbrow literacy. However, this literacy is part of her protagonist's "fake book," his freestyle method of middling highbrow literary knowledge, making it useful for a Chinese American writer with countercultural ambitions. Her protagonist's very name, Wittman Ah Sing, is a repurposing of literary knowledge, a set of allusions that exceeds the sum of its parts. Wittman yearns to make literature that is useful. Specifically, he wants his literary knowledge to help him both remake himself and reclaim the city of San Francisco from the know-nothing bohemians that flooded it in the 1960s.

What is inspiring about *Tripmaster Monkey* is the way Kingston injects literary value into such neglected urban spaces as the San Francisco Tenderloin, answering the question "what use is a liberal arts education?" with a demonstration of the capacity of literary knowledge to enrich a city-dweller's encounters with public space. But Kingston's intentions are not entirely altruistic. She also uses her novel to settle an old score. *Tripmaster Monkey* is set in the very milieu into which Kingston came of age as a writer (early 1960s San Francisco) and follows Wittman, a Berkeley-trained "Chinese Beatnik," as he confronts the barriers that Bay Area bohemians have placed between themselves and the ethnic diversity and urban materiality of "the City" (82).[3] Kingston's San Francisco is overrun by bohemians whose allegiance is not to the City but to the foggy haze of community that has been left behind by the frenetic cultural sensibility of the Beat generation. Through such fog, San Francisco's ethnic diversity appears to be little more than colorful wallpaper on a city-sized rumpus room.

But Kingston's satiric representation of bohemian life in the early 1960s is not a postmodern reaffirmation of Norman Podhoretz's argument in "The Know-Nothing Bohemians." Instead, Kingston's satire is affectionate, delivered in a spirit that rescues the liberatory potential of the very road novels that inspired the bohemian migration west. In fact, *Tripmaster Monkey* affirms the narrative sensibility found in Kerouac's earliest fiction, the sensibility I referred to in chapter 2 as "delocalization." This sensibility is lost on the San Francisco Renaissance. Instead of emphasizing the interchangeability of urban experience, Renaissance practitioners simply transcend (that is, ignore) the multiethnic urban realities of the City. From Kingston's point of view, this transcendence equals an erasure, a segregation tactic. *Tripmaster Monkey* thus rescues Kerouac's narrative sensibility in order to counteract the provincialism of his followers.

An example of Kingston's satiric representation of bohemian provincialism occurs at, of all places, an LSD party. As Wittman admires some "cat" for asking an apropos multicultural question —"How do you reconcile unity and identity?"— and strokes his Fu Manchu, he is interrupted by a "hippy girl" who marvels loudly at his epicanthic fold (105). Shocked to find himself suddenly an "anthro specimen," Wittman slouches away from the conversation, the sad "Homo epicanthus" of the bohemian scene (106). In this small episode, Kingston satirizes the oscillation between the abstract universalism of bohemian ideals and the ethnocentric particularism of bohemians' actual encounters with racial difference.[4] As the asker expands the horizon of inquiry, the tripper closes in on Wittman, making his racial markings into a liability. Joined in this way, the asker's question and the tripper's observation illustrate the crude identity politics of bohemian provincialism.

This unintentionally racist form of provincialism, the target of many such sardonic vignettes, contrasts against the provincialism of East Coast intellectuals, a provincialism that has always been anti–West Coast. Indeed, New York's literary gatekeepers have been taking shots at "California writers" ever since Edmund Wilson wrote *Boys in the Back Room* (1941). In that monograph, Wilson weighs the California literary scene and finds it wanting: "All visitors . . . know the strange *spell of unreality* which seems to make human experience on the [West] Coast as hollow as the life of a troll-nest where *everything is out in the open instead of being underground*" (57, my italics). Wilson's accusation that the West Coast has no "underground" becomes his denial that California has any real cultural depth.

Kenneth Rexroth, a famous hater of East Coast cultural trusteeship, ironically agrees with Wilson. California *is* depthless, and it is this lack of depth, this fact that (in Rexroth's words) there is "nothing underground about" San Francisco, that makes the City a prime spot for a literary rebirth. The City offers refuge from the "dense crust of custom" under which such cities as New York produce their art ("San Francisco," 179). As Rexroth explains in his afterword to Frank Norris's famous "story of San Francisco," *McTeague* (1899), the City is "spared the westward radiation of the great light from Plymouth Rock" (Afterword, 347). Like the lost generation who followed Stein and Toklas (two Bay Area natives) into their Paris salon, Rexroth tries to exile himself from the American cultural history. The difference is that Rexroth tries to take San Francisco with him. He confesses that, if it were not for the City's special status as a virtually non-American territory, he "would leave the United States for someplace like Aix en Provence — so fast!" To further the international zone analogy, Rexroth claims that he feels like he "ought to get a passport every time [he crosses] the Bay to Oakland or Berkeley" ("San Francisco," 180). In other words, Gertrude Stein was right: "There is no there there."[5] Hence, an insular Renaissance is erected as a defense against the nothingness that lies beyond the Bay Bridge.

Rexroth began developing this provincial logic while working for the Federal Writers' Project. During his tenure with the FWP, Rexroth wrote an essay titled "The Possibilities of an Intelligent Regionalism in California," which argues that regionally self-aware art breeds dynamic democratic citizens. Rexroth biographer Linda Hamalian cites this argument as the spark of the "Whitmanian" regionalism that would act as a governing principle of the Renaissance. In his review of *Leaves of Grass*, Rexroth applauds Whitman's ability to find "cosmogony under his heel" (quoted in Hamalian, "Regionalism," 220). This universalization of the particular, this looking at specific soil and thinking about the cosmos, is what Rexroth calls San Francisco Renaissance poets to do. Michael Davidson affirms this universalizing principle when he acknowledges that the subject of San Francisco Renaissance art is "the ground of numinous presence," rather than the ground of urban materiality (quoted in Hamalian, "Regionalism," 222). It is this irreversible leap from the specific to the universal that makes possible the bohemian provincialism that so plagues Wittman Ah Sing, if not also Kingston.

As Rexroth and company find cosmogony under their heels, Chinese American writers find Rexroth on the toes of their literary moment. In response to the universalization of the local, these writers turn to the gritty specificity of San Francisco's Chinatown. As Elizabeth Wheeler claims, with Chinatown comes a "diaspora [*sic*] sense of place" wherein "'home' [is] triangulated among multiple sites" (177). This is the minority response to the cosmic provincialism of Rexroth's cosmogony. In this sense, then, the Chinese American fiction that grows separately from but equally to official San Francisco Renaissance literature is actually more "numinous" than San Francisco Renaissance poetry, as it represents a social space that contains more than one reality. Chinatown is China and America at once. It involves (in novels from Louis Chu to Fae Myenne Ng) multigenerational negotiations of the immigrant's relations to American social space.[6] More importantly, these multiple intersecting senses of place, when embodied in a single text, provide a point of view that grounds a rootless subjectivity in a specific place.

In this chapter, I will examine the way Kingston realizes this delocalizing potential in her fiction. Specifically, I will show how her novel engages the street-level confluences and incongruities of urban space. Surprisingly, Kingston suggests that it is Kerouac who best models a sense of place that encompasses multicultural realities. Versifying an obscure passage from his first novel, *The Town and the City* (1950), Kingston evokes Kerouac's ingenuity and his insensitivity at the same time. She uses this paradox to counteract the contradictions of bohemian provincialism. On its face, the Kerouac passage is notable for its rapid-fire racial slurs. Its presence in *Tripmaster Monkey* thus appears to be Kingston's invitation for readers to condemn Kerouac, as Wittman himself does—"Fuck Kerouac and his American road anyway" (70). However, Kingston's use of the passage is part of a complex referential logic, a logic (as I discuss in section 3) that allows Kingston both to reclaim the urban hues of San Francisco and to dramatize her position within the renewal of the American canon. In section 4, I will discuss some of the objections to Kingston's novel, if not also to her place in the American canon. These objections range from Asian American writers who feel that Kingston is an accommodationist to academics who feel that Kingston's performance of literary knowledge is a betrayal of the "ethnic memory" she explores in her memoirs.[7] What these two objections overlook is the fact that *Tripmaster Monkey* restores transpacific, cosmopolitan realities to San Francisco. In the first section, I will demonstrate how Kingston involves Kerouac in this restoration.

I

By limiting the application of Wittman's literary knowledge to one city, Kingston revisits a tension between moving and settling that Kerouac never resolved. In *On the Road*, Sal goes crazy every time he has to stay in one place for too long, especially when that place is San Francisco. For Kerouac, San Francisco represents an "end of land sadness" about which his roving narrators must be wary (Kerouac, "Railroad Earth," 659). For instance, in *On the Road*, while rooming with Remi Boncoeur for ten weeks, Sal becomes a sociopath. He fantasizes about shooting out jewelry store windows or frightening "queers" in "bar johns" with his night watchman's pistol (73).

Kingston satirizes this madness born of settling in the opening sentence of *Tripmaster Monkey*: "Maybe it comes from living in San Francisco, city of clammy humors and foghorns that warn and warn — omen, o-o-men, o dolorous omen, o dolors of omens — and not enough sun, but Wittman Ah Sing considered suicide every day" (3). This grey atmosphere evokes the classic ennui of the urban flâneur. The sounding "o men" of the foghorn hints that such suicidal languor is conspicuously masculine. Under the weight of these classic dolors, Wittman's brain wants to "fly far apart in the scattered universe" (3). These suicidal tendencies are common to the male protagonists of city-set fiction. But Kingston's abrupt violent imagery evokes the somatic presence of Wittman's troubled brain. Wittman's suicidal impulses establish his carnality rather than his brooding invisibility. Readers are introduced to his "blood, meat, disgusting brains, mind guts" before we are introduced to his "skin arrangements" (Wittman's term for racial status) (3, 11).

In his suicidal state, Wittman ponders the Golden Gate Bridge. He recalls the suicides he has watched there. They all "take the side of the bridge that faces land. And the City. The last city. Feet first." Wittman decides that if he jumps, he will "face the sea. And the setting sun. Dive" (4). This commitment to the sea instead of to the "last city" signifies Wittman's refusal to credit "end of land sadness" (Kerouac's phrase, repeated often in his San Francisco sketch, "The Railroad Earth") for his suicidal tendencies. Indeed, in Kingston's hands, San Francisco is not the last city of bohemian migration. It is the first city of Asian America.

One of the peculiarities of living on such contested terrain is the literary "airs" of everyday life: "The air of the City is so filled with poems, you have to fight becoming imbued with the general romanza." Wittman's romanza is, in chapter 1, aimed at Nanci, a former classmate and fellow Chinese American, a girl with "a leotard and tights like an old-fashioned Beat chick." Wittman fantasizes about "the two of them making the scene on the Beach, like cruising in the gone Kerouac time of yore." This fantasy gets interrupted when Wittman starts to try to impress Nanci. He takes her to a paperback bookstore, a fictionalization of City Lights. He hopes that among its "homemade books, . . . mimeo jobs, stencils, and small-press poetry that fit neat in the hand" Nanci will discover the copy of his one-act that he snuck onto the shelves (20). Nanci doesn't notice it. Next, he takes her to his apartment and reads her some of his poems. He throws a fit when she tells him he sounds "like a Black poet. Jive. Slang. Like LeRoi Jones. Like . . . like Black" (ellipses in original). This evaluation of his work enrages Wittman. He fires back: "Monkey see, monkey do?"— angry that he is not allowed to express urban realities of the City without being labeled "Black" (32).

In this spirit of rejection and isolation, after he gets fired from his department store job for having displayed a Barbie doll and a toy monkey in a compromising position, Wittman takes to the job of "boulevardier" (68). Near the beginning of the third chapter, as he walks down Market Street at dusk, Wittman remembers these lines from Kerouac:

> *Soldiers, sailors,*
> *the panhandlers and drifters,*
> *[no] zoot suiters, the hoodlums,*
> *the young men who washed dishes in cafeterias*
> *from coast to coast,*
> *the hitch-hikers, the hustlers, the drunks,*
> *the battered lonely young Negroes,*
> *the twinkling little Chinese,*
> *the dark Puerto Ricans, [and braceros and pachucos]*
> *and the varieties of dungareed Young Americans*
> *in leather jackets*
> *who were seamen and mechanics and garagemen*
> *everywhere . . .* (Kingston, *Tripmaster*, 69)

These lines seem to float above Wittman like some rudely hung advertisement for the Tenderloin district. He cringes on cue at the lame racial slur, “twinkling little Chinese,” and, through pangs of betrayal, sighs, “Et tu, Kerouac” (70). Wittman will never be one of “Kerouac’s people, tripping along the street” (69). The most he can hope for is to be Victor Wong, the “Chinese-American guy who rode with Jack and Neal” (21) and who is referred to repeatedly in *Big Sur* as “little Chinese buddy Arthur Ma” (Kerouac, 88).[8]

According to Derek Parker Royal, the real sting of Kerouac’s racial insensitivity is that it is counterproductive. His anti-coolie diminutives expose the insincerity of the “anti-establishment sentiments” of Kerouac’s writing. At best, when accompanied by racial slight of hand, these sentiments become “another apology for the status quo, . . . the white all-American poet, is trapped within the same master narratives from which he attempted to free himself.”[9] Royal is probably right to say that Kerouac “marginalizes those very subjects with which he desires to identify” (151). But he overlooks the fact that Kerouac, the son of French Canadian immigrants, is far from “all-American” and is furthermore not likely to consider marginalization to be a liability. What’s great about Kingston’s resurrection of Kerouac’s marginalizing comments is that she reminds us that they are the comments of one whose own Americanness is tenuous. Indeed, Wittman shoots back at the Kerouac in the sky an equally marginalizing comment — referring to him as “twinkling little Canuck” (*Tripmaster*, 70).

In addition to Royal’s article, other articles that address this section of *Tripmaster Monkey* acknowledge Kingston’s nod to the racial slurs of the so-called Kerouac poem. None of these scholarly works, however, acknowledges that this text is in fact no “Kerouac poem,” but a versification of a sentence from part 4 of *The Town and the City*, a sentence that describes the sights and sounds of Times Square, not the Tenderloin. Below is the passage as it originally appears in Kerouac’s novel:[10]

> He wandered into Times Square. He stood on the sidewalk in the thin drizzle falling from dark skies. He looked about him at the people passing by — the same people he had seen so many times in other American cities on similar streets: soldiers, sailors, the panhandlers and drifters, the zoot-suiters, the hoodlums, the young men who washed dishes in cafeterias from coast to coast, the hitch-hikers, the hustlers, the drunks, the battered lonely young Negroes, the twinkling little Chinese, the dark Puerto Ricans, and the varieties of dungareed young Americans

in leather jackets who were seamen and mechanics and garagemen everywhere. (361)

In addition to the fact that this passage appears in a little-read novel, a possible reason why no one has bothered to find out where the "Kerouac poem" originates is that Kingston is so effective at introducing her versification into the world of her novel as an explanatory textual artifact. As a so-called poem it becomes a curated object, an epigrammatic assertion fixed onto the horizon of the Tenderloin. In effect, Kerouac's words seem like the specter of what started the whole problem of bohemian provincialism, even if they are not Kerouac's words to begin with, as, indeed, they are not Kerouac's words for those who find them only in the pages of *Tripmaster Monkey*. If they are Kerouac's words, the Kerouac whose words they are is a member of Kingston's fictional world. He is "Jock Kerouac," the honorary captain of a social scene that makes Wittman feel like a freak (70).

Kingston's versification turns Kerouac's words into a lyric inventory of disparaged types. She highlights the essentialism of the passage, fixing racial epithets into separate line units. Her versification puts on display what is deplorable about the Kerouac passage. It breaks Kerouac's sentence into lines that couple non-racially-specific types, such as "soldiers, sailors," and "panhandlers and drifters," and that isolate into separate lines the racialized figures of the passage. As such, "the battered lonely young Negroes, / the twinkling little Chinese" become barbs in our, and Wittman's, eyes. The bracketed words and phrases Kingston adds to the passage, updating it for the 1960s West Coast: the zoot suit had been out of fashion since the mid-1940s and the "braceros and pachucos" are West Coast terms, referring to migrant farmers and the rebellious youth, respectively.

Rather than reaffirm Wittman's indignation toward this sorry excuse for a "poem," we should ask why Kingston relocates and versifies the passage in the first place. Why hang an obscure description of Times Square on the horizon of the San Francisco Tenderloin? It's not as though Kerouac never wrote any similarly racially problematic description of San Francisco streets. My contention is that, by using Kerouac's description of the underground realities of Times Square to describe those of the Tenderloin, Kingston accomplishes two things: (1) she alludes to what is possibly Kerouac's first instance of delocalization, and (2) she affirms the minority presence central to the urban origins of both the East and the West Coast Beat movements.

In its original context, the Kerouac passage is part of the initial reaction of Peter Martin, the protagonist of *The Town and the City,* to seeing Time Square after having traveled extensively. The passage follows two vignettes about New York's status as a city "where everything is different from anywhere else" (350). In the first vignette, George, Peter's father, takes a train to Manhattan. He assumes the train will "go underground" as it approaches the Harlem River and is surprised when he "realized that it was going to go over and soar in the morning sun" (353). This is the way the father encounters Manhattan, as a sudden, totalized skyline. Peter, on the other hand, "penetrate[s Manhattan] by degrees" on a bus down from Galloway (the fictionalized name of Kerouac's hometown of Lowell, Massachusetts) via Connecticut. From this bus, one witnesses the "magnitude, the beauty, the wonder of the great city" (354), a city of "a million street corners" (355). It is Peter's incremental, street-level exposure that Kerouac represents as beautiful, not the mystifyingly sudden skyline perspective of the father. Approaching the city gradually allows Peter to experience the granular weight of urban materiality, the weight that unfixes New York from its exceptional self-perception.

A look at the sentences before and after the fragment that Kingston versifies reveals that the passage has been excised from between two delocalizing assertions. The first precedes the fragment: "He looked about him at the people passing by — the same people he had seen so many times in other American cities on similar streets." The second constitutes the sentence-long paragraph that follows the versified fragment: "It was the same as Scollay Square in Boston, or the Loop in Chicago, or Canal Street in New Orleans, or Curtis Street in Denver, or West Twelfth in Kansas City, or Market Street in San Francisco, or South Main Street in Los Angeles" (361). Enveloped thusly, the passage Kingston versified appears to have originally presented itself as part of an interchangeably urban and multicultural terrain.

San Francisco often offered Kerouac a special occasion to consider such an omnipresent sense of place. As Wheeler indicates, "Wandering the streets of San Francisco, Sal [narrator of *On the Road*] has an ecstatic vision of being everywhere at the same time" (250). In the passage to which Wheeler refers, Sal finds himself "frozen with ecstasy" on the sidewalk: "I looked down Market Street. I didn't know whether it was that or Canal Street in New Orleans: it led to water, ambiguous, universal water, just as

42nd Street, New York, leads to water, and you never know where you are" (Kerouac, *On the Road*, 172). Kingston's relocation of Kerouac is less of an antiessentialist move and more of an extension of the delocalized urge of Kerouac's prose, an urge to embrace the euphoria of being lost among familiar city sounds.

It is thus Kerouac's ability to delocalize specific places — to represent a sense of place that doesn't fall prey to either coast's provincialism — that Kingston alludes to through citing this passage. Furthermore, her relocation of the passage from Times Square to the Tenderloin reminds us that, at least in the early days of Kerouac's adventures in delocalization, Beat zones are not rooted in specific places. Rather, they are interchangeably urban, if not also multicultural.[11] Not surprisingly, just after Kerouac describes the Times Square underground, the three prototypically Beat generation characters of *The Town and the City* swagger onstage. A "strange trio" of Leon Levinsky (a.k.a. Ginsberg), Junkey (Huncke), and an ambiguous character referred to only as "Jack the hoodlum" meet Peter on the sidewalk (364).

Through versifying Kerouac, Kingston evokes the auspicious, inaugural moment of the Beat movement. More importantly, she frames this moment in such a way that we cannot help but notice the urban materiality and racial diversity of the moment's context. Following Wittman's progress, Kingston's novel represents San Francisco the way Kerouac represents Times Square, as a space charged with multicultural vitality. Through Wittman, who gets around either by walking or riding the Muni bus, the streets come alive with the sights and sounds of the books he's read. His observations easily blend literary and local knowledge; they allow Kingston to reassert Kerouac's lesson about the delocalizing experience of penetrating the city by degrees. In effect, Kingston's fiction reintroduces to readers the diverse urban environments in which Beat literary innovations originally developed. In the process, she saves urban materiality from the bohemian eclipse.

This stylistic correspondence between Kingston and Kerouac is conspicuously underexamined. As I will explain in the following section, this literary-historical blind spot may be a result of the fact that, according to the prevailing narrative of twentieth-century American literature, each writer serves as spearhead to his and her particular literary sect: Kerouac is so-called King of the Beats, and Kingston is the pioneer of "multicultural recanonization." By panning out from the Kerouac reference to the novel's referential logic as a whole, I will demonstrate Kingston's self-knowledge of her literary-historical position, a self-knowledge that has, surprisingly, been coolly received.

II

While the designations of Kerouac as founder of the Beat movement and Kingston as founder of the multicultural movement are historical, their usefulness at the dawn of the twenty-first century is questionable. In fact, there is a way to view Kingston's references to Kerouac and her adoption of his delocalizing agenda as a sign of an interest among contemporary writers in reevaluating the regional cosmopolitanism that has revolutionized the way America's contested terrain gets fictionalized.[12]

The spirit of delocalization in both Kerouac and Kingston counters the provincialization of local specificity and increases the potential for fiction to represent multiple simultaneous local affiliations. The multiply-affiliated narrators of Kerouac's road novels produce a transcontinental reach that simultaneously inventories American places and reduces the capacity of Americans to be "from" any one part of the country. Kerouac's regional cosmopolitanism thus combines community building and flight from community into a single act. *Tripmaster Monkey*'s dialog with this attempt to free Americans from their roots ultimately endorses Kerouac's urge, but not without criticizing the cultural forms that this urge engenders, namely the bohemian groups around which Wittman orbits.

In light of Kerouac's antiprovincial aesthetic, it seems ironic, if not downright contradictory, that the Beat movement would take root in San Francisco — that those influenced by delocalization would become squatters. As the final destination of the "hippie" movement, San Francisco becomes a veritable reservation of the nation's disaffected (and mostly white) youth. As demonstrated by Ed Sanders's unwavering affection for the reactionary drunk that Kerouac devolved into by the mid-1960s, hippies believed themselves to be in direct lineage with the Beats.[13] From Kingston's point of view, the contradiction between Kerouac's narrative innovations and the hippie reinvention of provincialism is far from an amusing irony. It is a segregation tactic.

Indeed, as they congeal into a "Renaissance," San Francisco Beats become, in Jack Spicer's words, "a coast people [with] nothing but ocean behind

[them]" (quoted in McClure, 44). In short, the provincial self-perception of the San Francisco Renaissance could not register the urban realities of the City. Rather than the gridiron organization of its streets, Renaissance practitioners see, through Sal Paradise's eyes, the "eleven mystic hills" of the "fabulous white city" (Kerouac, *On the Road*, 169). The hills are mystic because they represent the western limit of Sal's imagination. By turning this naïve marveling into a cultural principle, San Francisco Beats erase the possibility that San Francisco is not the end of the road but the first city of transpacific exchange. They construct a provincial logic that shuts out writers, such as Kingston, who had come of age in the Bay Area.

Set at the dawn of the San Francisco Renaissance (with talk of the *Howl* obscenity trial still looming in the air) and starring a Chinese American parody of the beatnik artist as a young man, *Tripmaster Monkey* represents San Francisco as a city charged with literary significance. The question of the civic life of the literary is especially important to Kingston who, after winning the National Book Critics Circle award and the National Book Award for back-to-back memoirs, became known more as an arbiter of transpacific cultural knowledge than as the Berkeley-trained student of literature that she considered herself to be. The goal of the novel, for Kingston, was to discover a way out of having to be a translator of culture. More specifically, she wanted to imagine the civic life of "people that were created by books" (quoted in Skenazy, "Kingston," 140). With a name like "Wittman Ah Sing," Kingston's protagonist is indeed an embodiment of literary retention, and his objective is to use the tools of literary reference to return San Francisco to its status as an urban space.

Indeed, in *Tripmaster Monkey*, Kingston continues a process of reflexive canonicity that David Leiwei Li sees emerge in her earlier memoirs. According to Leiwei Li, Kingston's memoir writing, specifically *China Men*, "deliberately blurs the boundaries of history as the master record of events and the canon as the container of privileged literary texts." This blurring is part of Kingston's conviction that "the law of inclusion and exclusion operating in the structuring of both history and canon . . . needs to be dealt with simultaneously" (482). Where, in *China Men*, Kingston follows suit with Williams Carlos Williams's agenda in *In The American Grain* (1925) and expresses American historical moments from the perspective of a poet, in *Tripmaster Monkey* she intervenes into a specific geographical site of literary-historical moment.

For instance, she sets the novel at a point just before male Asian American writers begin to construct an alternate, Asian American literary canon. As Viet Thanh Nguyen explains, by the late 1960s, such male writers as Frank Chin, Gus Lee, and Jeffery Paul Chan, developed a racialized artistic sensibility similar to that of the Black Arts Movement.[14] These writers appropriated the rhetoric of counterculture and forged a counter-hegemonic front that competed directly with standard literary history. Indeed, "1968 signaled a change in consciousness for Chinese Americans, as many of the younger generation in college became radicalized around the antiwar and anti-imperialism movements, and began to connect those issues with the cause of domestic racial empowerment" (130).[15] Incorporating the embers of antisegregation actions, these writers answered the isolation of such midcentury Asian American writers as John Okada, Toshio Mori, and Carlos Bulosan with a generationally self-aware literature. According to Jonna Mackin, the premises of the "*Aiiieeeee!* group" (named after their anthology of Asian American literature) include "(1) promoting Chinese American cultural hegemony; (2) engaging in an aggressive war of position with another Chinese American author [normally Kingston herself]; and (3) asserting gender dominance" (514).

Tripmaster Monkey represents a San Francisco just before this masculinization of Asian American literary production occurs. If viewed in such a context, the novel becomes an active manipulation of the production of canonical memory, a manipulation that corrects a gender binary that Elaine Kim argues has long plagued both Asian American literature and Asian American literary studies. According to Kim, the "sacred texts" of the Asian American canon have always been (and were especially in the 1960s) dominated by "'dead yellow men' instead of 'dead white men'" and that "Asian American literary studies usually did not question the concept of canonization but simply posited an alternative canon" (13). *Tripmaster Monkey*, a novel about a male Chinese American artist trying to punch his way onto the literary-historical register and written by a female Chinese American artist whose memoirs have helped change standard historical (and literary-historical) memory, is, if nothing else, a complication of the binary understanding of Asian American literary history as split between those who seize power via aggressive, homosocial methods (the *Aiiieeeee!* group) and those who passively accept being (as Amy Tan once sighed) "in the canon, for all the wrong reasons."[16]

In addition to the more subtle ways that Kingston intervenes into canonical memory (that is, through her versification and relocation of an obscure passage from Kerouac), the more obvious evidence that Kingston intentionally intervenes into canonical memory is her protagonist's name. By calling him Wittman, Kingston pits bohemian provincialism against what Diane Wakoski calls the "Whitmanian tradition" of literary production in the American West (36). The reference to Walt Whitman is clear enough, not only in the homophony but also in the novel's chapter titles, the first two of which are phrases from "Song of Myself" ("Trippers and Askers" and "Linguists and Contenders").[17] Indeed, Wittman's artistic agenda mirrors that of "the poet that his father tried to name him after" (161), as both Walt Whitman and Wittman Ah Sing try to enliven the correspondence between the simple separate person and the public spaces that they loiter among. The "Ah Sing" of Wittman's name is a conjoined reference to both the Whitman poem I just alluded to ("One's Self I Sing") and the name of the "Heathen Chinee" from Bret Harte's popular late nineteenth-century local color poem.[18] This reference to frontier local color, with its questionable racial politics and masculine-inflected humor, calls up Wittman's proximity to the garish stereotype local to the American West, the very type to which the "hippy girl" at the LSD party calls attention.

However, Wittman is both an embodiment of literary references and an agent that mobilizes the civic functionality of his literary knowledge. As such, he resembles not a racist stereotype but a "marginal man," a sociological category that James Kyung-Jin Lee resurrects in his article "The City as Region." According to Lee, when writers represent the confrontation of a disaffiliated central figure and a modern city, they revitalize Robert E. Park's century-old concept of the "marginal man," a "social type freed from bonds of tradition and custom, enabled by his cosmopolitan vision to observe different cultures and communities without the imprimatur of any one group's social control" (Lee, 148). The marginal man is thus a literary device used to represent the world through the eyes of one who has no group affiliation.

This "man" has taken on "many other names" since he entered, under somewhat false pretenses, the world of literary criticism. These other names, among them "Benjamin's *flâneur* [and] George Simmel's 'stranger,'" have obscured the marginal man's origins as a concept used to describe the experience of fitting racial otherness into urban social structures. No matter what his name is, Park's marginal man is always a "detached walker of the city" through whom a conception of urban complexities emerges. According to Lee, this walker "shares the common attribute of its ability to observe through detachment, to experience the city without falling prey to its forces. He makes uncanny what appears familiar in the mundane life of the urban; he himself is uncanny, a personification of the landscape's repressed, which brings to light the darker forces that gird and energize the city" (148).

Interestingly, Park's earlier name for this uncanny personification of the urban landscape was "hobo," whose credentials are not drawn from his detachment and invisibility but from his ground-level familiarity with the nooks and crannies of urban space. Not unlike Charlie Chaplin's character in *City Lights* (1931), who escorts a blind woman around downtown San Francisco, the marginal man is one who has no group affiliation but who is not also (as he becomes in the novels of Rilke, Sartre, and Camus) a detached loner. He is at root a public servant, directing traffic and collecting the vital signs of the city.

Wittman assumes this job, though Kingston makes it clear that he has no authorial relationship to his built environment. The fact that Wittman, a fifth-generation immigrant, is materially detached from the labor of production in the City is evident in the fact that Kingston mentions twice in the first two pages of the novel that he had no hand in "building the city." This observation would appear to be a non sequitur had Kingston's intention not been to rebuild the city that her protagonist's white cohort has rendered numinous. As a Chinese American artist who is also a classically trained humanist, Wittman performs his renovation from the materials he has at hand: deep reserves of literary knowledge and the audacity to think of himself as an artist.

Thus equipped, Wittman takes to the street and joins the tradition of young male artists who ponder "what they will do and what they will not do." In other words, he "Daedalates," as Kingston's narrator explains in a not-so-subtle reference to James Joyce's artist as a young man. But Kingston doesn't allow Wittman the arms of silence, exile, and cunning. Instead, his job for most of the novel is to worry over physiological banalities: "How to make a living. What to eat." Asian Americans with no recognizable trade (such as Wittman, who insists that his unemployment record read that he is a "playwright") can work in fast food, or, "if you're the more imaginative type . . . build yourself a cart or stand, sell umbrellas on rainy . . . days" (67). The job of "boulevardier," the option available to most young artists in the Western canon, is not open to Wittman, who muses: "How am I to be a boulevardier on Market Street? I am not a boulevardier; I am a bum-how, I am a fleaman" (68).[19] Wittman may not be a man about town, but he can pretend to be one of "Kerouac's people, tripping along the street" (69). He can remake his environment by commingling his literary knowledge with local, geographical allusions, even if he's on a bus to the unemployment office.

On the street, Wittman discovers shards of references to novels he's read. For instance, as he walks around Golden Gate Park, he sees "an old white woman . . . sitting on a bench selling trivets." She has no eyes, only "eye sockets . . . wide open." Wittman turns away in horror, only to catch sight of "a pigeon and a squatting man, both puking." At this, the narrator asserts that Wittman's morning stroll "was turning out to be a Malte Laurids Brigge walk" (4). The reference to Rilke here and elsewhere is significant for a number of reasons. As opposed to the Bay Area "bohemians," Rilke is an actual "Bohemian poet": he was born in present-day Prague before the dissolve of the Bohemian Kingdom. The novel alluded to, *The Notebooks of Malte Laurids Brigge* (1910), represents an earnest version of the ironic existential mood that Kingston uses to begin her novel.[20]

Kingston is deliberate and humorous when revealing the confluence between Wittman's street knowledge and his knowledge of the Western canon. For instance, he hears in the cables of the Muni railway a sound similar to Beckett's mantra "I can't go on, I go on" (7). Though Beckett's presence in the bus cables echoes Wittman's malaise at being what he calls "racinated" (34), Kingston makes sure not to imply that her protagonist is on a level with great men of letters.[21] Instead, these great men are on a level with other forms of urban data. A line from Rilke or Beckett and the local fact that "the Orpheum [was] once 'the best vaudeville house in the West'" mean about the same thing to Wittman (7). Both are synaptic accidents that happen on a bus ride to unemployment. In this spirit of horizontal partnership between the literary and the local, Wittman's bus rides up and down Market Street call up an assemblage of literary and local references told on the surfaces of San Francisco's cityscape. Kingston thus finds a cultural and historical depth in the semiotics of a city in motion, a city that represents both the beginning and the end of the American continent.

In the third chapter of *Tripmaster Monkey*, the same chapter wherein the versification of Kerouac occurs, Wittman walks down Market Street, near the bus depot, through the heart of the Tenderloin. The place where Kerouac and Snyder used to drink rotgut from paper sacks and pretend to be homeless, the Tenderloin is an area described in the *San Francisco Chronicle*'s city guide as "the worst neighborhood in San Francisco." It boasts "loads of drug dealers, addicts, prostitutes and mentally unstable street people" but is nevertheless "one of the city's most exciting and diverse locales."[22] From the vantage of its poorest place, an area where the reader might imagine herself slumming, Kingston represents San Francisco as a two-dimensional film set, the type of phony self-representation Sal Paradise encounters during Wild West Week in Cheyenne. Her narrator remarks ominously that a "storm will blow from the ocean or down the mountains, and knock the set of the City down. If you dart quick enough behind the stores, you'll see that they are stage flats propped up. On the other side of them is ocean forever" (67).

This vision of the city as a construct of a ghost town — a set of "stage flats"— takes Kerouac's point about the interchangeability of American places to an absurd extreme. She forces the reader to consider what is missing, rather than just what familiar amusements and illusions the city has to offer. Kingston here is not just delocalizing San Francisco, she is renovating the idea that American cities are at heart self-conscious spectacles wherein the beholder plays witness to an unanswerable performance. This assertion is reminiscent of Alan Trachtenberg's argument in *The Incorporation of America* that the twentieth-century American city presents itself as a "frank illusion" or "an admitted sham" that dislocates any orienting "vision of the real" (231).

To deepen this contemplative moment and to make explicit the consequences of Kerouac's delocalization, Kingston asks a series of rhetorical questions that highlight the tenuous existence of the transpacific cityscape: "And what for had they set up Market Street? To light up the dark jut of land into the dark sea. To bisect the City diagonally with a swath of lights. We are visible. See us?" (67). Mimicking the blindness of non–Asian American writers to the cultural resonance of the Pacific, the false idea that transplanted San Franciscans have "nothing but ocean behind us," Kingston introduces Kerouac's delocalization to the task of illuminating the contested terrain of American cultural influence. To signal to the ocean that the city does in fact exist is to indicate that there is something or someone to signal to, that there is some cultural agency West of San Francisco.

From this renewed spirit of delocalization, Kingston starts to carve a home for her protagonist. Wittman reads his Rilke out loud on the bus from Golden Gate Park to downtown. The Rilke passage that Wittman reads, which runs for more than a page of Kingston's novel, describes in nauseating detail the stillness of a bourgeois family dinner. Filling the silence of a bus with a description of the silence of a dining room, Wittman gives himself some form of a home. In turn, he is met with the same brand of complacency that Rilke narrates: everyone ignores him. This complacency, this passive acceptance of Wittman's eccentricity, is what remains of "Walt Whitman's 'classless society' of 'everyone who could read or be read to.'" Nevertheless, Wittman hopes that some passenger will "write to the Board of Supes and suggest that there always be a reader on this route." He hopes to begin a "tradition that may lead to [a] job as a reader riding the railroads throughout the West," "through Fresno — Saroyan; through the Salinas Valley — Steinbeck; through Monterey — *Cannery Row*; along the Big Sur ocean — Jack Kerouac; on the way to Weed — *Of Mice and Men*; . . . through the redwoods — John Muir; up into the Rockies —*The Big Rock Candy Mountain* by Wallace Stegner" (9).

This interest in translating literary knowledge into an actual day job is pervasive throughout the novel. More importantly, and notable in light of the above roll call of male writers, Kingston indicates that to translate literary knowledge into a way of earning a living is to level the hierarchy of literary value. Cast as soundtracks to their corresponding places, Saroyan, Steinbeck, Kerouac, Muir, and Stegner earn a status parallel to that of Rilke and Beckett as writers who texture the experience of public life and introduce "the public" to the vital living ground of its daily life. In effect, Kingston's railroad reader literally mobilizes literary fiction.

It's fitting, then, that Wittman finds in his wife, Taña, an unlikely literary companion. As part of her initial reaction to Wittman's off-kilter personality, Taña recites a kitschy local color poem, "The Men That Don't Fit In," by frontier balladeer Robert Service. At this recitation, Wittman marvels at the apparent uselessness of his English-major credentials: "Four years of Chaucer and Shakespeare, Milton, and Dickens, Whitman, Joyce, Pound and Eliot, and you shoot me right through the heart with Robert W. Service." Taña's middlebrow literacy makes Wittman's humanities training into a form of kitsch. It dissociates Wittman's generation from the bohemian generations that come before the 1960s: "Bloomsbury did not recite Robert Service. Neither did Gertrude Stein's Paris salon. Neither did the Beats. But Wittman Ah Sing's friends — . . . his generation — did" (113).

By coupling the lover of Rilke and the lover of Service, Kingston produces a situation that interrogates the everyday value of literature and weighs literature alongside other public services and social rites. Beginning with Wittman's roll call of public reading material, Kingston uses her novel to rethink the literature of the American West not as some racist conspiracy threatening Asian Americans but as a natural resource, an organic canon whose chaff can be winnowed out, a task exemplified by Wittman's decision to "refuse to be a reader of racist Frank Norris. He won't read Bret Harte either, in revenge for that Ah Sin thing" (9–10). Kingston thus democratizes high literary fiction and poetry. Ironically, *Tripmaster Monkey*, with its ultimately liberatory system of literary reference and manipulation, has been ambivalently received in academic circles.

IV

Rather than welcoming the novel's referential density, some readers claim that its allusions unfairly reward canonical literacy. As one audience member at a conference at the University of California, Santa Cruz, put it: these allusions are "only available to very literate people" (quoted in Skenazy, "Kingston," 143). Kingston responds by reminding her audience that readers of *The Woman Warrior* or *China Men* do not feel excluded by the obscure cultural references in them, references that are far more difficult to ferret out than are the literary references in *Tripmaster Monkey*. The reason is obvious. Readers of Kingston's memoirs can chalk up their confusion to cultural difference. An audience member at the same conference echoes this position: "if you're not Chinese American, you don't have to feel like you should have known the allusions." Kingston argues that these allusions are there to enfranchise readers of canonical literature, to give them some sense of how their literary knowledge can intervene into public life. "But," Kingston responds to the Santa Cruz audience, "the way that you're all talking, it seems like I put those allusions out there to give you pain" (144). Regardless of whether she is earnest when she says that she assumed her reader would welcome Wittman's book smarts, Kingston gives her protagonist's liberal arts training some street value, some way of applying Kerouac and Rilke to his daily life.

She also makes herself a key player in the evolution of literary realism, an evolution spurred on by discourse about literary representations of urban experience. The point, then, of the complex interaction among literary and local knowledge is to reclaim the democratic social space of urban zones, the space wherein the performance of literacy is a civic act.[23] Kingston's choice to inhabit this space and not what Marshall Berman calls the space of "ethnic memory" that she so expertly occupies in her memoirs seems counterintuitive, especially considering how commercially and critically successful her memoirs continue to be ("All That Is Solid," 334). But, as Kingston explains it, *Tripmaster* was "a great relief. In the first two books, I felt that I was translating a culture for everyone.... It felt like a burden to me.... [With *Tripmaster* I] wanted to use everything that I know, to use the language at the hardest level that I can work it, the American language, the language that I hear and speak" (quoted in Skenazy, "Kingston," 144). Thus, the goal of *Tripmaster Monkey* is to carve a place for a Chinese American artist within a language and cultural sensibility that the generation that misread Kerouac has managed to eclipse.

Yunte Huang sees this effort as a mode of assimilation. Specifically, Huang criticizes Kingston's reliance on realism. By stooping to such a mainstream American literary tradition, Kingston foils "the formation of radical, transnational models of American literary studies" (142). Speaking more generally about Asian American literature, Huang observes that "the generic preference for realist, personal narratives is too obvious for anyone to miss" (144). This preference earns writers like Kingston a place in the canon at the same time as it stunts the development of more overtly transpacific literary traditions. From Huang's perspective, Kingston uses her cultural knowledge to season her realist narratives, thus providing readers with a safe, readily consumable form of an exotic culture.[24]

While I can concede that Kingston's memoirs are consumable and that such consumability may be a sign of Kingston's deference to a mainstream audience, I think that to consider realism "Western" is both to traffic in an unstable dualism and to deny "non-Western" writers the very tool that might, as it does for Kingston, allow them to control the conversation about their relationship to literary history. In short, to think of Kingston's realism as a whitening of Kingston is to overlook the fact that the definition of "realism" has changed in the past few decades and that this change has been affected by such novels as *Tripmaster Monkey*, novels that are "realist" only insofar as they "anthropoligize" literary history. Patricia Lin refers to this method of negotiating literary knowledge as brand of realism that "exposes the constitution of everyday or taken for granted realities" (335). Kingston's commingling of literary allusion and local knowledge is thus both realist and overtly transpacific.

Huang is wary of realism because it is a literary aesthetic that presupposes the centrality of the self in the context of democratic social space. This readymade social agenda, if not at odds with the aims of Asian American literature, is at least an agenda that Asian American writers did not themselves articulate. In the context of contemporary fiction, a "realist" is one who explores the impact of social space on individual identity. *Tripmaster Monkey* does engage the presuppositions of realism. However, the novel is not a "personal narrative." Its realism has its roots not in the Western tradition of confession and autobiography but in Walt Whitman's expansive project of defining American identity by compiling an immense paratactic set of observations. There are many "Whitmanian" catalogs in *Tripmaster Monkey*.[25] Indeed, the sheer amount and complexity of the world Kingston presents are as evocative as the world Whitman presents in "Song of Myself." The problem is that the paradigm through which readers understand Kingston is rigid. Her offerings can be as liberatory as Walt Whitman's, but they will always be received as either an act of assimilation or an externalization of a "Chinese American" sensibility. In short, misreadings of Kingston begin with an assumption that her work ethic and ambitions are always somehow racially specific.

Luckily, such ghettoization of intent is going out of favor. In her introduction to the *PMLA* special issue on "Cities" (2007), Patricia Yeager contends that literary representations of the "city" have helped rewrite the social contract agenda of realism. As Yeager explains, one of the tasks of recent urban literature is "to give body and voice to the multiplying subaltern publics that struggle to transform the spatial politics of cities." Advancing this argument, Yeager critiques Henri Lefebvre's theory of city space. Lefebvre denies "the possibility of any working connection between 'mental or literary "places"' and space 'of a purely political and social kind.'" Yeager claims the city as a trope of literary representation, rather than a psychosocial conundrum to be pondered from a distance. She disagrees with

Lefebvre's assertion that literary texts "can do little to assess the contradictions of place," countering this assertion with the more optimistic claim that "literature has an advantage" in negotiating the politics of city space. The assets of literary meditations/representations of the city include "the intertwining of codes; the habit of overdetermination; the multiple mapping that accompanies condensation and displacement; the layering that comes with the use of compound plots, points of view, tonality, atmosphere, and meter; and the dense range of figurative speech" (21). The city thus needs literature in order for its fractured realities and multivalent social possibilities to become visible.

Yeager's critique of Lefebvre opens a window onto the politics of academic discourse about the city. Theorists such as Lefebvre have the impulse to separate city spaces into categories: representations of space (manifested through planning and architecture) and representational space (manifested in the activities of inhabitants). The former is a source of oppression, whereas the latter is a site of resistance. Literary critics, on the other hand, tend to conceive of public space as a malleable container of activity. For instance, Morris Dickstein draws from Kafka's "leopards in the temple" parable to explain the plasticity and unpredictability of public space.[26] While Lefebvre agrees that leopards can rearrange the daily goings on of the temple they invade, their presence doesn't automatically mean that the temple and what it represents dissolve. Such arguments, posed by Dickstein and other critics, overstate the disruptive agency of literature. To think of transgressive use of public space as revolutionary is to traffic in a homology that mistakes behavior similar to revolution with behavior that actually rewrites the social contract. Like Foucault, who understands the administration of public space as dictating urban subjectivity, Lefebvre demonstrates the futile provincialism of such transgressive behavior.[27]

My point in bringing up this debate between theorists and critics is not to indicate that literary critics are more provincial and social theorists more cosmopolitan when it comes to the question of urban space. Even if it were somehow useful, this reductive thinking would not change the fact that recent city fiction has rewritten the rules of realist representation. In contrast to the legacy of the disorienting, spectatorial city notable in many realist American novels since Dreiser's *Sister Carrie* (1900), "inner-city" fiction since mid-twentieth century has reoriented the spatial reality of cityscapes. Ann Petry's *The Street* (1946), Ralph Ellison's *Invisible Man* (1952), Saul

Bellow's *The Adventures of Augie March* (1953), Harriette Arnow's *The Dollmaker* (1954), N. Scott Momaday's *House Made of Dawn* (1968), Joyce Carol Oates's *them* (1969), John Edgar Wideman's Homewood trilogy (1981–1983), and Sandra Cisneros's *The House on Mango Street* (1984) are just a few urban-set novels that present a localized alternative to the city novels of spatial disorientation. These novels suggest that, as a literary trope, "the city" has given way to more socially responsive issues.

But it is a mistake to think of multiethnic, city-set fiction as an appropriation of a dominant literary trope. In fact, minorities may have gotten to the city first. The first major thrust toward thinking of the city as a laboratory through which to investigate the interrelationship of environment and sensibility comes from Robert E. Park's "marginal man," a sociological category Park derived from his "investigation of the 'Oriental' and 'Negro Problem'" (Kyung-Jin Lee, 148). In other words, what has become known as the white man's burden of disorientation and identity crisis is actually a result of serious inquiry into racial subjectivity.[28] The marginal man is the regional cosmopolitan perspective personified. He is an "urban ethnographer," who has "permission to bring objective credence to subjective perception" (149). Kingston grants Wittman such permission. With it, he redefines himself. He makes indistinguishable the signs that locate one as literate and the signs that locate one as part of a particular identity group.

Kingston tests this proposition in her characterization of Wittman. Readers learn early on that Wittman was "born backstage in vaudeville" and raised in a "theatrical trunk" (13). Because he was born and raised at the epicenter of American popular culture, Wittman understands his parodying racial identity as a birthright. He understands his race to be as much "burlesque" as it is "Chinese." It's no surprise, then, that the final chapter of *Tripmaster Monkey* takes place on the stage of Wittman's one-man show. The stage allows Wittman to demonstrate his literacy in a way that controls his audience's understanding of his racial identity.

Kingston's interest in the stage is notable throughout the novel. The novel's first chapter ends with Wittman deciding to write the one-man show he performs in the last chapter. Also in chapter 1, as Wittman performs his talk-stories and poems for Nanci, the narrator makes this enigmatic interruption: "*a door had swung open before you, and now you were among the alembics in the firelight. . . . Your theater came into being*" (16, ellipsis and italics in original). This line is actually an uncited passage from

The Notebooks of Malte Laurids Brigge. It is Rilke's address to an unnamed poet-turned-playwright (likely Henrik Ibsen).[29] The Rilke quotation is an impressive meditation on the power of the realist aesthetic to expose the fluidity of identity markers. In the passage, Malte Laurids Brigge addresses the burgeoning realist playwright directly:

> Since your blood drove you not to form or to speak, but to reveal, . . . you made the enormous decision to so magnify these tiny events, which you yourself first perceived only in test tubes, that they would be seen by thousands of people, immense before them all. Your theater came into being. You couldn't wait until this life almost without spatial reality, this life which had been condensed by the weight of the centuries into a few small drops, could be discovered by the other arts. . . . You couldn't wait for that; you were there, and everything that is barely measurable — an emotion that rises by half a degree, the angle of deflection, read off from up close, of a will burdened by an almost infinitesimal weight, the slight cloudiness in a drop of longing, and that barely perceptible color-change in an atom of confidence — all this you had to determine and record. (Rilke, 82–83)

In his excitement about small-scale ranges of reference, Rilke's narrator glorifies the ability of realism to illuminate the scarcely measurable details of everyday life. The "tiny events" are in effect a residue of "emotions." The playwright's realism is a slight caress that makes iridescent the borders of identity. Rilke praises realist art for its use of the increments of "barely measurable," "half a degree," and "angles of deflection" that are recognizable only at close quarters. This condensation is a capsule of tenderness that is available to "the other arts," by which Rilke here (in the middle of his first and only novel) likely means the various literary arts. The unnamed writer's ability to put on the stage these minutiae is applauded by Rilke and will be applauded by Kingston throughout *Tripmaster Monkey*.

Playwriting becomes Wittman's form of becoming visible. It becomes a way of making racial identity into a uniquely visible "angle of deflection" (Rilke 83). In other words, the *fact* that the focal point of a one-man show is a Chinese American man is a matter of physical presence, not a matter established through the writing of any script. The writer of drama is relieved of the burden of ethnic self-presentation, as the burden of recognizing racial identity is transferred onto the audience. Ultimately, Kingston's turn to the stage allows Wittman to obscure the precise location of his Chinese Americanness.[30] Instead of blowing out his brains — as per his wish from the opening page of the novel — Wittman finally unfolds the contents of his brain in a productive, not self-destructive, manner.

This unfolding fuels Wittman's dream of social welfare. Wittman's decision to write a play vitalizes his desire to make a living on his literary knowledge. In addition to bus-ride renditions of Rilke and his other schemes for integrating literature into public transportation, Wittman's one-man show is a kind of public service. His wish to revive "deep-roots American theater," to perform plays that last for days, plays that "leave room for actors to do improv, a process as ancient as Chinese opera and as far-out as the theater of spontaneity that was happening in streets and parks," is a wish to produce plays that are woven into the fabric of everyday life (141). In order to finally realize his dream of an FWP-type job as a public artist, Wittman has to spike the dream of social welfare with a healthy dose of Chinese theater. The only salaried patronage available to a Chinese American artist in 1960s San Francisco is that of the "corporate playwright," the writer who "scripts industrial shows and hygiene films for the educational-military-industrial complex" (239). Wittman is so completely redlined out of the San Francisco Renaissance that he has to beg a Chinese Benevolent Association to let him stage his play in the Association hall. To convince the Association president that his play is socially useful, Wittman reminds the president just how central theater is to Chinese culture. The narrator translates the Chinese synonyms for "theatrical play," words that signify "To make air. To give to airy nothing a local habitation and a name." Kingston adds to this idea about the correspondence Chinese art makes between theater and public space when she gestures to a statue of Gwan Goong, sitting on the Association mantel. Gwan Goong is the "god of actors and writers and warriors and gamblers and travelers" (255). In apposition, these "occupations" imply that the performance artist and the rootless drifter are one and the same. Placed in such a horizontal alignment, the actor and writer become synonymous with the Chinese drifters who first came to the U.S.

As with all of her gestures at Chinese cultural knowledge, Kingston does not mystify the status of Chinese language, mythology, or history. These details emerge in the midst of Wittman's attempt to convince the Benevolent Association president that his play meets the Benevolent Association's mission. A fraternal order chartered by first-generation Chinese immigrants, the Association represents both the antiquated old guard of Chinese American bachelors and the makeshift ingenuity of Wittman's lot. The Association is a cooperative. Wittman asks, in broken Chinese: "Else, what Association for, huh? Collecting dues? . . . You bury old men. You be nothing but one burial society" (255). Without Wittman's fervor for public art, the Chinese immigrant experience will amount to little more than a co-op with no socially useful goal, save interment.

In her chapter on the play itself, Kingston oscillates between Wittman's logorrhea and the narrator's insights into the larger significance of the play. Wittman's improvised soliloquies are combined with spectacles of racial and cultural parody, including a biracial Cheng and Eng routine, magic tricks, juggling, trapeze artists, and a geriatric cancan performance. As the show reaches its climax, the narrator lists Wittman's "theatrical ancestors," others who have "perform[ed] without a permit" (301). A nearly two-hundred-person list, this catalog includes "flimflammers of tourists, wildcat miners, cigar makers without the white label, . . . cubic air breathers, miscegenists, landsquatters . . . crowders into single-family dwellings . . . un-Americans, red-hot communists, unbridled capitalists . . . and exploders of fireworks" (301–302). Everyone in the catalog is named for the crime that he or she commits. To think of these lawbreakers as "performers" is to make a bold statement about the nature of democratic action. On the one hand, this catalog is absurd, especially since the one principle that holds it together is that the actions named are difficult to understand as "performances." On the other hand, calling these practitioners of civil disobedience "performers" asserts a common argument in postmodern philosophy, namely that it is impossible to perform disobedience without making the performance mistakable for the real thing. As witnessed in Jean Baudrillard's command to "Go and organise a fake hold-up," Kingston's semantic play highlights the absolute affront that certain kinds of public performance pose to civil society (Baudrillard, 408).[31]

Kingston follows this inventory of civil disobedience with another list, a catalog of tragic fires associated with American theater houses. The list ends with revolutionary fervor: "We'll do anything for lighting, die for it, kill for it" (302). The fire catalog functions quite differently from the preceding catalog. It names facts as facts, rather than interpreting civil disobedience as performance. The fire catalog is less of an affront to polite society than is the civil disobedience catalog. It names disasters, the destruction of the places of performance rather than the possible innovations one can apply to the very idea of performance.

Together, these catalogs prove prescient, as Wittman's one-man show attracts a fire truck. Though Wittman's fire is not real, Kingston's narrator's dedication to thinking that Wittman is a fiery revolutionary is real:

> Of course, Wittman Ah Sing didn't really burn down the Association house and the theater. It was an illusion of fire. Good monkey. He kept control of the explosives, and of his arsonist's delight in flames. He wasn't crazy; he was a monkey. What's crazy is the idea that revolutionaries must shoot and bomb and kill, that revolution is the same as war. (305)

This passage — and many others like it — positions Wittman as a marionette, a monkey who dances to a concertina and who might "let us tweak [his] ear, and kiss [his] other ear" (340). Kingston establishes dominance over her male artist in this way. She implies that the real revolutionary writer is the observer of such manic behavior, the one who can contextualize it into a larger cultural and literary context. Such writers I have been calling "regional cosmopolitans."

Extra vagance! it depends on how you are yarded.
— Henry David Thoreau, *Walden*

There is a moment of equipoise, a widespread flowering of the imagination in which the thoughts and feelings of the people, with all their faiths and hopes, find expression. . . . Then gradually the mind, detached from the soil, grows more and more self-conscious. Contradictions arise within it, and worldlier arts supplant the large, free, ingenuous forms through which the poetic mind has taken shape. What formerly grew from the soil begins to be planned. . . . What has once been vital becomes provincial; and the sense that one belongs to a dying race dominates and poisons the creative mind . . . is not this the story of New England?
— Van Wyck Brooks, *The Flowering of New England*

FOUR

The Deflowering of New England

Russell Banks and the Wages of Cosmopolitanism

Van Wyck Brooks concludes his landmark study of New England literature, *The Flowering of New England* (1936), with a series of vignettes about the deaths of the region's literary giants (Thoreau, Hawthorne, and Emerson). These deaths mark a shift in the creative imagination of New England, a shift away from the extravagant force of nature under whose influence Hawthorne rummaged through the Salem Custom House and Thoreau built his cabin in the Concord woods. In the place of this raw, masculine productivity comes a "self-conscious" mode of literary production, an imitation of the "worldlier arts" of Europe. Brooks bottom-lines the shift like this: "The Hawthornes yield to the Henry Jameses" (*Flowering*, 527). There is a grain of truth to this literary-historical shorthand. Self-consciousness does become a distinguishing feature of New England fiction. Starting with Edith Wharton's novella about the doomed love affair between Ethan Frome and Mattie Silver, New England fiction becomes home to characters who know full well that they belong to a "dying race." To recent New England writers, this provincial self-knowledge provides either a late twentieth-century version of the cultural elegy cache of first-wave regionalism or a means to imagine a version of cosmopolitan detachment that might also revitalize the region.

Despite reports of the region's death, or perhaps — thinking of Brodhead and Foote's explanations of late nineteenth-century regionalism's popularity — because of these reports, regional fiction has lately started to matter to literary culture.[1] In the first decade of the twenty-first century, the regional works to win Pulitzer Prizes — Richard Russo's *Empire Falls* (2001), Marilynne Robinson's *Gilead* (2004), Elizabeth Strout's *Olive Kitteridge* (2008), and Paul Harding's *Tinkers* (2009) — all feature small-town socioeconomic histories and reflections on aging among the debris of past vitality. However, this fiction does not signal a return to nostalgia. In fact, these books are prime examples of a regional cosmopolitanism that is back in vogue. In this chapter, I will argue that this kind of fiction deserves to be rewarded. Its accomplishments at the level of plot and voice are enhanced by a sophistication that represents the cosmopolitan hues of a region whose spirit is reported to have died sometime back in the nineteenth century. I will examine Banks's answer to the question of what it means to be a "New England writer" at the turn of the millennium. The short answer is that it means that the writer has his work cut out for him. The New England writer has to squeeze global significance out of a region whose vitality has been buried for over a century. The reflexively provincial sensibility of Banks's fiction, which both owns up to and rages against limitations that accompany regionalism, creates a reconciliatory alternative to the reductive regional imagination of those who have decided that New England is over.

In *Empire Falls*, Richard Russo reminds us that cosmopolitan fantasies are native to the minds of New England men. Like such yearning seafarers as Sarah Orne Jewett's Captain Littlepage and Elijah Tilley, Russo's old men want to lift anchor and leave.[2] Max Roby dreams of being a "conch" in Key West; Max's son Miles dreams of owning a bookstore in Martha's Vineyard. Everyone else in Empire Falls dreams of the day the Empire Shirt Factory, closed for thirty years, finds a new investor and reopens. Horace, the town newspaperman, describes the collective dream this way:

> They came to invest millions. For a while they were thinking about tech stocks, but then they thought, Hell, no. Let's go into textiles. That's where the *real* profits are. Then you know what they did? They decided not to build the factory in Mexico or Thailand where people work for about ten bucks a week. Let's drive up to Empire Falls, Maine, they said, and look at that gutted old shell of a factory that the river damn near washed away last spring and buy all new equipment and create hundreds of jobs, nothing under twenty dollars an hour. (Russo, 25)

This theme of dreaming among the ruins suggests that contemporary writers, "New England writers," are not uninterested in global vistas. However, their representations of a region that modern capital has abandoned refract back to the reader some of the more poignant economic injustices brought about by globalization.

In contrast to the affability of Russo's small-town narrative voice, Banks's voice is dark. His narrators' voices are marked by the weathered sensibility of one whom inertia has nearly defeated. This quality of voice is the result a life spent straining against regional limitations, a life spent indulging the impulse to flee provincial America without first untethering himself from the ties that bind him to home. Banks's voices mobilize undesired local knowledge, encyclopedic comprehension of a hated hometown, into a matter of character. He approaches provincial self-knowledge as something to *use*, not simply a precondition of fiction that is set somewhere off the beaten path. Banks thus understands the "regional" modifier of his fiction not as an announcement of local and cultural limits but as the descriptive material he uses to tell his story.

Instead of using local knowledge to enhance the descriptive fidelity of his fiction, Banks uses it to engage "self-enactment" (Banks, Interview 1986). Writing fiction is his way of struggling with who he is, specifically a way of reconciling the fact that he is a former union plumber with the fact that he has dedicated his life to a "bourgeois art form" (Interview 1986). Banks does not rebel against the "bourgeois" nature of the novel. Indeed, his novel *Affliction* (1989) is a kind of middle-class attack on rural America. What troubles him is the bourgeois assumption that a fiction writer can simply choose to transcend his background, either by fleeing and never looking back or by "writing what you know" and thereby converting local knowledge into a salable good.[3] The "self" that Banks "enacts" in his fiction is always to some degree indistinguishable from the place from which that self speaks. But that self is always also freed from its local conditions and, by extension, it frees the place that produced the self.

Banks credits Carl Sauer and William Carlos Williams for this uniquely autobiographical use of regional fiction. Sauer's cultural geographies and Williams's modernist localisms "invited," in Banks's words, "a deep investigation into the 'local'" (quoted in Niemi, 69). "By keeping things local," Banks explains, "I could also keep them personal, without being 'autobiographical.'" The contrast between personal and local is thus "resolved by means of my immersing myself in New England . . . history, geology, economics, geography[,] etc." (69). Thus Banks's interest in local color is an interest in dealing with his own past as a plumber. His narrators handle the details of working-class identities the same way laborers might handle the rusted tools of their trade. Banks has described this particular method of regional fiction writing as a "kind of violence [or] heroism" through which he battles against "entropy" (Interview 1986). The entropy that Banks battles against is the entropy that visits the working-class writer as he tries to survive in a genre whose conventions are not natural to him.

More than any other writer I examine, Banks self-identifies as white and working-class. Indeed, his early book blurbs ended with the assertion that "he grew up in a working-class environment, which has played a major role in his writing." This writerly identity has become, to some degree, synonymous with the regional writer, especially when that writer is white and male.[4] In the following section, I will discuss the possible reasons why this parallel has emerged in contemporary literature. My sense is that redefining identity categories as literary categories is fairly common practice: African American writers often write "African American fiction"; Latina/o writers write "Latina/o fiction," etc. What's curious about the white male writer writing regional fiction is that the category does not take the name of the writer's identity group. Instead, the category actually gives content to the otherwise empty signifier of "white male."

I

Regionalism is central to the literary production of the Program Era. As Mark McGurl sees it, the resurgence of regional fiction is spearheaded by men; many contemporary male writers, including Wallace Stegner, William Kennedy, and Cormac McCarthy, "have staged their careers in the continuing tradition of literary regionalism" ("Program Era," 119). Stegner has not only sustained a long career via the regional tradition, he has also produced a generation of American writers who capitalize on their regional inflections. Having founded and run the Stanford University writing workshop, Stegner shaped the careers of such influential writers as Edward Abbey, Wendell Berry, Ken Kesey, Thomas McGuane, and Larry McMurtry. McGurl sees these writers staking claim to the genre because it "has always been cultural pluralist," always "a form of appreciation of diversity." Regionalism thus allows white men an "alignment by analogy" with some of the more pressing issues of diversity in the literary marketplace (119).

Unlike McGurl, who views the resurgence of regional writing as a reaction to the ascendancy of identity politics, Sally Robinson sees attempts at "marked" embodiment as part of a white, male impulse to remain relevant in an era of "visibility politics" (2).[5] According to Robinson, the "disenfranchised white man" is a product of an oscillation of desires, an oscillation between the invisibility that affords white men refuge from accountability and the "fully embodied, particularized identity" that current cultural paradigms value (4). The "disenfranchised white man" emerged in the late 1960s, when white men began to see themselves as the victims of history.[6] According to Robinson:

> From the late sixties to the present, dominant masculinity appears to have suffered one crisis after another, from the urgent complaints of the "silent majority" following the 1968 presidential election, to the men's liberationists call for rethinking masculinity in the wake of the women's movement in the 1970s, to the battles over the cultural authority of "dead white males" in academia, to the rise of a new men's movement in the late 1980s. (5)

Notice how Robinson explains each movement in literary terms. Each mass assertion of masculinity comes with a "language of crisis" and a "vocabulary of pain" (5).[7] White men have reacted to this changing tide of history by *marking* themselves. In fact, white men have become so specialized a group that the "enduring image of the disenfranchised white man has become a symbol for the decline of the American way" (2). Robinson sees recent white masculinity "most fully and convincingly represent itself as victimized by inhabiting a wounded body" (20). Such bodies are typical of recent regional fiction.

In many ways, Banks is representative of the masculinization of regional fiction; he is white and working-class, and his use of local color marks his male characters with a "Nordic register" reminiscent of Sarah Orne Jewett's female characters.[8] For instance, in describing the faces of "Whitehouse men," the family name that both the narrator and the antihero of the novel *Affliction* share, Banks evokes an ancient, ethnic inflection:

> We wear a face shaped by thousands of years of peering into firelight, into cold mists rising off salt marshes, into deep waters where huge sturgeon cruise slowly past; a face tightened . . . from having pursed thin lips thoughtfully for millennia over animal tracks and droppings. (*Affliction*, 56)

Banks highlights the Whitehouse tie to Nordic masculinity. He marks his character's whiteness as an ethnic category, exposing what Pheng Cheah calls the "privative ethnic identity that disguises itself as a universalism" (21). In fact, though this passage describes the ingrained marks of the Whitehouse face, it debunks the place-based logic of identity considered common to regional writing. Even as the Whitehouse men's "ancient habits of expression" arrive as signs of Nordic masculinity, their faces betray an "intimacy and a tenderness, a melancholic vulnerability . . . [that] gives the impression of intelligence and sensitivity" (56). The point of noticing the markings of both masculinity and sensitivity is to define both as *impressions*, or markings that aren't totally the property of either the object being described or the writer himself. Rather than trying to forge a place for white men within a literary culture that values diversity, Banks demonstrates the place of provincial self-knowledge in the context of contemporary fiction. He provides a manner of representing the local in a way that is amenable to the delocalizing thrust of globalization.

Being a "New England writer," Banks is in dialogue with a long, fraught tradition of American regionalism. In the following section, I will survey Banks's relationship to this tradition, including his contribution to a now century-old backlash *against* regionalism. Assuming that the Jewetts and Freemans of the late nineteenth century have given way to the Bankses and Russos of the late twentieth century, I read a general shift in New England fiction toward masculinization, toward male writers who need the markings of diversity that regional knowledge allots. The reason I look to New England for an example of this shift is twofold. First, since New England regionalism has long been considered the territory of women writers, the recent proliferation of male writers who have taken root there provides an ideal occasion for reading the type of boundary blurring that is unique to regional writing. Second, New England is a special site of cultural polarity in America. The sacred ground of Matthiessen's "American Renaissance" has been, in Dwight MacDonald's words, "pushed aside by history [and is] dwindling to provincial gentility" (34–35). A byproduct of this fall from cultural prominence is an ambivalence regarding the bucolic features of New England. After it inters its literary leviathans, New England earns the emasculating distinction of center of idyllic rurality in America. In the heyday of regional fiction, the preservation of idyllic rurality was legislated by the *Atlantic* group. These days, the preservation is a mode of self-preservation.

Banks's New England novels signify a career-long meditation on the virtues and limitations of local knowledge. Looking closely at two of them, *Hamilton Stark* (1978) and *Affliction*, I examine Banks's reiteration of a tradition of subverting the dichotomizing cultural logic of nostalgia for bucolic New England. As originally engineered by Edith Wharton, this antinostalgia was supposed to shift interest away from the backward provinces and toward the fashionable (if not also tribal) pockets of urban high society.[9] Banks, on the other hand, does not propose that writers abandon rural for urban tribes. Instead, he is interested in dramatizing the complexities of placing local knowledge in fiction, of calling attention to the love and violence that accompany any honest representation of a ruined place.

II

New England fiction has, to some degree, always exposed nostalgia as a self-destructive impulse. Kent Ryden reminds us that archetypical New England regionalism, such as Mary Wilkins Freeman's "The Revolt of the Mother" (1890) and "A New England Nun" (1891), "explored the tensions hidden beneath the popularly accepted façade of New England village life, offering a harsh critique of the social, imaginative, and emotional stresses and limitations placed upon small-town residents, particularly women." Ryden goes so far as to say that New England regional writing "prefigured the social criticism" of the post–World War I "revolt from the village" (205). It was the first literary genre to represent the proportionate decline in the region's culture and its agriculture. By the 1920s, cultural commentary, conventional wisdom, and even state policies had caught up with literature:

> Regional and national commentators fretted that New England, seen as the cultural hearth of the nation and the repository of national strength and virtue, was losing its vitality and going to seed.... The remnant rural population came increasingly to be seen as shiftless, inbred, and morally bankrupt, their continued residence in shabby villages now seen as a sign of fecklessness rather then [*sic*] of incorruptibility. (205)

Donna Campbell demonstrates how New England regional writing hovers between the twin themes of cultural decline and self-destruction. Campbell uses the example of Rose Terry Cooke, whose stories include "horrifying infant murders, and... beatings and a suicide" (184). Campbell recognizes the absence of a very specific kind of violence: that of "men in groups acting against each other." This "suggestive absence" evokes the presence of the type of violence that is missing. (21) Where first-wave regionalism "purposefully explores... varieties of absence" in order to set such facts as physical violence into relief, twentieth-century New England local color highlights the agency that comes with violence (21).

Indeed, man-on-man violence is precisely what bubbles up in Banks's fiction. As Banks often suggests, tearing the world to pieces is sometimes the only way that working-class men can understand themselves as unique and not a product of a system they had no hand in creating. This proposition, as writers as early as Wharton and as recent as Banks have asserted, is valid because the kind of fiction that prohibited violence also produced a sentimental attachment to a New England that never existed but that nevertheless is the inspiration of many small-town social rites. The object of critique is thus the type of provinciality whose myopia denies the existence of destructive impulses that nostalgia engenders.

The gendered logic of regional fiction was originally shaped via a debate in late nineteenth-century periodicals about the place of masculinity and femininity in a realist tradition. In an 1897 issue of the *Atlantic Monthly,* James Lane Allen defined the "Feminine Principle" and "Masculine Principle" in American fiction. This division is similar to the traditional understanding of the split between local color and naturalist fiction.[10]

Such naturalists as Frank Norris, Jack London, and Stephen Crane—Campbell includes Wharton in this list—rebelled against the popularity of preservation-centered regional writing. They disliked, among other things, the unquestioned assumption that it's a good idea to preserve rural folkways. Campbell provides an insightful reading of Stephen Crane's "The Monster" as a story that evokes conventions of preservation in order to subvert them. As I'll discuss below, Banks's New England fiction does the same thing: it dramatizes the violent self-destruction that looms under the surface of even the most innocent preservation impulse.

More important than Crane's critique of local color is Wharton's more famous version. In the well-known climax of *Ethan Frome* (1911), Ethan and Mattie steer their sleigh down a pretty hillside in Starkfield, Massachusetts, straight into an elm tree. This suicide attempt marks the beginning of antinostalgic regionalism in New England. It is the culmination of Wharton's effort to "contradict the 'rose and lavender' pages of native writers" (Wharton, quoted in Hamblen, 239). *Ethan Frome* is a "blackly comic joke, a vision of the genre so extreme as to border on private parody" (Campbell, 172). By using the trappings of New England's idyllic landscape (the sleigh, the snowy hill, the innocent lovers) as instruments of violence, Wharton "confront[s] the genre of local color fiction on its own terms . . . disrupt[ing] and transform[ing] its narrative conventions" and thus revealing a New England as a region crippled by its own quaintness (162).

As Wharton herself explains in her introduction to the novella, she hopes this self-destruction will catch on as the New England fiction writer's "siren-subject." She hopes local color writers will abandon the woman's work of representing the delicate, irrelevant hues of the region, crash their "cockle-shell to the rocks." The characters in *Ethan Frome* are deliberately colorless, characters Wharton refers to as "*granite outcroppings* . . . half emerged from the soil, and scarcely more articulate" (vii). They are recounted from the detached, sober perspective of a "looker-on," a narrator who has "scope enough to see it all, to resolve it back into simplicity, and to put it in its rightful place among his larger categories" (viii–ix).

Wharton thus replaces interest in the delicate, exotic, and endangered details of regional difference with a crude essentialism, wherein difference is reduced to proto-elemental categories like rock and soil. Despite its tragic plot, *Ethan Frome* implements a very liberating approach to local knowledge. Wharton reminds other writers that local knowledge is an element of the writer's representational palate, not a nonnegotiable category of reality that must be honored. Judith Fetterley and Marjorie Pryse criticize Wharton for having treated regionalism with such "extreme hostility and even fear" (58). While I disagree with the spirit of this critique, I agree that Wharton feared regional writing. It was claustrophobic and regressive.

In short, Wharton was no fan of the "Feminine Principle." This isn't a surprise, especially considering that her strong suit is the urban social novel. As Fetterley and Pryse imply, Wharton's New England novellas are cautionary tales. But Wharton's brief relationship with the rural had a research methodology that deserves acknowledgment. Wharton's method has been criticized by critics of regionalism for whom nonnative perspectives are always suspect. Wharton has been accused of knowing too little about New England to write about it. However, she insists that her two New England novellas are the result of ten years of "explorations among villages still bedrowsed in a decaying rural existence" (quoted in Hamblen, 239). Despite what she says, Wharton was no James Agee. Her ten years in the country were spent as summers in a fully staffed mansion called "The Mount."[11] The class-inflected context of this "fieldwork" notwithstanding, Wharton's criticism of rose-colored New England is valid. Her critique is of reader and writer interest in idyllic representations of New England, representations that find roses and lavender where there may be only stark granite. Wharton pushes rural America toward extinction. The impact of her tragic vision is multivalent. Her goal is to devalue fiction about provincial niceties and thus to mobilize the production and consumption of urban social novels.

Banks's objective contrasts with Wharton's. Rather than abandon the rural, Banks wants to find a way to value the rural while also escaping it. He produces a divided narrative sensibility that both loves the monsters of New England and frees itself from them. Unlike Wharton's unnamed narrator, whose cosmopolitan credentials are assumed, Banks's narrators are never automatically detached from their region.[12] They are natives who want somehow to be outsiders. They try to attain cosmopolitan credentials either by becoming writers and thereby expressing distance through metafiction (as does the narrator of *Hamilton Stark*) or by going to college and moving to the suburbs (as does the narrator of *Affliction*). Banks's career represents a steady shift from metafiction to realism, a shift from an unresolvable ambivalence about the purpose of representing the rural to a clear-eyed accounting of the late twentieth-century remains of the rural. Banks's early metafictional pretensions display a tone of sophistication that contrasts with the raw materials on which *Hamilton Stark* focuses so heavily. This juxtaposition recalls Agee's reflexivity, which also juxtaposes introspective sophistication against provincial thoughtlessness. But Banks's metafiction is not the play of self-reference that one expects from the genre. Though referentiality does play into the structure and sensibility of the narrator, the purpose of the novel's "meta-" component is to dramatize the awkward position of a novel writer who chooses to handle local color long after it's outlived its value.

Unlike Wharton, Banks doesn't do violence to local color. Instead, he dramatizes the relationship between local color and violence. He eventually abandons metafiction for a more conventional form of fiction, because metafiction tends to mystify more than dramatize. If the writing process itself the takes center stage, as it does in a metafictional narrative, the larger cultural point gets obscured. Therefore, in more recent novels, Banks transforms metafictional logic into a logic of characterization that exists firmly in the world of the novel. Banks begins to tell the story not *of* "granite outcroppings" but *through* "granite outcroppings." Characters suffer the same familial and cultural failures and external sentimentalisms as do the Fromes, but the narrators of these stories are not detached observers.

His narrators are almost Conradean in their insistence on "immersing" in the "destructive element," and their agency, however intense, is occupied solely in tasks that respond to their collapsing legitimacy.[13] Banks thus treats local knowledge not as a set of disposable facts but as an obstacle that his characters and narrators alike are wholly absorbed in negotiating. For his characters, local knowledge overwhelms and is thus a source of pain that "marks" them as distinct. For his narrators, local knowledge is a way out of the local, a way of gaining the evaluative means to explain why violence is so central to writing about the overlooked sites of America's most beloved region.

The divided allegiance of Banks's narrative sensibility has been characterized as "self-consciously postmodern" (Niemi, 17). According to Robert Niemi, *Hamilton Stark* is less of a novel than it is a "fictive journal about the entire cognitive, emotional, and investigative process of novel writing" (70). Its prose style is reminiscent of *Let Us Now Praise Famous*

Men — formal introductions, self-reflexive digressions, elaborate studies of geography and regional history, transcriptions of tape recordings, and various addenda. Like Agee, Banks represents the nexus between rooted and detached subjectivity. For instance, in a chapter titled "The Matrix," Banks elaborates on the "geographic, historic, economic, and ethnic factors" that have produced the colorless "outcroppings" of the region (*Hamilton*, 21). Here Banks draws complex parallels between the title character's violent behavior and the glacial and colonial violence that produced the region and its settlements. He overemphasizes the message that northern New England is "only for tough, heavy-coated, pugnacious, stubborn animals" who submit neither to sentimental fantasy nor to the movement of industrial capital (29). Those who want fantasy and prosperity "inevitably drift to the south and west" (30).

Hamilton Stark's life in rural New England is not so quiet and desperate that Stark attempts suicide. He does, however, cut himself on the rough edges of his world. He takes a decidedly masochistic delight in, to quote Wharton's introduction to *Ethan Frome*, crashing "his cockle-shell to the rocks" (vii). Stark regularly destroys his own furniture. After divorcing a wife (he has five in the course of the novel), Stark shoots holes in whatever domestic remains she's left behind and throws them in a great junk heap, "making bets, and usually winning them, that he could lift and throw a sofa over the fence . . . or that he could carry a refrigerator in a broken wheelbarrow for a quarter of a mile over a rough surface under a hot August sun" (6). Stark here is disposing of sentimental attachment. Anthropomorphizing Cather's call to "de-furnish" the novel —"How wonderful it would be if we could throw all the furniture out of the window"— Banks represents the destructive pleasure of fiction that abandons its responsibility to represent material conditions (Cather, 51).

Unlike Ethan Frome, who can't escape provinciality except through smashing himself to pieces, Stark chooses violence as a way of inhabiting provinciality. He relishes his granite features and labors (as a plumber) in filthy working conditions, among "cobwebs, dust, soot, mucky water, shit and garbage." The biographical reading here is clear: both Stark the plumber and Banks the plumber-turned-writer are "trying to make an old piece of equipment work like a new one," to make art out of rusty junk (107). This understanding of literature as labor is analogous to Banks's plans for local knowledge, which he wants to fit onto the pipeline of cosmopolitan citizenship.

Unlike Wharton, who represents the destructive element of rural New England as evidence for why people should stop caring about the rural, Banks deals with the wreckage of the rural as though it were the stuff of autobiography. Indeed, *Hamilton Stark* is a record of a working-class writer's flight into writing, into the kind of self-conscious language acts that are both a welcome contrast to physical labor and a way of aestheticizing the inelegant details of a laborer's life. Banks's narrators have to work for their cosmopolitan credentials. This, as I will argue in the following section, is a process of embedding the thumbprint of provinciality onto the very consciousness of one who considers himself "cosmopolitan."

III

In *Affliction*, Banks's "deep investigation into the 'local'" finally delivers on its promise to be "personal without being 'autobiographical'" (quoted in Niemi, 69). In this novel, Banks splits the working-class sensibility into two parts: the embodiment of provinciality (Wade) and the voice of hard-won cosmopolitanism (Rolfe). This dynamic frees Banks up to explore the violent self-destruction that exists at the heart of a masculinity that has been abandoned by the movement of history. Rolfe Whitehouse, the narrator of *Affliction*, is a high school history teacher. He narrates the majority of the novel from the safe distance of the Boston suburbs. Rolfe was a reluctant member of the Whitehouse family. He "fled the family and the town of Lawford when [he] was little more than a boy" (4). His training as a historian affords him a keen view of the violent self-destruction that defines his brother, Wade. Through Rolfe, Banks historicizes self-destructive masculinity. Through Wade, he exemplifies it. The interaction between the two adds up to the kind of oscillation between native knowledge and detachment.

However detached he tries to be, Rolfe is subject to the same categories as his brother: "I was no more or less adapted than Wade to the soil and climate we were both born into — stingy soil, rocky and thin, and a mean climate. . . . I was as much a tough little lichen as he" (201). Banks's narrators always have this kind of native knowledge of landscape. They speak of moraines and monadnocks (geological vocabulary found in *Hamilton Stark*, *Continental Drift*, *Affliction*, and *Cloudsplitter*). This literacy of terrain makes for beautiful scenic description. For instance, in *Affliction*, Rolfe describes the regional coordinates of New Hampshire as being geologically and meteorologically bifurcated. He tells of an "unmapped line" between the impoverished rural region to the north and the suburban fields of Concord and Manchester to the south (61). North of the line, the weather is characteristic of eastern Canada; to the South, it is characteristic of the Northeast. Rolfe presents the class division this way:

> There are . . . two crucially different climate zones that are divided by an invisible line running across New Hampshire, drawn from Vermont in the southwest corner of the state near Keene, through Concord in the center of the state to the lakes north of Rochester in the east and on into Maine. . . . The land is tilted higher in the north, is rockier, less arable, with glacial corrugations like heavy-knuckled fingers reaching down toward the broad alluvial valleys and low rolling hills of Massachusetts and Connecticut and the coastal plain of eastern New Hampshire and Maine. (60–61)

The reference to the knuckle-print of glacial violence shows Rolfe's working-class roots. He thinks about region by enlarging the scale of thinking about labor. Aside from this reference to the narrator's working-class imagination, the above description is void of figurative language. The division between the disparaged poverty of Rolfe's youth and the affluent suburbs of his adulthood is simply a fact. Natural patterns like the "unmapped line" are ready-made; the narrator's only job is to present them. The intended effect of such presentation — to assert that violence and injustice have geological coordinates — is already built into the form. Things are bad in Lawford simply because Lawford is too far north. No amount of reform could overcome the problems north of the line, at least that's what Rolfe wants to believe. Rolfe's description of northern New Hampshire is thus an object lesson in how to mobilize knowledge as information in order to escape responsibility.

Aside from being a manifestation of Rolfe's desire to rely on an unjust geography of economic disparity, this map of a bifurcated New Hampshire is reminiscent of other, more canonical representations of New England. Like Robert Frost's *North of Boston* (1914) and Wharton's "North Dormer" in *Summer* (1917), Lawford has a "northness" to it that seals its fate. Unlike the nineteenth-century local color writer, who would treat the zone north of the "unmapped line" as though it were in need of preservation, Rolfe criticizes the citizens of Lawford for not moving away. Those south of the line "have reflected the generosity and temperance of the climate there," and those north, obviously, "have reflected in their daily lives the astringency, the sheer malignity and the dull extreme of the climate there" (61).

Rolfe's reliance on the geography of economic disparity continues when he rescales this dichotomized logic from region to nation. As the history teacher explains, the split between northern and southern New Hampshire is analogous to "the difference . . . between China and Mongolia, or between England and Scotland, Michigan and Manitoba" (61). Differences like these make regional difference look like a miniature version of national difference. By naturalizing the split between north and south, Rolfe casts an economic problem as a regional matter of fact. He fails to politicize divisions that, in the case of England/Scotland and China/Mongolia, are precisely political.

But, in *Affliction*, the political narrative always gets subsumed by the personal narrative. Dedicated to Banks's father, Earl Banks, whom Banks has identified as abusive, the novel circles the theme of paternal violence throughout. As a parable of paternal violence (which it certainly becomes in Paul Schrader's film adaptation), *Affliction* projects itself as a vehicle for a universal theme and thus a novel that has abandoned the small themes of regional fiction. Even Banks's decision about the novel's title highlights the book's nonregional focus. The manuscript was originally titled "The Dead of Winter," a title that asserted the prominence of the "unmapped line." The title "Affliction" has no regional connotations. A reference to his favorite philosopher, Simone Weil, who supplies the novel's epigraph —"*The great enigma of human life is not suffering but affliction*"—"Affliction" connotes permanence. With a central theme of paternal violence, Banks evokes one of the most ubiquitous, regionally nonspecific, literary themes. Even Wade knows that he is a regionally nonspecific type: he "was shrewd and honest enough to know that he would be in his forties and lonely, poor, depressed, alcoholic and violent anywhere" (83).

A formerly abused child (though he never directly admits it), Rolfe has strong negative feelings toward everyone in his story. But he also has the training of a historian. As a historian, Rolfe presupposes that paternal violence has a history and a cause. On the one hand, as evidenced by the "ancient" terminology used to describe Wade's face, Rolfe blames peasant masculinity for the violence that runs in his family. On the other hand, as evidenced by Rolfe's insistence on disparaging his hometown, Rolfe blames the willed ignorance of the town. Rolfe announces the impact of his affliction on his perspective on the story he is telling: "I despised Wade's life. Let me say it again. I despised Wade's life" (4). Nevertheless, the story of Wade's life continues to "displac[e] all other stories" (48). Rolfe must identify the cultural disease of Lawford before he can be free from it. He must figure out how Wade, high school football hero and favorite son of Lawford, turned into such a beer-fat, abusive failure. It is through this afflicted historian that Banks produces his most complex critique of provincialism.

Rolfe is no storyteller. His story is hard for him to write. He is a history teacher and relies heavily on sober facts to tell even the most personal and traumatic experiences. He recounts Wade's story as though it is a matter of procedure, beginning the novel simply: "This is the story" (1). He does not mystify or moralize the violence that has been so central to his life. He simply criminalizes it, asserting that even the most ancient and enduring form of paternal violence is a simple matter of crime and punishment. From Rolfe's perspective — the affluent Boston suburbs — paternal violence is not a rich literary theme but simply a misdeed answerable to law enforcement. If only the people of Lawford could see it this way, they might banish the monsters from their midst.

The real problem, then, must be the town itself. Rolfe breaks his disinterested historian's affect when considering the idiocy of Lawford residents, who so poorly run their town that they appoint its resident monster, Wade Whitehouse, as its sole police officer. Rolfe insults the citizens of Lawford, whom he calls "remnant people," for having stayed in a worthless place, a veritable lawless zone of drunken masculinity (6). He is unsympathetic about the "sad jumble of families huddled in a remote northern valley," hiding from the monsters that their own stupidity has begotten (180). But, like the people of any local color story, the citizens of Lawford have no interest in being part of the larger nation. Their "willed conservatism," the pride they take remaining in a place that has outlived its economic reason for being, helps them "cope with having been abandoned by several generations of the most talented and attractive of its children" (6). Noticing this cultural logic, Rolfe revises the "affliction" of paternal violence from its status as a universal inevitability to a regionally specific type of behavior.

The people of Lawford resurrect for special occasions the "rose and lavender" idea of New England. They have been "tricked . . . by the wider, sentimental culture" to preserve the region's rich legacy, even if that means doing nothing to stop the monsters terrorizing its interior (6). Thus, Lawford clings to "bits and shards of social rites that once invested their lives with meaning: . . . bridal showers, weddings, birthdays, funerals, seasonal and national holidays" (5). Without these "half-forgotten misremembered ceremonies," the people of Lawford would be "no longer a people." Mawkish rites like bridal showers and Christmas dinners "affirm a people's existence, but falsely" (6). Even at the level of word choice, Rolfe indicts Lawford for the crime of paternal violence. He describes bridal-shower social rites as "bits and shards," while he describes the evidence of Wade's violence as "bare scraps and bits" (5, 48). The former has dangerous ("sharp") edges that can actually do violence, whereas the latter is "bare" and fleshy, more a surface to be scratched than an implement for scratching. Also, the "bare scraps and bits" are not strange to Rolfe but are pieces of historical knowledge that fit into "coherent, easily perceived patterns" (48). It seems ironic that Rolfe gives sharp edges to the innocuous social rites and a fleshy innocuousness to violent rampage. Lawford's provincialism is in some way more dangerous than Wade's violence. Where violence can be criminalized, the people of Lawford will always have the right to uphold their seemingly innocent social rites, even though these rites actually reproduce the conditions that drive away those, like Rolfe, who might save the town from its monsters. It is not a crime to be sentimental about rural culture, and that is exactly the problem.

Partly because of his focus on indicting Lawford and partly because he is a traumatized storyteller, Rolfe delays, for nearly two hundred pages, any direct discussion of Wade's having been beaten by this father. In an extended flashback about Wade's high school courtship, Rolfe recalls that "it was the same summer that Wade first spoke to anyone of our father's violence" (182). This narrative delay forces the reader to decide whether the new information ought to override the character profile of Wade that Rolfe has already produced. By retroactively labeling Wade a victim of child abuse, readers run the risk of understanding Wade's own violence as an inevitable feature of his character. Such a post hoc character analysis might obscure the complexity of Banks's critique of local knowledge. Nevertheless, this father-centric reading has become dominant. For instance, Paul Schrader's film adaptation focuses steadily on paternal violence, which feeds into a deer hunting murder mystery plot that is far more central to the film than it is to the novel. All the film's publicity photos (and all the tie-in trade paperback covers) feature James Coburn, as Wade's father, looming above Wade's shoulder like a diabolical reminder of the lineage of Wade's titular affliction.

Though it's tempting to align all the plot elements under the centering theme of paternal violence, the father's late arrival produces a crisis in reading, wherein paternal violence arrives as one of a string of horizontally related causes of Wade's criminal behavior. When read this way, paternal violence is just another in a series of masculine dilemmas that represent the laboring man at risk. For instance, when Wade's father tries to kill Wade, Rolfe describes the scene with the same pacing and tone as, elsewhere, he describes Wade plowing snow. It's as though filicide were another kind of labor common to the region. The father's face had "no expression other than one of mild disgust . . . of a man compelled to perform a not especially pleasant task, the decision to do it having been made long ago" (342). Then, in the spirit of parataxis, Rolfe catalogs a number of other violent acts of labor:

> wooden mallet to pound a circus tent stake into the ground, to slam the gong that tests a man's strength, to split the log for a house, to drive the spike into the tie with one stroke, to stun the ox, to break the lump of stone, to smash the serpent's head, to destroy the abomination in the face of the Lord. (342)

Fragmenting the signs of ancient inevitability, Banks here and elsewhere disregards the purity of big themes. But he doesn't devalue them. On the contrary, he pieces together the signifiers of the weighty theme, both questioning the use-value of male violence and disputing its claim to universality.

Instead of assuming its permanence, Banks calls up an index of causes of what looks like inevitability. In doing so, he proves Sally Robinson's point that "the forced embodiment of whiteness and masculinity is often represented as a violence" (4). When not working or being violent, Lawford's men have little value. Their natural occupation seems to be to destroy the world. Such destruction is the one form of labor that remains recession-proof in Lawford, as exemplified by Gordon LaRiviere's well-drilling business. "Lawford's only success story," LaRiviere has made his company motto: "OUR BUSINESS IS GOING IN THE HOLE" (11). The basic metaphor here is that the labor of rural workingmen is a kind of willed self-destruction, of spending more of oneself than is available—"going in the hole." Wade's position in the production of holes is key. He is the one who drills most of the wells in Lawford. Everything about his work annoys him, makes him feel like a boy negotiating the trivialities of the world over which he has no control. For instance, he is always worried that he will not be able to get from his school crosswalk job to his snowplowing job in time to get the good, heated snowplow. Wade is "humiliated" to have to drive the uncomfortable grader, a "huge lumbering ridiculous machine" (113). Giving violent manual labor the emotional resonance that comes to a child who is denied a favorite toy, Banks is implying here that rural masculinity is stuck in a perpetual state of petulant childhood.

Wade's perpetual toothache both underscores this condition of masculinity and rescales the drilling metaphor. His injury has an interesting impact on Wade's self-perception. It is a crippling pain that leaves him remarkably *unmarked*. Wade looks at himself in the mirror during an intense fit of pain and notes the irony of how unlike a wounded man he appears to be. Wade's toothache, along with his employment as a well driller, evokes the tradition of American literary naturalism, as a not-so-veiled reference to Frank Norris's famous tooth-obsessed monster, McTeague. The reason why teeth and toothaches are important to writers like Norris and Banks is twofold: they dramatize the question of scale in relation to the violence of physical labor, and they present the perpetual, invisible pain of men.

As such, Wade's "affliction" is not something that a disinterested observer can see. This invisible pain is contrasted against the paralysis of Wade's divorce lawyer, J. Battle Hand. As opposed to Wade's internal afflictions, Hand's relation to violence (in his case, that of a drunk driver) is explicit. Hand's body cannot perform physical labor. It is the result of violence but cannot reproduce violence. Wade has essentially the same agency as does the broken lawyer, that of *disability*. Going through the formal moves of law is as uncomfortable for Wade as going through the normal moves of daily life must be for Hand. All either man can do is adapt himself to disability's limits and develop "wholly reactive" lives (177).

By the end of the novel, the entire town of Lawford has to adjust to its transformation from a quaint hamlet into a ski resort town, an adjustment that everyone but Wade can execute. In the end, Rolfe's investigation is not what banishes Wade from New England; it is the operational logic of venture capitalism. It is the selling of a key piece of real estate in Lawford, the seven-thousand-acre "monadnock" of Parker Mountain, that ultimately saves Lawford (50).[14] The Abenaki word for the erosion-resistant hills that exist independent from the White or Green Mountains, monadnocks are for Banks what granite outcroppings are for Wharton. They are geological accidents that become the lodestones of rural New England.

Disgorged by thousands of years of retreating glaciers, Parker Mountain (named after the colonial officer who "bought" it from the Abenakis for some trunks of sundries) was bequeathed to Parker's children, who sold it to a logging corporation and "moved south to Concord and Manchester, where they disappeared into Victorian bourgeois respectability, setting the precedent for a later pattern of migration" (50–51). During the Depression, the corporation went bankrupt, taking from communities like Lawford their economic reasons for being. The aggregate of banks that acquired Parker Mountain auctioned it off "in large slabs for one hundred dollars an acre." By the late 1980s, the mountain belonged to a hundred different families "barely aware of the existence of their few acres of useless stony northern New Hampshire countryside, except when the tax bill came in" (51). Banks expounds on the fragmented state of this foraged piece of rural New England:

> By now, deeds, bills of sale, surveyors' reports, maps and tax assessments were so tangled . . . it was difficult if not impossible to ascertain who owned how much of what. Consequently, . . . more than two centuries after Major Parker's purchase of Parker Mountain from the Abenaki Indians, proprietary rights had come full circle. Once again, ownership of the land was determined more by use than by law. (51)

The irony here, that corporate logic returns the landscape to its "natural" state, is compounded by the fact that two shrewd businessmen (Gordon LaRiviere and Evan Twombley) silently buy up the mountain to convert it into a ski resort, turning Lawford into the kind of "thriving economic zone" that Wade cannot continue to terrorize (353). This side plot about the mountain adds to the central theme of self-destructive masculinity in that the side plot presents a version of local knowledge that, like Rolfe's historicization of paternal violence, renders provinciality into a grainy set of conditions that can be "revitalized."

In short, though paternal violence is an ancient and universal theme, it has a face that tells the history that has led to its present state: "a face shaped by thousands of years of peering into firelight" and a body "evolved over tens of thousands of years of holding the reigns of another man's horse . . . the kind of body that made it possible for European princes and popes to wage war" (56–57). By producing a universal theme from a collection of symbols that imply both masculinity and its ever-diminishing power, Banks engages a debate about the value of white male fiction in a way that neither mirrors the anxieties of devalued white men nor suggests who is really "holding the reigns" of power. The very idea of who has access to power starts to look unanswerable. The Parker Mountain side plot thus finally demystifies paternal violence.

Banks implies here that rural New England is in trouble partially because of how afraid of corporate facelifts it is. The long tradition of New England local color has produced a culture that would rather inbreed monsters than join a narrative of economic and cultural "progress." Banks thus suggests that readers and writers of local color should reconsider the tendency to think that standardization is a universally bad thing. The point is not that standardization produces better communities but that standardizing logic roots the revenant monsters out from the New England wilderness.

In a sense, the novel's deus ex machina reminds regional writers that the old storylines are over. The forces of standardization are no longer the unqualified antagonist of the regional narrative. Banks's point is not to endorse the forces of standardization but to call for an examination of the global resonance of rural tragedies. Banks's novels try to keep alive conversations about the continued relevance of rural America. His more recent novels demonstrate the parallels between the local traumas of rural America and those of the so-called Third World. In the next section, I will examine this more explicitly global form of regional writing.

IV

In *The Darling* (2004), Banks applies his no-nonsense regional voice to a remarkably worldly narrator: Hannah Musgrave, a former member of the Weather Underground and a former wife of a Liberian politician. A onetime domestic terrorist, Hannah knows a lot about how to abandon local ties. As she learns in her tenure as a housewife, she knows very little about how to settle. The novel begins long after the end of Hannah's radical past. It begins even after her time as the wife of Woodrow Sundiata, friend and political partner of Charles Taylor. (Yes, that Charles Taylor.) As if Banks hadn't globalized his scope enough, he begins *The Darling* the day after Hannah has a dream that compels her to leave a small farm in the Adirondack Mountains and return to her chimpanzee sanctuary in Monrovia. He ends the novel on September 10, 2001, the day before "the story of my life could have no significance in the larger world," the day before the history of America would be rewritten so that her story would seem "merely the story of an American darling" (392).

Thus, despite its global scope, *The Darling* is a return to the elegiac mode of regional fiction. The narrator knows that her relevance is waning and that her mode of radical politics is as quaint as a Patty Hearst reference. Despite this waning relevance, many recent novels have centered on the figure of the role of women in revolutionary or radical politics. These novels, arguably beginning with Julia Alvarez's *In the Time of the Butterflies* (1995), also interact with historical events and figures. So many of these kinds of novels have been published recently that "women revolutionaries — fiction" has earned its own Library of Congress subject heading. A short list of American fiction cataloged under the "women revolutionaries" heading includes *Erased Faces* by Graciela Limón (2001), *No One to Trust* (2002) by Iris Johansen, *Blood Diamonds* (2002) by Jon Land, *The Maquisarde* (2002) by Louise Marley, *American Woman* (2003) by Susan Choi, *The Wild Irish* (2003) by Robin Maxwell, *The Tree Bride* (2004) by Bharati Mukherjee, and *Rosa* (2005) by Jonathan Rabb. This list offers a fairly even sample of popular historical fiction, crime fiction, romance novel, and "literary" fiction, marking "women revolutionaries" as a bountiful subject in contemporary fiction. An interesting offshoot of the "women revolutionaries" category is the recent boon of novels featuring the kidnapping of Patty Hearst. In addition to Choi's excellent novel, Christopher Sorrentino's *Trance* (2005) and Dana Spiotta's *Eat the Document* (2006) have meditated on this particularly spectacular "woman revolutionary." The fact that Banks's narrator labels herself a "darling" signals Banks's awareness of the titillation of such narratives, if not also of the shelf life.

After reading about how the New Deal dream of social welfare evolved into the nightmare of early 1970s radical politics from Hannah's perspective, it becomes clear that Hannah's generation was the last to actually be moved by the dream, the last to have something other than a passively consumerist relationship to the dream. What's different is that what Banks, via Hannah, elegizes is not a dying region but a dying sensibility. The dream of social welfare that James Agee tried to save from the reductive regional imagination of documentary art and that Jack Kerouac planted into his roving hobos and that Kingston revitalized through Wittman's civic literacy is now a defanged "darling." The dream is over and *The Darling* is Banks's process of discovering what killed it.

The answer has something to do with the botched connection between poverty and privilege, with the white, middle-class misunderstanding of its obligation to the "less fortunate." Unlike *Let Us Now Praise Famous Men*, which indicts the bourgeois American tendency to pity poor people, *The Darling* goes a step further and criticizes white managerial control over the way the deep injustices of slavery get repaired. Hence, Banks's choice of setting. Liberia is a nation created by abolitionist Americans in the early nineteenth century as a way of "freeing" manumitted slaves by removing them from America. As Banks explains, "the whole theme of Liberia . . . became important to me when I was researching *Cloudsplitter* [Banks's novel about John Brown] . . . I got into the early history of the antislavery movement and the creation of Liberia and its intimate and ironic connection with American racial history" (Interview with Birnbaum, 2005).

The plot of *The Darling* touches on many points of a standard civil liberties timeline. It starts with Civil Rights–era initiatives managed by privileged white men like Hannah's father, a fictionalized version of Dr. Benjamin Spock. (Yes, that Dr. Spock.) Hannah hates her father's self-righteous liberalism. He is a physician, best-selling author, and activist, who makes news every time he attends a protest with the likes of Arthur Miller and the Berrigan brothers. Hannah's radical activism is a reaction against her father's visible, safe mode of activism, his walking "arm in arm with like-minded, earnest white men of a certain age and position" (144).

As opposed to her father, who "believed in nonviolence because he himself was incapable of committing a violent act," Hannah believes in violence because violence assures her that she is a proactive manager of social welfare rather than a privileged kid who can only react to what chance inheritance has granted her (147). Violence here, as in Banks's earliest fiction, serves as a mode of self-enactment for Hannah.

What is fascinating about *The Darling* is that Hannah's tone casts an air of easy reflection over the most nightmarish places and events. Like Marilynne Robinson's *Gilead*, minus the homiletic resonance and plus a lot more sex and drugs and violence, *The Darling* captures the intimate drawl of a narrator in the midst of reflecting on her life. Like all of Banks's first-person narrators, Hannah's literacy of self is secondary to her literacy of her surroundings. Since she is a woman, this literacy at first looks like a gender stereotype. Hannah alludes to this fact when she reveals, somewhat abruptly, her gender: "I sometimes think it's because I *am* a woman . . . that I was able to adapt so easily to the pace and patterns and rhythmic repetitions of nature's clock and calendar" (4, italics in original). Though this sounds like Banks is typecasting Hannah, the truth is that all of Banks's storytellers have this talent. They all understand what Hannah calls "the requirements of soil" long before they understand how to tell a decent story (4). Narrative control — the ability to shape historical and regional knowledge into a coherent narrative — is something that Banks's narrators acquire within the pages of the novels themselves.

In *The Darling*, which focuses on global vistas and not on a single, blasted region, this reflexive approach to narrative control has the effect of making cosmopolitan credentials seem like something anyone can acquire. By placing the familiar drawl of a regional narrator into the mouth of a political-radical-turned-West-African-housewife, Banks makes an almost unthinkably "global" person sound like the girl next door. The ease and familiarity of Hannah's voice makes her radical past seem safe. Through her voice, unimaginable places become palpable. Once palpable, these places can be assimilated into a reader's worldview. They become places that actually exist in the same world in which the reader lives.

Hannah's voice is thus quite the consumable delivery mechanism for a post-national elegy of social welfare. Through her voice, Banks delivers what Amitava Kumar calls for in *World Bank Literature*: stories that do not simply showcase the diverse cultures that have sprung from economic globalization but that "forge new connections and elaborate on . . . new coalitions and emergent subjectivities" (xxiii). By engaging both the Liberian Civil War and the Weather Underground, *The Darling* brings forces of radical rebellion in the third- and first-worlds, respectively, into close proximity. What's more, Banks's experience with New England fiction helps his West African milieu seem real.[15] Both settings are economically devastated. Just as Lawford has been stripped of its original purpose as a logging village, so has Liberia outlived its usefulness to a U.S. that has found a cheaper supplier of bananas and rubber. Banks's accounting of the aftermath of this abandonment applies the regional-cosmopolitan objective of expressing uncommon interrelationships to a global context.

But the interrelationship that Banks is after differs from, for example, the global interrelationships dramatized in the popular movies released around the same time as *The Darling*. Unlike Paul Haggis's *Crash* (2004) or Alejandro González Iñárritu's *Babel* (2006), which cashed in on the post-9/11 upsurge of interest in global interrelations, *The Darling* is not an exercise in interlocking plotlines. Banks's interrelationships are not simultaneous but are rooted in a history of global interrelationships that date back to the founding of Liberia. Hannah's journey to Liberia is a trip back in time, to the beginning of U.S. managerial control over the lives of African slaves and their descendants.

Indeed, the only way to Liberia is through the American South. Banks begins this trip by placing the origin of Hannah's dream of social welfare in the segregated South. Reminiscing about her college days, Hannah describes herself as a white, middle-class youth bent on placing herself onto the sites of social injustice. (It is worth suggesting here that Hannah's fervor may have been fueled by the 1960 reissue of *Let Us Now Praise Famous Men*.) Hannah remembers feeling an unexpected jolt of white supremacy when she and other white college students were asked to cede their managerial authority to the very black people for whose rights they had traveled south to fight. She explains:

> For years, ever since the Civil Rights movement got taken over by blacks, and the white college kids like me and the white lawyers and clergymen were sent home from the South, leaving us with only the splinters that

were left of the antiwar movement . . . I'd felt somehow cheated out of my true mission, as if in my chosen line of work I'd been deprived of an essential tool, and that tool was black people. (56)

This confession implies that the dream of social justice is sometimes indistinguishable from a dream of managerial control. The form of authority that Hannah craves is akin to coalitionism, by which a majority group approaches a minority group and asks for its help realizing demands that the minority group never articulated. This form of mercenary political activism is the very kind Hannah craves as an undergraduate. The fact that adult Hannah winds up marrying a centrist Liberian official whose political ambition it is to reinstate trade relations with the U.S. is thus unsurprising. Liberia shares many traits of the American South.

Because of her undergraduate wish to be the boss of social welfare, Hannah has always been attracted to the South. Explaining her "first journey into the American South," Hannah describes herself as

> a college girl using her summer vacation to register black voters . . . an innocent, idealistic, Yankee girl whose vision of the South had arisen dripping with magnolia-scented decay and the thrill of racial violence from deep readings of William Faulkner and Flannery O'Connor. A newly minted rebel, fresh faced and romantic . . . confident that we were about to cleanse our parents' racist, oppressive world. (12)

The South for Hannah was a stage upon which to indulge in idealism. It's the place of Flannery O'Connor, the place wherein "the fact that we shall always have the poor with us is a source of satisfaction."[16] Introducing it as the first site of white managerial control over poor black people, Banks sets up Liberia as an incubated form of the antebellum social system. Hannah explains that Liberia originated as an "alliance between northern white Christians and anti-slavery advocates and slaveholders from New York State to Georgia" as a way to export "enslaved blacks — especially the more troublesome ones." The West African terrain upon which Liberia was founded was "impenetrable jungle, mangrove swamps, and malaria-infested estuaries, a plot of super-heated, saturated ground that no one else wanted" (87). It was not a nation so much as a zone beyond the reach of even the most radical abolitionist's sense of duty.

It was a quick fix for a "*race* problem" that even abolitionists, who had "noticed the presence of a growing number of ex-slaves on the streets of northern cities," feared (86). In short, Liberia was "the first U.S. colony . . . a covert surrogate, clamped tight to the white-skinned leg of its North American founding fatherland" (88). Hannah explains:

> By the end of the nineteenth century, just as in parts of the deep South and the Caribbean at the end of the eighteenth, one percent of the population of Liberia . . . owned the other ninety-nine percent, and a huge chunk of the profits generated by the back-breaking labor of that ninety-nine percent went straight to the board rooms of America. (89)

But by the mid-twentieth century, the U.S. had found cheaper suppliers of rubber and bananas in Latin America, meaning that "our man in Africa got left behind" (89). In the wake of this abandonment, Liberia solidified its caste system as a way to maintain social and economic stability. Liberian appreciation of Hannah's good intentions is not likely to expire; no one will ever kindly ask her to leave Liberia to the Liberians. No one except Charles Taylor and the civil war he produces.

It is at the edge of an impenetrable jungle, midway between the city of Monrovia and the interior bush, that Hannah realizes her complicity in the injustice of wanting to manage social welfare initiatives. She is riding in her fiancé's limousine, the very kind of "air-conditioned chariot" she had, as a member of the Weather Underground, fantasized about blowing up. Out the window, she sees "poor people eking out their day-to-day livings." After all that she has done in the name of justice, she remains on this side of the glass barrier between poverty and privilege. Hannah screams internally: "let me be one of *them*, not one of *you*! Let me walk unnoticed with them along this dusty road to the market and not ride smoothly over it" (119, italics in original). She jumps out of the limo and comes face to face with a frightened goat. She hugs the goat. The goat is indifferent to her good intentions. Looking at the goat, Hannah experiences a moment of interspecies intersubjectivity. The goat's "pathetically scared gaze" becomes "for one brief moment . . . the central reality of my world" (120–121). The goat's face ignites an uncanny shock. Hannah realizes that she needs the goat more than it needs her. In fact, her comforting embrace is a source of discomfort to the goat. Fleeing the chariot is thus not an act of empathy but an act of self-preservation.

What Hannah realizes here is that she has been fleeing one chariot or another her whole life. She has been thrusting herself onto the sites of injustice in a way that only makes those sites less habitable for the victims of injustice. Hannah admits, "when I fled from the safety and comfort of the ministry car and embraced that poor, pathetic, female goat, it was not to comfort her, but somehow to induce her to comfort me" (125). By embracing the goat, Hannah engages in what looks like an act of comfort for a less fortunate being but what is actually a last-ditch effort at managerial control.

Is it surprising, then, that Hannah starts a chimpanzee sanctuary? Considering that her travels had opened the door to many new kinds of injustice and victims, it might seem odd that Hannah chooses chimpanzees. But, insofar as needy figures have, since the sharecropper, been represented as unassimilable into mainstream society, the chimpanzee is as good a candidate as any. Like the sharecropper, whose visibility answers the question of *who* is beyond the reach of New Deal welfare, the chimpanzee answers the question of *what* lies beyond the boundary of the human. The name "chimpanzee" itself marks this boundary. As Hannah points out, chimpanzee means "'mock-man' . . . derived, not from the creature's own nature, but from its relation to us, to humans, as if its essential nature were a lesser version or a negation of ours." The chimpanzee is "the only species named in such a purposefully distancing way. It's the not-human. The not-us. The un-man" (21). Hannah's chimpanzees allow her to exert managerial control. The fact that they are caged allows for her to make safe emotional commitments to their welfare. Even the names she gives them exemplify this need for emotional commitment. The names "were sounds that for mysterious reasons I liked saying to myself, sounds that were keys capable of unlocking blocked memories, lost sensations, ignored associations" (185).

For Hannah, animal welfare is a more feasible form of social welfare.[17] The chimps matter to Hannah because they allow her a scaled-down version of her fantasy to control the distribution of justice. Because she recognizes that her significance is diminishing, that "when my politics disappeared, my only hope for an autobiographical narrative had disappeared," Hannah knows she has few options outside of the chimpanzee sanctuary (165). Her life without the chimps has been punctuated by acts of abandonment. From the chimps she learns how to value the stability of confinement, the safe comfort of cramped spaces:

> It may seem strange to you, but something about prisons, jails, cages comforts me. All my life I've run from confinement and tried to keep others, even animals, from being imprisoned. Yet whenever I come close to an actual place of confinement, whenever I'm physically in its proximity, something inside me clicks off and something else clicks on. (291)

What "clicks on" here is the ecstasy of "limitation theology," the storyteller's excitement at finding a world that is at once articulable and transcendable.[18] Confinement confirms the idea that place is something to inhabit and eventually to imagine one's way out of — not something to be defined by. Because so little of her life has been defined by her local ties — and more by her choice to flee these ties — the idea of limitation is a curious comfort to Hannah.

This ironic turn of events, wherein a former member of the Weather Underground winds up wanting to be in jail, is Banks's way of reasserting his career-defining mantra that local knowledge can be a generative tool — that by "keeping things local," a writer can "keep them personal, without actually being 'autobiographical'" (quoted in Niemi, 69). Because Hannah fled too soon, because she sought to bomb the air-conditioned chariots of her past without first exploring these chariots' contours, she never properly escaped the chariots. This reminder about the virtues of reflecting on one's roots, one's conditions of confinement, is arguably the key legacy of the New England literary imagination. Indeed, it is only through reflecting exhaustively on the manner in which he is "yarded" that Thoreau finally escapes the entropy of daily life in Concord.

EPILOGUE

Jonathan Franzen and the Unity of Discord

Part of what makes Jonathan Franzen infuriating to so many of his contemporaries is that he acts as though he invented the desire to have a big audience for literary fiction, as if his decision to write readable social novels is part of some private, Promethean urge to consolidate the otherwise niche reader communities of contemporary America. Franzen disapproves of the recent popularity of regionalism. This disapproval amounts to a finicky caveat to his desire to have a big audience. Though regional fiction makes best-seller lists and wins big literary prizes, it's the wrong kind of widely read fiction, Franzen suggests, because it diminishes the possibility that widely read fiction will be widely read in nonpolarized ways, in ways that don't simply group together like minds.

Indeed, Franzen's reticence about having *The Corrections* (2001) chosen for Oprah's Book Club is a sign of his fear about having his own work met with the wrong kind of big audience. Audiences made of like minds—even Oprah-level numbers of like minds—are always just niche gangs hunting for that consumption-centric experience of "identifying with" and thus assimilating into a narcissistic self-perception the product of an author's hard work.[1] According to Franzen, any fiction that marks itself for group specificity, be that mark a regional inflection or an O-shaped logo on a novel's cover, is inviting a readership that looks like a community but that is actually an insulated comfort zone. Indeed, a close look at Franzen's career reveals a career-defining anxiety about the possibility that groups of readers might start to think that the experience of like-minded consensus is the same as, if not an adequate replacement for, the not altogether comfortable experience of real community.

To put this assertion in the terms of my argument, Franzen works against the idea that cultural polarity will be "solved" by an interpretive principle that values consensus above all else — one that appears to serve depolarization but that actually reboots the dichotomizing cultural logic of elitism vs. populism. In his *Slate* recap of the elitism/populism debates that Franzen's career has initiated, Jess Row reminds us how the reaction against Franzen, specifically Ben Marcus's aggressive nose-thumbing, represents "an unnecessary, and disingenuous, attempt to repolarize American literary culture." While Marcus is trying to rekindle an air of contention that actually, according to Row, "ended decades ago," to drag literary culture back into an age of manifesto writing, Franzen is trying to drag into the twenty-first century the kind of broadly read middle-class realism that Gordon Hutner sees peaking in the first half of the twentieth century.[2]

This is the impression one gets from reading the flak around Franzen's success. A closer look at Franzen's fiction reveals something similar but more nuanced. Franzen is actually, slowly coming to terms with the fact that he must please the identification-seeking reader. He must satisfy the reader's age-old desire to see himself in and thus to "care about" the characters and their worlds. Franzen has to learn the lesson about the centrality of "identification," a lesson that Timothy Aubry articulates in his book, *Reading as Therapy* (2010):

> Your urge to identify with fictional characters, though dangerous in its favoritism, covert narcissism, and concomitant cruelties, will nevertheless enable you to transgress your own boundaries, apprehend unfamiliar modes of subjectivity, and thus begin the dialogue necessary to constitute a more inclusive community. (68–69)

Franzen's effort to force onto the literary scene a renaissance of digestible social fiction is our sign that he's arrived at this realization. As Paul Charles Griffin notes, with the publication of Franzen's novel *Freedom* — Oprah Winfrey's pick for the final installment of her book club — comes Franzen's "complete transformation . . . from a more experimental status novelist to a traditional contract novelist." The goal of this transformation, and probably also the goal of Franzen's reconciliation with Winfrey, is to unify a reading public that has been divided along lines that grow from the fallacy that experimentation is a kind of audience aversion.

What will eventually bring about this renaissance is some kind of truce between New York and the Midwest, a truce that will not come easily. In his much talked about trend piece (and soon-to-be book), "MFA VS. NYC," Chad Harbach reminds us that New York–orbiting writers like Franzen are pretty insular. He also reminds us that these insular writers have to live daily with the discomforting reminder that they must please readers beyond the five boroughs. They have no choice but to write for red America and blue America alike, to produce "clear and lyrical long novel[s]" that both hockey moms and hipster moms will want to read (10). Books that, like Harbach's own, are simultaneously about baseball and homosexuality and Herman Melville. The reason is obvious: "fierce market pressure toward the middlebrow, combined with a deep authorial desire to communicate to the uninterested" (9). So, as NYC writers make novels designed for this new "violet" American market, Franzen acts as if he invented the market. Which brings me to the second reason why people hate Jonathan Franzen.

He's trying to have it both ways. He wants to be able to say with a straight (if not slightly red) face during his *Paris Review* interview, "I'm an old egalitarian Midwesterner" (Franzen, Interview) and be able to conclude his dust-jacket author notes with that obligatory "He lives in New York City." Of course, this sentence has recently expanded to read: "He lives in New York City and Santa Cruz, California," which means that now Franzen is claiming bicoastal zip codes *and* a flyover-state sensibility. Add to that the fact that he acts as though he invented the desire to have a big readership — *and* that he's actually achieved this readership — and it's safe to assume that Franzen's *Time* magazine cover photo is pocked marked with dart holes in more than one west-central Brooklyn apartment. The best case one can make against this self-fashioned poster boy for Violet

America is thus that he is successful despite the fact that all he's really done is reinvent the wheel. He is a career-minded writer who follows the pressures of the market and then calls this market-directed path his brilliant solution to a polarized reading public.

What follows is a brief comparison of Franzen's earliest intervention into polarized America to his most recent intervention into an America that seems to have depolarized itself in the wrong way. In his first novel, *The Twenty-Seventh City* (1988), Franzen poses a "crackpot" solution to cultural polarity. More recently, he has tried to use his fame, born as it has been from debates about elitism vs. populism, to articulate the role of literary fiction today. What this comparison will show is that Franzen's solution to his fear of a falsely consolidated readership is an earnest defense of the idea that literary fiction can create possibilities for cultural depolarization — specifically for a reconciliation between red and blue America.

IN THE *NEW YORKER* review of *The Twenty-Seventh City*, Terrence Rafferty criticizes Franzen for not doing what first novelists usually do too much of: beginning his career with a "heartfelt, solipsistic coming-of-age novel." While the "scrupulously maintained air of objectivity" through which Franzen renders his hometown of St. Louis, Missouri, is a pleasant surprise to Rafferty, the novel's lack of "emotional resonance" is finally unsettling. The fact that Franzen writes about his hometown "as if he were a city-planning consultant from out of town" convinces Rafferty that Franzen is too interested in demonstrating his detachment from the Midwest to be a convincing storyteller (101). In fact, Franzen's objective manner of telling his story amounts to "tactics for evasion," reasons to dismiss *The Twenty-Seventh City* as a soulless demonstration of skill (103). Rafferty prefers the more successful, if less skillful, "first novels" from the fall 1988 list — among them Michael Chabon's self-consciously bildungsromanian, *The Mysteries of Pittsburgh* (104).

In his recent *Paris Review* interview, Franzen admits that Rafferty was right. *The Twenty-Seventh City* is a novel written by a twenty-five-year-old who is wearing "the mask of a middle-aged postmodern writer" (Franzen, Interview). The novel takes on the air of postmodernism that is characteristic of a genre of fiction that Melvin Jules Bukiet (borrowing from Richard Powers) calls "crackpot realism." According to Bukiet, such realism carries enough counterintuitive flights of fancy to mislead readers into thinking they are reading a writer who agrees with DeLillo's assertion that the contemporary world lacks "a sense of a manageable reality" (quoted in DeCurtis, 48), when in fact they are being taken into what Bukiet calls an "orbit where the imagination changes the political, the emotional, and occasionally, the physical ground rules of existence."[3] These "orbits" qualify the fiction as "realist" because they tether plot and character to a cohesive scenic and narrative logic. Crackpot realists (Bukiet names Pynchon, Franzen, and Powers) flirt with but don't finally submit to metafictional digression. Instead, they "find pattern and meaning . . . beyond the welter of random, inchoate experience" (14). Their hunts for meaning always involve a narrow escape from the web of signification to which metafiction generally submits. Crackpot realists create and solve the technical challenges that arise from the minutiae of such counterfactual situations as, to use the example of *The Twenty-Seventh City*, a Midwestern city under siege by a Marxist Indian police force. Such brands of realism also reveal the capacity of literary fiction to act as a laboratory through which to experiment with causes and solutions to cultural polarity.

The world of *The Twenty-Seventh City* is a disconcerting clash of Midwestern banality and Eastern exoticism. The novel's plot is an improbable, ultimately failed, conspiracy to consolidate the tax bases of St. Louis City and St. Louis County. The conspiracy plot is complemented by a scenic landscape dotted by the exotically dressed Indian immigrants who occupy the abandoned built environment of downtown St. Louis. This plot and setting add up to an opportunity for Franzen to indict the antiurban sentiments that animate city-planning paradigms in the Midwest. For instance, the inability of newly arrived Indian families to inhabit in any natural way the public space of downtown St. Louis is revealed not as a matter of the insolubility of Indian and Midwestern culture but as a matter of poor architecture:

> Indians were noticed lounging with no evident purpose on the skybridge between Dillard's and the St. Louis Centre. They were observed spreading blankets in the art museum parking lot and preparing a hot lunch on a Primus stove, playing card games on the sidewalk in front of the National Bowling Hall of Fame. (6)

Such imagery calls attention not to the fact that the people are out of place but to the fact that there is no place for people. Such transitional spaces as skybridges, parking lots, and sidewalks are designed to convey individuals, not to help sustain human community. Franzen's grammar reinforces the nonhuman scale of the city's built environment. Franzen's passive voice removes city dwellers — the would-be noticers and observers — from the sentence. The Indians "were noticed" and "were observed" by no one and from nowhere in particular. By placing visuals that read as foreign into an environment that reads as vacated, Franzen brings into relief the extent to which cultural polarity is hardwired into the very urban materiality of the Midwest. Public space belongs to nobody, and that's just who has moved in.

Before zooming into this surreal, counterfactual version of St. Louis, Franzen provides a hand-drawn map of the city. From this lofty vantage, the reader sees a cluster of suburban municipalities with such sylvan names as Kirkwood, Crestwood, West Wood, Brentwood, Rock Hill, Webster Groves, Richmond Heights, Ladue, Creve Coeur, Frontenac, Des Peres, and Clayton, separated from the desolate set of superblocks that represents downtown St. Louis. The map thus incites an explanation of this municipal oddity. Readers want to have answered the question of why what we think of as "St. Louis" is actually a cluster of small municipalities parked next to a relatively small city. In his second chapter, Franzen offers an answer in the form of long passages about the city's history.

In that chapter, Franzen recounts the past hundred years: In 1870, it was "America's Fourth City . . . a booming rail city, the country's leading inland port, a wholesaler for half a continent. Only New York, Philadelphia and Brooklyn had larger populations." (24). By citing these facts, Franzen alludes to the fact-bending rationalizations that Midwestern city boosters have been using since Sinclair Lewis imagined "Zenith" in 1922:[4]

> Granted, there were newspapers in Chicago, a close Fifth, that claimed the 1870 census had counted as many as 90,000 nonexistent St. Louisans, and granted, they were right. But all cities are ideas, ultimately. They create themselves, and the rest of the world apprehends them or ignores them as it chooses. (24)

But the problem with St. Louis's ascent is not the dishonesty of its boosters but the line between city and county, which boosters actually opposed. In fact, city boosters tried to reduce county superiority. They tried to bypass the county's "archaic" administration and court system, whose "'judges' were notoriously corrupt and insensitive to urban needs" (24). Franzen details a "secession scheme" in which the city offers to let the county buy its way out of thinking about "urban matters" for the price of forty acres of farmland for "tomorrow's parks and industry." The scheme passed and the County Court dissolved. Forty acres, however, turned out to be nowhere near the amount of land needed, and "as early as 1900 the city was running out of space." As a result, industrial interests fled the city, and new business interests settled in the county. In the 1930s, suburban white flight began as "poor black families arrived from the rural South, hastening the migration of whites to the suburbs." In the 1940s, the city's tax base dwindled to next to nothing. The housing projects of the 1950s (most famously Pruit-Igoe) "failed spectacularly" and imploded in the 1960s (25). By the 1970s, St. Louis entered its "Era of the Parking Lot" (26). By the 1980s, the decade in which the novel takes place, the city's population was half what it had been in 1930. This recap of the city's post-Depression decline presents St. Louis as a case study into the way post-Depression cultural polarity can become a geographical matter of fact.

Just before he introduces this historical explanation of the dividing line between county and city, Franzen introduces an unlikely unifying force—"one S. Jammu," a character he creates through combining nonfictional local knowledge about St. Louis and a fictional back story for Jammu's character (5). This combination of fictionalized and nonfictional local knowledge establishes the correspondence between actual and counterfactual history that qualifies *The Twenty-Seventh City* as a work of crackpot realism.

For instance, Jammu's arrival in St. Louis coincides with "another, more familiar Eastern visitor to St. Louis, the Veiled Prophet of Khorassan" (6). The Veiled Prophet Organization, an actual secret society in St. Louis, is made up of the families of county business leaders. It takes its name from a Thomas Moore poem titled "The Veiled Prophet of Khorassan" (1817).[5] Franzen's narrator notes that the novel's opening night is the same night as the Veiled Prophet Organization's debutante ball — an annual occurrence that features a lavish parade as well as an appearance from the prophet himself (a costumed business leader) and attendants adorned in Persian regalia.[6]

Following the gloss about the Veiled Prophet is a transcription of a fictional newspaper profile of Jammu, in which we learn that she had formerly been an enforcer of Indira Gandhi's quasi-socialist policies in Bombay in the 1970s. We also learn that, from Jammu's perspective, St. Louis is best understood less as a city than the center of a regional block. The criminal element she's been hired to eradicate is, in her words, part of "a *regional* problem" to which county leaders ought to start attending (11, italics in original).

Most of the novel's action consists of Jammu's luring these leaders into a "'State'" wherein they become so preoccupied with previously dormant personal and professional problems that they begin to act against their better interests (30). Once in the State, the men start to do uncharacteristic things, like buying up abandoned buildings in the slums of St. Louis City for the "blighted area" tax abatements (83). During the political phase of her consolidation scheme, Jammu initiates a grassroots movement known as "Urban Hope," a competing force of the "Municipal Growth" movement from the County. This rift eventually develops into a City/County merger referendum that — despite a lot of pro-Jammu fanfare from young people in St. Louis County — fails miserably. What Jammu hadn't bargained for is the fact that political support in the form of young people wearing tank tops with photogenic Indian policewomen on them is not the same thing as actual political support.

Despite Jammu's popularity as an icon for the 18 to 24 County demographic, only fifteen percent of the voting public turns out on election day. Only twenty percent of that fifteen percent vote for the merger. In the end, it's too much to ask even the hippest County kid to undo a municipal logic that has safely insulated him from the unsavory realities of the poor black families in the City. As for youth culture's love of Jammu-headed tank tops, it turns out that the sons and daughters of the "well-to-do white people [who] were never going to permit their children to attend schools with dangerous black children" are hip to change but are simply too enlightened to participate in the democratic process. Indeed, Franzen represents Reagan-era youth as a generation that is "outgrowing the age of action" (503). In the place of civic engagement comes an acculturated form of Eastern enlightenment:

> Americans seeking purity wisely left the toxic wastes and consumer complaints and labor unrest and bankruptcies to other nations, or to the remnants of the original merchant caste. The path to enlightenment led through the perception that all communal difficulties are illusions born

> of caring and desire. It led through non-action, non-involvement, and individual retirement accounts. The new generation had renounced the world in return for simplicity and self-sufficiency. Nirvana beckoned. (504)

According to this solution to "all communal difficulties," the way to overcome cultural polarity is simply to fall into a collective state of inaction, to inhabit the very comforting fog of nonengagement that had finally wafted from the West Coast of the 1960s to the Midwest of the 1980s.

In addition to being hippie wannabes, the youth of *The Twenty-Seventh City* are products of what Samuel Cohen calls the "triumph-restoring amnesia" of the 1980s, an amnesia that has recently given way to more proactive forms of forgetfulness (Cohen, 132). In his 2011 Kenyon College commencement address, Franzen admonishes students for one such form of forgetfulness: social media. This great evil, says Franzen, transforms that triumph-restoring amnesia into a firewall against any real form of commitment, political *or* personal:

> to say to yourself, "Oh, I'll get to that love and pain stuff later, maybe in my 30s" is to consign yourself to 10 years of merely taking up space on the planet and burning up its resources. Of being (and I mean this in the most damning sense of the word) a consumer. ("Liking")

To put it in less curmudgeonly (no less generation-damning) words, millennials have traded the painful experience of "growing up"— that process of extending oneself into a world that might reject that self— for access to technology that remakes the world into a safe and affirming place. After all, the point of technology, says Franzen, is "to replace a natural world that's indifferent to our wishes . . . with a world so responsive to our wishes as to be, effectively, a mere extension of the self" ("Liking").

In the quarter century between Franzen's faux-middle-age damnation of young people to this actual middle-age damnation of young people, social media have indeed emerged and placed most of us into a "State" similar to the one into which Jammu places her twelve businessmen. We're all happily inside what Frazen, in 1988, called a "spherical enclosing screen on which pictures were projected," and Franzen couldn't be more upset about it (Franzen, *City*, 219). This is why he's been writing novels that try to force us out of our States, force us into an unmediated world of alienation wherein we have to experience something close to the analog pain of such beautiful failures as Chip Lambert and Patty Berglund.

Indeed, in the wake of the death of Franzen's good friend (and real life beautiful failure) David Foster Wallace, Franzen insisted that the one common trait of both experimental fiction (à la Wallace) and middlebrow fiction (à la Franzen) is nostalgia for intimacy: "The point of agreement that [Wallace] and I eventually reached was the notion of loneliness: that fiction is a particularly effective way for strangers to connect across time and distance" (quoted in Kirsch 22). Adam Kirsch takes Franzen at his word and sees Wallace and Franzen as part of a generation that believes "that literature should be positive, constructive, civically engaged, a weapon against alienation" (22). Where Wallace immersed himself in the sinkholes of alienation that litter technocratic landscape of late twentieth century, Franzen reminds readers that the internet era has no special purchase on alienation.

Consider the episode in *The Corrections* wherein a young, petulant Chipper Lambert gets consigned to his seat at the dining room table for refusing to eat his liver and rutabaga. It's here in the crepuscular light of a suburban home, with "the sound of someone else's Ping-Pong" in the distance, wherein Chipper acquires a taste for that self-destructive alienation that he so relentlessly stalks in the first 130 pages of the novel (263). Chipper "grows up" at this long moment of confinement. As his fingertips explore the underside of the dining-room table, he has the painful realization that the material reality of the table's underside "would be puny" compared to the world he's imagined it to be (265).

> He'd see crannies he hadn't yet discovered with his fingers, and the mystery of the realms beyond his reach would be dispelled, the screw holes would lose their abstract sensuality and the boogers would shame him. (265)

The Corrections tells the story of three adult children whose lives will not be complete until they return, kicking and screaming, back to these Midwestern sites of shame. For Denise Lambert, the sign is etched under her father's workbench. For Gary, it is in that electric drill he still fails to operate correctly. These signs of shame, for Franzen, are a central paradox. As evidence of tactile interaction with the world that does exist, they are testaments to the fact that these people have actually lived. Chip finally experiences the shock of his existence when he returns home in time for Christmas breakfast. As he helps his father to and from chairs, he experiences the simple fact that he is a person with a body—"somebody was *clinging* to him, as if he were a person of substance, as if there were something to him" (542). Like a good Midwestern mother, Franzen makes his characters feel bad for their flights and failures. And he makes these characters use their shame to save the lives of the people who deserve to be saved — be they Al or Enid Lambert or Walter Berglund.

This is Franzen's answer to polarizing forces he couldn't plot his way out of in *The Twenty-Seventh City*: plant into the Midwest a sensibility that is antithetical to the region's cultural logic but that is ultimately the region's only hope. It's a reverse of the revolt from the village. What makes this answer effective is that it gestures at a kind of sectional reunion between what's become known as "red and blue America" that doesn't devolve into a reaffirmation of flag-waving exceptionalism. This nonexceptional method of unification can be seen in Franzen's contribution to *State by State* (2009), Matt Weiland's homage to the WPA State Guide series. Franzen was (surprisingly?) assigned to write the New York entry in that anthology, and his essay is (surprisingly) winsome, a transcript of an almost unsuccessful attempt to interview the state of New York, which Franzen personifies as a popular girl with a deep entourage. Musing about his childhood crush on New York, Franzen makes the following reconciliatory claim:

> There's a particular connection between the Midwest and New York. Not just that New York created the market for the goods that made the Midwest what it is. And not just that the Midwest, in supplying those goods, made New York what it is. New York's like the beady eye of yang at the center of the Midwest's unentitled, self-effacing plains of yin. And the Midwest is like the dewy, romantic, hopeful eye of yin at the center of New York's brutal, grasping yang. ("New York," 333)

Franzen takes seriously Weiland's proposition that the states of America are "united" in a profoundly contentious way, that America is "bound together . . . as tightly as any confederation on earth" but that it also "stubbornly resist[s] blending into a single undifferentiated whole" (xii). It's this stubborn resistance that Franzen hopes to see continue to govern American cultural and intellectual life in the twenty-first century. This utter refusal to settle on a particular paradigm to govern everyday life unites us. It even connects America today to the public bickering and civic engagement that characterized the autonomy-seeking colonies of the prenational era.[7]

What's changed is that stubborn resistance has become a set of predictable postures. These postures only sharpen the lines between red and blue America. By forcing the "beady eye" of New York into the Midwest's "unentitled, self-effacing plains," Franzen's fiction dramatizes the kind of cross-cultural pollination that he hopes a big, different-minded audience might help to bring about in America culture. By making the kind of widely read, serious fiction that gets him on the cover of *Time* magazine — and by having the kind of public career that gets him disinvited *and* reinvited to Oprah's Book Club — Franzen has become a catalyst for public discourse about the role of novel reading in the twenty-first century.

His alliance with Oprah is a sign that the tension between the contract model of reading (wherein books entertain) and the status model (wherein they challenge) has given way to a new set of possibilities. The fact that Oprah intervened into the reception of both *The Corrections* and *Freedom* should not be misunderstood as a distraction from serious debate about these novels. Instead, it's a condition of the way we have to talk about these novels, a condition that foregrounds the question of what kind of public life literary fiction ought to have. Franzen's disinvitation from and reinvitation to what is the de facto touchstone of contemporary novel reading add up to the very kind of fracas that draws different-minded readers out of their interpretive comfort zones and into a common line of discourse. In effect, the Oprah/Franzen alliance — stranger than fiction as it may be — may prove to be emblematic of the very acts of depolarization that have, until now, been imagined only in the pages of the kinds of books I've examined in *Violet America*.

NOTES

Introduction

1. A couple of examples of this spike in interest: Wiley published the massive *A Companion to the Regional Literatures of America* in 2003 as part of the Blackwell Companions to Literature and Culture Series; in 2009, *Modern Fiction Studies* published a special issue on regional modernism.

2. See Bill Brown's *A Sense of Things* (84–92) for an interesting discussion of the parallels between Jewett's fiction and museum curatorship, both of which, according to Brown, reproduce place "as knowledge" (86).

3. See Martha Nussbaum's "Patriotism and Cosmopolitanism" for more on the concentric logic of cosmopolitanism.

4. The phrase "practices of everyday life" is a reference to Michel de Certeau's book *The Practice of Everyday Life* (1984). For more on Hegeman's notion of "spatiality" in the formation of modern conceptions of "culture," see *Patterns for America* (32–65).

5. For some great work in this vein, see the *Modern Fiction Studies* special issue "Regional Modernism" 55.1 (2009).

6. Lutz corrects his periodization almost immediately after he makes it. He also has a chapter in *Cosmopolitan Vistas*, titled "After 1930," that surveys the persistence of regional cosmopolitanism in American fiction.

7. See Glazener's appendix on the *Atlantic* group of periodicals for more discussion of this commitment to centralizing their cultural trusteeship (257–266).

8. Brodhead's *Cultures of Letters* and Foote's *Regional Fictions* are both mainstays of this line of scholarship on regional fiction.

9. See Anthony Hilfer's classic *The Revolt from the Village* (1969) for more on these writers' crusades against provincialism.

10. Hilfer is making an obvious reference to an often-quoted, enigmatic passage in chapter 20 of Joseph Conrad's *Lord Jim* (1900), in which the German trader Stein advises Marlow to "immerse" himself in the "destructive element," suggesting that the only way to understand the self in the context of the turmoil of modern life is to submit totally to the turmoil.

11. "Program era" is Mark McGurl's term for fiction produced in the context of creative writing programs.

12. This "poem" is printed in the front matter of her collection of craft essays, *The Faith of a Writer* (2003), and is reprinted on so many of her lecture-tour pamphlets.

13. Oates has long been an advocate for a renewal of regionalism in contemporary fiction. In her introduction to *The Oxford Book of American Short Stories*, Oates answers the question —"Is American literature at its core a literature of *regions*?"— in the affirmative. Contemporary writers resemble one another "along lines that have less to do with traditional American themes than with . . . highly specific, brilliantly realized American *places*" (6).

14. See Foer's interview with Robert Birnbaum for more on Oates's role in Foer's career.

15. For more on O'Connor's formative role in the Iowa Writers' Workshop, as well as her academic credentials, see McGurl's "Understanding Iowa: Flannery O'Connor, B.A., M.F.A."

16. Here's how limitation theology works: a writer "transcends its limitations only by staying within them" (O'Connor quoted in McGurl, *Program Era*, 154). This idea of transcendence carries religious connotations, which is to say that it is obviously polarizing. O'Connor's commitment to transcendence is likely a result of her Catholicism. See Paul Elie's *The Life You Save May Be Your Own: An American Pilgrimage* (2003) for a discussion of O'Connor's Catholicism.

17. The essay fetched an entire anthology of rebuttals, *For Love of Country?* (Cohen, 1996).

18. I'm alluding to the title of Pinsky's recent contribution to the Rice University Campbell Lectures, *Thousands of Broadways: Dreams and Nightmares of the American Small Town* (2009).

19. Even in Brooks's time, these kinds of celebrations were reserved for such disillusioned reformers as Granville Hicks, who, in the wake of the Hitler-Stalin pact, gave up on progressive politics and embraced small-town conservatism. In 1939, Hicks resigned from the Communist Party, and in the 1950s he was a cooperative witness before the House Committee on Un-American Activities. In 1946, he published *Small Town*, his celebration of island-community parochialism.

20. "Against Theory," by Steven Knapp and Walter Benn Michaels, which originally appeared in *Critical Inquiry* (8.4), incited a number of responses. Those responses are collected in *Against Theory: Literary Studies and the New*

Pragmatism (1985). The most accessible and direct example of Michaels's "against multiculturalism" position can be found in *The Trouble with Diversity: How We Learned to Love Identity and Ignore Inequality* (2006).

21. For discussion of this overlap, see Fredric Jameson's lengthy discussion of *The Gold Standard* in *Postmodernism* (1991, 181–217). Jameson sees the book as symptomatic of "New Historicism," which is marked by "a return to immanence and to a prolongation of the procedures of 'homology' which eschews homology's theory and abandons the concept of 'structure'" (188). *The Gold Standard*, according to Jameson, is mostly engaged in the work of establishing homologies. However, Jameson finds a "second impulse . . . , which (most often in the footnotes) draws active and protopolitical consequences from the more neutral work of the establishment of homologies" (200).

22. See Deborah Tannen's "Agonism in the Academy: Surviving Higher Learning's Argument Culture" for more on "agonism," or the ritualized debate of academic culture.

23. For a useful overview of these debates, see Jess Row's "Marcus vs. Franzen: The Latest Literary Wrangling in *Harper's* Leaves Everyone Confused."

24. Ginsberg recalls this as Kerouac's career-long mantra, and perhaps the mantra of the Beat generation at large. The quote originally appears in Kerouac's novel *Visions of Cody* (1959). Ginsberg's reminiscence about that line appears in the documentary film *What Happened to Jack Kerouac?* (1986, redistributed 1998).

25. In his "Notes on the Franzen Wars," Paul Charles Griffin voices, then explains this readerly bicker as follows:

> the only structural innovation in the novel outright fails: Patty's nearly two-hundred-page "autobiography" . . . sounds exactly like Franzen's authorial voice that both precedes and follows it. Many reviewers have noted this flaw; nobody was fooled. And that's because Franzen didn't put enough effort into actually inventing an original prose voice for Patty. Apparently, that would have been too hard, too experimental. In a word, too *interesting*.

1. *Specific Soil*

1. Jones's *American Hungers* includes a discussion of *Praise* as this very kind of literature (116–120).

2. See Robert Vanderlan's *Intellectuals Incorporated* (2010) for a fuller description of the publication history of *Praise* (159–164).

3. The quoted passage comes from Flannery O'Connor's essay, "The Teaching of Literature." Here is the entire passage:

> I am very much afraid that to the fiction writer the fact that we shall always have the poor with us is a source of satisfaction, for it means, essentially, that

he will always be able to find someone like himself. His concern with poverty is with a poverty fundamental to man. (131)

4. Though Haraway's quote is not about documentary writing per se, it is applicable in that it relates to the subject position that pseudoscientific writing normally silently assumes.

5. See Jonathan Harris's *Federal Art and National Culture* for more on the consequences of Congress's defunding of "Federal Project Number One," the "collective name for the visual art, music, theater and writing projects created by the Works Progress Administration" (130).

6. Stott argues that, without documentary art, the Depression would have been hard for many Americans to experience: "Not only was the Depression easy for the casual eye to miss, but those who should have brought it to public attention — the Hoover government, the business community, most of the media — overlooked or minimized it, hoping thus to restore confidence" (68).

7. MacLeish's documentary photo-book *Land of the Free* was published, with Roy Stryker's blessing, in 1938. As John Tagg explains, MacLeish's goal in *Land of the Free* "was to find ways to shape public opinion through the direct and public use of poetry, hybridizing his writing with forms drawn from mass media" (31). MacLeish describes the accompanying poems in *Land of the Free* as a "choral voice," an overbearingly populist mix of what Tagg refers to as "Southern Agrarian themes of the betrayal of Eden with quasi-Marxist themes of capitalist exploitation in a way that seemed convincing at the time to so many east coast intellectuals" (31). According to Tagg, MacLeish's project was to establish a "metaphoric unity" among photographs for photographers who had no idea of the "metonymic realism of their archival Project" (32).

8. In the editor's note, Laughlin acknowledges that "it has been obvious for some time now that the photograph was destined to play a far greater role in literature than ever the simple art illustration did" (145). Alluding to MacLeish's essay, Laughlin claims something like editorial ownership of the "fusion of photograph and soundtrack (words)" (145). This fusion produces a "third experience" independent from hearing words or seeing images. Laughlin claims that the prose "attempt[s] to fix things in immobility, in the way that a great lyric can fix an ephemeral mood for all time" (146).

9. Though its titles focus on provincial America, the "American Scene" section of the New Directions anthology reinforces the cultural trusteeship of New York. Morris had moved to Connecticut only two years earlier, in 1938.

10. See my article, "Revising the Great Depression," for more on the standard narrative about the Depression. In that article, I discuss memoirs and history books about the Depression, examining the emergence in recent years of a neoconservative conceit about the self-sufficiency of poor people.

11. See Lauren Coats and Nihad Farooq's "Regionalism in the Era of the New Deal" for more on the regional imagination of New Deal art and for more on the TVA, which "many . . . regionalist contemporaries lauded as the great regionalist experiment" of the New Deal (81).

12. Cordell Hull was Roosevelt's Secretary of State and a Tennessee native.

13. This bad reputation is especially true of regional fiction (cf. Jewett's "The White Heron" and Chesnutt's "The Goophered Grapevine").

14. *Children of Crisis* was a five-volume study (1967–1977). Volume two, which along with volume three won the Pulitzer Prize for general nonfiction in 1973, was titled *Migrants, Sharecroppers, Mountaineers* (1971). This volume is a multigeneration study of East Coast migrant farmers, southern sharecroppers, Appalachian mountain dwellers, and the "rural mind" in general.

15. The above quote from Stott is his biting reference to the work of Bourke-White, whom Stott accuses of just about every crime against documentary form.

16. See Paul K. Conkin's *The New Deal* (1967) for more on New Deal policies toward marginal farmers, specifically the failure to institute sufficiently progressive tax reform and the excessive generosity toward select business interests.

17. These two phrases—"nominal subject" (which refers to the sharecropper families and homes) and "on loan from the federal government" (which refers to the leave Evans took from the FSA to accompany Agee to Hale County)—appear in each of the many versions of the preface, which Agee revised more than any other section of *Praise*. That these two phrases show up in every version of the preface suggests that Agee's flip attitude toward the genre was painstakingly produced.

18. "Gudger" is the surname Agee gives the family. It's since come to light that the real family name is "Burroughs." Nevertheless, I use the name that Agee and Evans attributed to the family.

19. W. J. T. Mitchell is right, then, to call her the "Mona Lisa" of the Depression. But he's wrong to say that she is a Mona Lisa because we "find her fatigue, pain, and anxiety beautiful" (294). Instead, Annie Mae Gudger is a Mona Lisa because she registers the scopic carnality that exists at the point of contact between subject and artist.

20. The translation that Agee uses is this: "Workers of the world, unite and fight. You have nothing to lose but your chains, and a world to win."

21. There's another possible reason for the reissue and popularity of *Praise*: Agee's untimely death and posthumous Pulitzer Prize had created an uptick of interest in Agee. According to Stott, the reprinting of *Praise* is a result of a "cult forming around Agee because of his *Death in the Family*, film scripts and film criticism, and early death" (268). Indeed, my assertion that the shift in reception had something to do with the maturation of the country's attitude to social justice overlooks Loren Glass's assertion that American reading habits are usually

more responsive to celebrity than to an author's social commitments. See Glass's *Authors Inc.* for more discussion of American reading habits, as they relate to literary celebrity (1–27).

22. According to Szalay, Peter Bürger's principle tenets of the avant-garde are "fundamentally in accord with" New Deal Arts Projects: "unqualified hostility toward the individual production and reception of art as well as toward the distribution of art through laissez-faire markets and institutions" (68).

23. For instance, Bill Nichols reveals overlaps in documentary and avant-garde aesthetics in the 1920s and 1930s. His essay "Documentary Film and the Modernist Avant-Garde" examines the crossover career of Dutch avant-garde filmmaker Joris Ivens, who directed such documentary films as the Hemingway-narrated *The Spanish Earth* (1937) and the New Deal promotion of rural electrification, *Power and the Land* (1940). Similarly, art historians like Erika Doss see documentary and regional art in the 1930s beget the abstract expressionism in the 1940s and 1950s. See Doss's *Benton, Pollock, and the Politics of Modernism: From Regionalism to Abstract Expressionism* (1991) for a compelling look at the continuities between Thomas Hart Benton's aesthetics and those of his protégé, Jackson Pollock.

24. Du Bois was fond of the mock dignity of the French word for sharecropper (*Souls*, 146 and 156–158; *Negro*, 132 and 134). Du Bois uses the word to refer to black sharecroppers, tenants, and wage laborers.

25. This passage appears in the closing pages of "Colon: Curtain Speech," the ten-page hiatus between "Part One: A Country Letter" and "Part Two: Some Findings and Comments."

26. Critics have often assumed this companion to be Evans. Not only is there no evidence that Agee's companion is Evans, critics' assumptions confirm Agee's own suspicion that the men and women he tries so diligently to "praise" will, despite his efforts, remain churls with next to no intellectual capacity. However, in these critics' defense, Agee makes no effort to identify the rest of the group constituting the "we" of "On the Porch 3." The only other prevalent instance of Agee using the pronoun "we" occurs in the third section of "A Country Letter," when Agee repeats the ominous rhetorical question "How was it we were caught?" (72, 81). This "we" is likely Evans, if not the reader. The only indication that the other half of "we" in "On the Porch 3" is in fact Evans comes when Agee notes that the animal making the mysterious sound has "become a searcher with whom we had identified ourselves" (411). But assuming the companion is Evans based on this evidence assumes that "searchers" are by default documentary intruders, thus stripping the Gudgers of the very subjectivity that Agee tries to keep alive in his representation.

27. Boyle's subject, illegal immigration in Southern California, bears strong relation to Steinbeck's, especially considering Steinbeck's own conception of the

lineage of immigrant laborers in the California farm fields (more on this below). Boyle's novel also begins with an epilogue from *Grapes*: "They ain't human. A human being wouldn't live like they do. A human being couldn't stand it to be so dirty and miserable."

28. See Kevin Hearle's "These Are American People" for more on the relationship between Steinbeck's fiction and white supremacy.

2. *Pavement*

1. "Moloch" is a reference to part II of Allen Ginsberg's *Howl* (1956).

2. See note 24 of my introduction to this book.

3. One can see Agee's self-reflexive structural wackiness in David Foster Wallace's *Infinite Jest* (1996) and Dave Eggers's *A Heartbreaking Work of Staggering Genius* (2000).

4. Kerouac mimics this song's refrain, "mañana, mañana, mañana is soon enough for me," in his description of the Mexican workers Sal lives with for a time. Knowing no Spanish, Sal decides that "mañana" must be Spanish for paradise: "It was always *mañana*. For the next week that was all I heard—*mañana,* a lovely word and one that probably means heaven" (94). For more discussion of Kerouac's appropriation of stereotypes of Mexican peasantry, see Mark Richardson's essay "Peasant Dreams: Reading *On the Road*."

5. It is worth citing here the final paragraph of the scroll manuscript, if only to confirm the fact that the "Pooh Bear" pimple was premeditated:

> So in America when the sun goes down and I sit on the old brokendown river pier watching the long, long skies over New Jersey and sense all that raw land that rolls in one unbelievable huge bulge over to the West Coast, all that road going, all the people dreaming in the immensity of it, and in Iowa I know by now the evening-star must be drooping and shedding her sparkler dims on the prairie, which is just before the coming of complete night that blesses the earth, darkens all rivers, cups the peaks in the west and folds the last and final shore in, and nobody, just nobody knows what's going to happen to anybody besides the forlorn rags of growing old, I think of Neal Cassady, I even think of old Neal Cassady the father we never found, I think of Neal Cassady, I think of Neal Cassady. (408)

6. See Morris Dickstein's chapter "On and Off the Road" in *Leopards in the Temple* for a discussion of the "road" motif in midcentury fiction.

7. Although Sartre's novel was published in 1938, *Nausea* was not translated into English until 1949. See George Cotkin's *Existential America* (2003) for further discussion of the impact of Sartre and other French existentialists on midcentury American fiction. Cotkin describes the ways existential ideas played out

in American popular culture in the late 1940s and early 1950s (91–133). See Bill Brown's brief discussion of *Nausea* as the most famous modernist instance of literature that animates the physical environment to emphasize the radical otherness of physicality (*Sense*, 8).

8. *Blue Highways* opens with this explanation: "On the old highway maps of America, the main routes were red and the back roads blue" (ix).

9. I am thinking specifically of the branch of local color made popular by Bret Harte's *Overland Monthly* stories and poems, published from 1869 to 1870, all featuring sentimental depictions of gangs of noble gamblers and prostitutes. As Elizabeth Ammons notes in her introduction to the Penguin anthology of *American Local Color Writing*, local color in this vein "has the ability to challenge and deconstruct monolithic national, imperial, and racial agendas" (xvii). Kerouac had similar ambitions in his narrative of the West.

10. Morris Dickstein refers to *Adventures of Huckleberry Finn* as "one of the *ur*-texts of the postwar fiction" (90).

11. Stewart's *The Names on the Land* was initially published in 1946 and reissued in 1956, one year before *On the Road* was published.

12. The above is a reference to Huckleberry Finn's famous decision to "light out for the Territories" at the end of *Adventures of Huckleberry Finn*.

13. For more on such post–New Deal revitalization efforts, see David M. Wrobel's *The End of American Exceptionalism: Frontier Anxiety from the Old West to the New Deal* (1993). Wrobel argues that when New Dealers imposed comprehensive government regulation on the frontier economy, the goal was to create a "moral equivalent" to the standard view of the frontier as an "equalizer" of economic class.

14. See Robert Holton for a discussion of this and other scenes in *On the Road* as representations of a burgeoning postmodernist landscape. Holton characterizes the Wild West Week episode as a "manifestation of postmodern history . . . a parody of the past, a consumer spectacle without depth" (272).

15. See Jonathan Harris for more discussion of the New Deal "citizen-artist," specifically the way in which "the [Federal Art] Project employed artists as wage laborers, in the same way that other agencies employed plumbers, engineers or lumberjacks" (9).

16. It's noteworthy that Sal repeatedly sees "Indians," especially in Cheyenne, who "watched everything with their stony eyes" (33). Holton notes that this one "curious and repeated detail" suggests an "impenetrable depth wholly absent" from Cheyenne as well as from most of Sal's cohort (272).

17. In Central City, Sal evokes fond mental arrangements of Dean and Carlo, arrangements that rescue Sal from his realization that he is just another member of a frat party. He knows that the real Dean and Carlo would "be out of place and unhappy" in the frat party atmosphere and thus he envies and reveres them

all the more (54). In a state of despair, Sal blends these two bohemian figures into a messianic figure sent to oppose the "mad drunken Americans" (55) of Central City: "They were like the man with the dungeon stone and the gloom, rising from the underground, the sordid hipsters of America, a new beat generation that I was slowly joining" (54). The "man" of this simile is likely Florestan, the imprisoned hero of *Fidelio*, the opera Sal just watched. This coupling of Dean (the "west wind") and Carlo (the New Yorker), accompanied by the novel's first mention of the phrase "beat generation," suggests that the Beat agenda is to update the tragic solitude of classic imaginative literature. In addition to the Beat Florestan, Sal while in Central City imagines moving "over the Plains . . . an old man with white hair . . . walking toward us with the Word" (55).

18. See K. A. Cuordileone's chapter on "Postwar Liberalism and the Crisis of Liberal Masculinity" (*Manhood*, 1–36) for more discussion of the fear surrounding what Cuordileone calls a "doctrine of togetherness."

3. *The Chinatown and the City*

1. The National Book Critics Circle Award and the National Book Award, respectively.

2. Kingston's second attempt at fiction was foiled by a house fire, which consumed the only manuscript of her second novel. Kingston offers an extended "re-creation" of that lost novel in her book, *The Fifth Book of Peace* (63–238).

3. When capitalized, the "City" here and elsewhere refers to the city of San Francisco.

4. Martha Nussbaum uses this language in her essay "Patriotism and Cosmopolitanism."

5. The entire Stein quotation is of note here, if only to compare Stein's attitude toward Oakland to Rexroth's: "what was the use of my having come from Oakland it was not natural to have come from there yes write about it if I like or anything if I like but not there, there is no there there" (289).

6. See Juliana Chang's "Melancholic Remains" for a comparative reading of Ng's novel *Bone* and Chu's novel *Eat a Bowl of Tea*.

7. The term "ethnic memory" comes from Marshall Berman's discussion of Kingston's *The Woman Warrior* (334).

8. What Kingston doesn't indicate is that Kerouac explains his use of the adjective "little": "I keep saying 'little' George and 'little' Arthur but the fact is they were both small anyway" (*Big Sur*, 99). If nothing else, this recognition demonstrates that Kerouac had some clue about the diminutive effect of his modifiers.

9. Michael Davidson calls this internal split within communal identity a feature of a "California Orientalism" that has been around since the first anticoolie laws were passed in 1862. California Orientalism, according to Davidson, is a

tradition of displacing onto Chinese American men the exotic, seductive, and irrational impulses latent in Manifest Destiny (*Guys*, 76–99)

10. Two articles refer to the passage as "Kerouac's actual verse" (Royal, 151) and "his poem" (Maini, 259); one article claims that "Kerouac listed the figures he saw on a San Francisco street" (Lowe, 118).

11. Just as Kingston places Times Square in the Tenderloin, Kerouac relocates from New York City to San Francisco the more elicit, and potentially libelous, episodes of *The Subterraneans* (1958). See Charters's biography of Kerouac, which indicates that Kerouac made this decision either to avoid lawsuits or to cash in on the "San Francisco Renaissance" that journalists had been touting so much in the late 1950s (*Kerouac*, 360).

12. See Paul Giles's *The Global Remapping of American Literature* for more on the interrelation between American literature and the "contested terrain" of American geography (1–28).

13. Sanders' affection is notable in the 1968 episode of William F. Buckley's "Firing Line."

14. Gus Lee is of the same generation as Chin and Chan, and Nguyen groups him with them because the Black Arts movement similarly impacted Lee's sense of Chinese American masculinity. It is important to note, however, that Lee's first autobiographical novel, *China Boy*, which recounts Lee's fascination with black male youth culture in the 1950s and 1960s, was not published until 1991.

15. Nguyen isn't alone when he claims 1968 as an inaugural year of a generation of militant Asian American writers. Eric Lott reminds us that "[Paul] Berman and [Todd] Gitlin turn '1968' into a trope for What Went Wrong — in Berman's work [*A Tale of Two Utopias: The Political Journey of the Generation of 1968* (1996)], political authoritarianism and black criminal-leftism; in Gitlin's [*The Twilight of Common Dreams: Why American Is Wracked by Culture Wars* (1995)], a fracturing of the left into newer social movements — a.k.a. identity politics — that are no longer enraptured in the early- and mid-'60s idea of a New Left" (26).

16. The above quotation is the title of Amy Tan's 1996 *Harper's* article about multicultural authorship and the canon.

17. A later chapter title is "A Song for Occupations," after the Whitman poem of the same name.

18. The name of the Harte character is "Ah Sin." When originally published in the *Overland Monthly*, the poem was titled "Plain Language from Truthful James" (1870). It was pirated under the title "The Heathen Chinee." It tells of a gambler who attempts to cheat at cards against the Chinese character Ah Sin. The poem defends the Chinese minority in California but is often read as a polemic against Chinese presence there.

19. When Wittman visits his mother, she also refers to him as a "bum-how": "He read books when he was three years old. Now look at him. A bum-how"

(184). This word may be a phonetic spelling of a Chinese word or simply a slang word. Regardless, both seem to refer to the colloquialism "bum," as both uses name a Wittman who is not gainfully employed.

20. Compare the opening lines of each novel: (1) "Maybe it comes from living in San Francisco, city of clammy humors and foghorns that warn and warn — omen, o-o-men, o dolorous omen, o dolors of omens — and not enough sun, but Wittman Ah Sing considered suicide every day" (Kingston, 3); (2) "So this is where people come to live; I would have thought it is a city to die in" (Rilke, 3).

21. The quotation reads as follows: "By writing a play, he didn't need descriptions that racinated anybody" (304).

22. The Tenderloin's neighborhoods include Mid-Market, Civic Center, Theater District, Lower Nob Hill, Polk Gulch, and Little Saigon. See the Tenderloin entry in the travel guide section of the *San Francisco Chronicle* (Lisick).

23. See Philip Fisher for more on "democratic social space."

24. Kingston's own cohort echoes this criticism. In his introduction to *The Big Aiiieeeee!: An Anthology of Chinese American and Japanese American Literature* (1991), Frank Chin reminds readers that "every Chinese American book ever published in the United States of America by a major publisher has been a Christian autobiography or autobiographical novel." By choosing the genre of autobiography, Kingston is choosing to be "reborn in acculturation and honorary whiteness" (xii).

25. A standard example of Whitman's catalogs is section 33 of "Song of Myself."

26. Dickstein uses this Kafka parable as the title of his study of American fiction from 1945 to 1970, *Leopards in the Temple* (1999). Four years before Dickstein's book, Joseph Roach references the parable in *Cities of the Dead* (1996), to discuss those who, like the Zulu crew in New Orleans Mardi Gras, interrupt performances of origin and supremacy and resist the comfort of selective amnesia.

27. See Jeremy Crampton and Stuart Elden's *Space, Knowledge, and Power* (2007) for an example of the impact of Foucauldian theory on scholarship concerning urban planning.

28. Richard Lehan's *The City in Literature* (1998) offers the most exhaustive study of the modern city as backdrop for white male soul-searching. Taking his cues from T. S. Eliot, Lehan argues that the "unreal" city is the place of modernist innovation, a shape-shifting physical site upon which the psychological crises of modern life can take shape as formal innovations. Lehan relies on a "major figures" taxonomy to address the city, a figure who prefigures a new perspective on the built environment. Ultimately, then, Lehan's interest in the city is reducible to the common interest in this literary trope, to endorse "major figures" taxonomies, if not also to continue the list of "genius" men-of-letters in contemporary literature.

29. In the footnote to his translation of the novel, Stephen Mitchell indicates that the unnamed poet-turned-playwright is to be understood as Ibsen.

30. It is outside the bounds of this project to compare Kingston's decision to have Wittman be a playwright and the often-cited similarities between Wittman and Frank Chin. However, Wittman's final one-man show can be seen as a form of ventriloquism, wherein Kingston does for the militant Chinese American writer what he is unable to do for himself. However, Chin's *Chickencoop Chinaman* (1972) and *Year of the Dragon* (1981) are fairly well done meditations on the very identity questions Kingston has Wittman wrestle with.

31. In this context, *Tripmaster Monkey* dramatizes the spectacular intricacies and effects of problematic seizures of the public sphere. As W. J. T. Mitchell suggests in his essay, "The Violence of Public Art," in the year 1989 there was a spike of interest in representing "public sphere" debate and political activity. Commonly referred to as the "Year of Miracles," 1989 bore witness to both the end of the cold war and the Tiananmen Square protests. In the same year, *Tripmaster Monkey* was published and Spike Lee directed a comparable version of a racially charged, potentially violent public sphere, *Do the Right Thing* (1989).

4. *The Deflowering of New England*

1. See the introduction to this book (xii) for a discussion of Brodhead and Foote's take on regional fiction's popularity.

2. Captain Littlepage and Elijah Tilley are characters in Sarah Orne Jewett's *The Country of the Pointed Firs* (1896).

3. See the introduction (xiv–xv) for more on the program-era injunction to "write what you know."

4. His early book blurbs all end with the assertion that "he grew up in a working-class environment, which has played a major role in his writing."

5. Using regional writing as a way of breaking into the literary market is not a new tactic. As Richard Brodhead reminds us, late nineteenth-century authors (namely, George W. Cable, Sarah Orne Jewett, Mark Twain, Charles W. Chesnutt, Mary Wilkins Freeman, Abraham Cahan) who submitted regional fiction "typically had their first efforts published" ("Regionalism," 151).

6. See Susan Faludi's *Stiffed: The Betrayal of the American Man* for a historical study of this phenomenon.

7. Fred Pfeil's *White Guys* is the best book to elicit this counterintuitive victimization and its reactionary backlash.

8. See Sandra Zagarell's article "Crosscurrents: Registers of Nordicism, Community, and Culture in Jewett's *Country of the Pointed Firs.*"

9. See Tom Lutz (119–123) for a more detailed discussion of Wharton's cosmopolitan ambitions. The reference to "tribal" is a reference to Wharton's novel, *The Age of Innocence* (1920), which focuses of the "tribes" of old New York.

10. See Campbell's *Resisting Regionalism* (1–13).

11. Abigail Ann Hamblen's 1965 article in the *New England Quarterly* first expressed these inadequacies in Wharton's manner of gathering material for *Ethan Frome* and *Summer*. In it, Hamblen criticizes Wharton for knowing too little about rural New England. This lack of knowledge may be true, but Wharton's agenda is not verisimilitude but a formal manifestation of the crude essentialism presupposed in all local color regionalism.

12. The narrator of *Ethan Frome*, for instance, is in Starkfield on business. He's been sent on a kind of consultancy mission to a "power-house" somewhere in the hinterlands of northern New England.

13. I'm referring to the "destructive element" passage from Conrad's novel *Lord Jim*, which I describe in note 10 of the introduction. Banks's career has long been seen in Conradean terms, or at least in terms of masculine intrusion metaphors. The lead blurb for his most recent novel, *The Darling*, written by J. M. Coetzee, claims that the Liberia of that novel "is as hellish a place as Joseph Conrad's nineteenth-century Congo."

14. Banks enjoys the word "monadnock," using it to describe significant geological formations in both *Affliction* and *Hamilton Stark*. In *Hamilton Stark*, the narrator describes the landscape of rural New Hampshire as consisting of "deep furrows and mile-high moraines . . . here and there an isolated monadnock" (27).

15. Banks never stepped foot in Liberia. As he explains in an interview for *Guernica*: "I went to West Africa. I tried to get into Liberia. . . . I did an awful lot of prep work beforehand, library, reading, talking to people who had spent time there, Peace Corps volunteers, Liberians living in the United States and so on. I even spent an entire weekend with an old CIA hand who'd been stationed in Liberia."

16. The quoted passage comes from Flannery O'Connor's essay, "The Teaching of Literature." Here is the entire passage:

> I am very much afraid that to the fiction writer the fact that we shall always have the poor with us is a source of satisfaction, for it means, essentially, that he will always be able to find someone like himself. His concern with poverty is with a poverty fundamental to man. (131)

17. I may be overstating the case here. However, Banks does seem to have a very earnest affiliation with the Society for the Prevention of Cruelty to Animals (SPCA) and a collection of various NGOs dedicated to "saving chimpanzees from medical experimentation, abuse as entertainers and pets, and outright extermination" (*The Darling*, Acknowledgments, 393).

18. I discuss Mark McGurl's conception of "limitation theology" at length in the introduction of this book.

Epilogue

1. See Timothy Aubry's discussion of readerly tendency to "identify" (45–51).

2. See David Shields's much talked about *Reality Hunger: A Manifesto*, which includes some typical Franzen agonism (198–204), for evidence that Marcus's plan might be working. See Hutner's *What America Read* (2009) for more on the centrality of middle-class fiction, what Hutner refers to as "pedagogical realism."

3. In the above quote, DeLillo is referring to the period specifically between the assassination of John F. Kennedy and the time of the interview, 1988.

4. Lewis describes Zenith, the city setting of *Babbitt*, as a boomtown, a city of office building "grotesqueries," full of white-collar workers who make nothing in particular, "neither butter nor shoes nor poetry" but who hold fervent opinions about everything from settlement work and socialism, to entrepreneurialism and British entitlement (3–4).

5. The Veiled Prophet Organization is known primarily for its annual festival and debutante's ball. The Veiled Prophet Festival was renamed "Fair St. Louis" in 1992. The debutante's ball, or Veiled Prophet Ball, still occurs under that name, but in December, rather than in autumn (which is when it takes place in Franzen's novel). For more on the Veiled Prophet secret society, see Thomas M. Spencer's *The St. Louis Veiled Prophet Celebration* (2000).

6. The Persian costumes are based on Moore's representation of the real veiled prophet, al-Muqanna, an eighth-century heretical Persian Muslim, whose veil shielded his staggering holiness from his followers.

7. See Russell Banks's introductory remarks in *Dreaming Up America* (2008) for more on the special purchase that the English colonials had on autonomy (1–15).

BIBLIOGRAPHY

Abel, Marco. "Speeding across the Rhizome: Deleuze Meets Kerouac on the Road." *Modern Fiction Studies* 48.2 (2002): 227–256.

Agee, James. "The American Roadside." 1934. *James Agee: Selected Journalism*. Ed. Paul Ashdown. Knoxville: U of Tennessee P, 2005. 43–60.

———. "Colon." *New Directions in Prose and Poetry, 1940*. New York: Kraus Reprint, 1967. 181–192.

———. "J 6.3: LUNPFM Drafts: Introduction." *James Agee Rediscovered: The Journals of* Let Us Now Praise Famous Men *and Other New Manuscripts*. Ed. Michael A. Lofaro and Hugh Davis. Knoxville: U of Tennessee P, 2005. 143–155.

———. Letter to Archibald MacLeish. 18 November 1937. James Agee Collection. Box 11, folder 16. Harry Ransom Research Center. U of Texas, Austin.

———. "Tennessee Valley Authority." 1933. *Film Writing and Selected Journalism*. New York: Library of America, 2005. 631–646.

Agee, James, and Walker Evans. *Let Us Now Praise Famous Men*. 1941. New York: Mariner, 2001.

Altieri, Charles. "Whose America Is Our America: On Walter Benn Michaels's Characterizations of Modernity in America." *Modernism/Modernity* 3.3 (1996): 107–113.

Ammons, Elizabeth. *American Local Color Writing, 1880–1920*. New York: Penguin, 1998.

Anderson, Amanda. *The Powers of Distance: Cosmopolitanism and the Cultivation of Detachment*. Princeton: Princeton UP, 2001.

Anderson, Sherwood. *Winesburg, Ohio*. 1919. New York: Penguin, 1987.

Arthur, Jason. "Allen Ginsberg's Biographical Gestures." *Texas Studies in Literature and Language* 52.2 (2010): 227–246.

———. "Revising the Great Depression." *Minnesota Review* 71–72 (2009): 277–283.

———. "'Where Is the Dust?': James Agee's Lost Review of John Ford's Film Adaptation of *The Grapes of Wrath*." *The Grapes of Wrath: A Re-Consideration*. Ed. Michael Meyer. New York: Rodopi, 2009. 189–218.

Aubry, Timothy. *Reading as Therapy: What Contemporary Fiction Does for Middle-Class Americans*. Iowa City: U of Iowa P, 2011.

Austin, Mary. "Regionalism in American Fiction." *English Journal* 21.2 (1932): 97–107.

Banks, Russell. *Affliction*. 1989. New York: Perennial, 1990.

———. *Continental Drift*. New York: Harper, 1985.

———. *The Darling*. New York: Harper, 2004.

———. *Dreaming Up America*. New York: Seven Stories P, 2008.

———. *Hamilton Stark*. 1978. New York: Harper, 1996.

———. Interview by Robert Birnbaum. *identitytheory.com*. Identity Theory. 18 January 2005. Web. 19 November 2011.

———. Interview by Kay Bonetti. Columbia: American Audio Prose Library, 1986. Audiocassette.

———. Interview by Leigh Anne Couch. "Road Signs." *indyweek.com*. Independent Weekly, 29 Marcy 2000. Web. 19 November 2011.

———. Interview by Robert Faggen. "The Art of Fiction No. 152." *Paris Review* 147 (1998): 50–88.

———. Interview by Joel Whitney. "Telling Details." *Guernica*. Guernica, September 2005. Web. 19 November 2011.

———. *Success Stories*. New York: Harper, 1986.

———. *Trailerpark*. New York: Harper, 1981.

Barber, Benjamin. "Constitutional Faith." Joshua Cohen 30–37.

Barth, John. *The Friday Book: Essays and Other Nonfiction*. New York: Putnam, 1984.

Baudrillard, Jean. "Simulacra and Simulations." Trans. Paul Foss, Paul Patton, and Philip Beitchman. *Modern Criticism and Theory*. Ed. David Lodge and Nigel Wood. 2nd ed. New York: Pearson Longman, 2000. 404–412.

Benjamin, Walter. "The Author as Producer." *Reflections: Essays, Aphorisms, Autobiographical Writings*. Trans. Edmund Jephcott. New York: Schocken, 1978. 220–238.

Berman, Marshall. *All That Is Solid Melts into Air: The Experience of Modernity*. New York: Simon, 1982.

Berman, Paul. *A Tale of Two Utopias: The Political Journey of the Generation of 1968*. New York: Norton, 1996.

Berry, Wendell. *A Continuous Harmony: Essays Cultural and Agricultural*. New York: Harcourt, 1972.

Blake, Casey Nelson. *Beloved Community: The Cultural Criticism of Randolph Bourne, Van Wyck Brooks, Waldo Frank, and Lewis Mumford*. Chapel Hill: U of North Carolina P, 1990.

Bold, Christine. *The WPA Guides: Mapping America*. Jackson: UP of Mississippi, 1999.

Boyle, T. C. *The Tortilla Curtain*. New York: Viking, 1995.

Brodhead, Richard. *Cultures of Letters: Scenes of Reading and Writing in Nineteenth-Century America*. Chicago: U of Chicago P, 1993.

———. "Regionalism and the Upper Class." *Rethinking Class: Literary Studies and Social Formations*. Ed. Wai Chee Dimock and Michael T. Gilmore. New York: Columbia UP, 1994. 150–174.

Brooks, Van Wyck. *The Flowering of New England, 1815–1865*. New York: Dutton, 1937.

———. *On Literature Today*. New York: Dutton, 1941.

———. *Opinions of Oliver Allston*. New York: Dutton, 1941.

———. *The Ordeal of Mark Twain*. New York: Dutton, 1920.

———. *The Pilgrimage of Henry James*. New York: Dutton, 1925.

Brown, Bill. "Identity Culture." *American Literary History* 10.1 (1998): 164–184.

———. *A Sense of Things: The Object Matter of American Literature*. Chicago: U of Chicago P, 2003.

Bukiet, Melvin Jules. "Crackpot Realism: Fiction for the Forthcoming Millennium." *Review of Contemporary Fiction* 16.1 (1996): 13–22.

Bulosan, Carlos. *America Is in the Heart: A Personal History*. Seattle: U of Washington P, 1973.

Caldwell, Erskine, and Margaret Bourke-White. *You Have Seen Their Faces*. 1937. Athens: U of Georgia P, 1995.

Campbell, Donna. *Resisting Regionalism: Gender and Naturalism in American Fiction, 1885–1915*. Athens: Ohio UP, 1997.

Cather, Willa. *Not Under Forty*. 1936. Lincoln: U of Nebraska P, 1988.

Certeau, Michel de. *The Practice of Everyday Life*. Berkeley: U of California P, 1984.

Chabot, C. Barry. *Writers for the Nation: American Literary Modernism*. Tuscaloosa: U of Alabama P, 1997.

Chan, Jeffery Paul, Frank Chin, Lawson Fusao Inada, and Shawn Wong. *The Big Aiiieeeee!: An Anthology of Chinese American and Japanese American Literature*. New York: Meridian, 1991.

Chang, Juliana. "Melancholic Remains: Domestic and National Secrets in Fae Myenne Ng's *Bone*." *Modern Fiction Studies* 51.1 (2005): 110–33.

Charters, Ann. *Kerouac: A Biography*. New York: St. Martin's, 1994.

———. Introduction. *On the Road*. By Jack Kerouac. 1957. New York: Penguin, 1991. vii–xxx.

Cheah, Pheng. "Introduction Part II: The Cosmopolitical — Today." *Cosmopolitics: Thinking and Feeling beyond the Nation*. Ed. Bruce Robbins and Pheng Cheah. Minneapolis: U of Minnesota P, 1998. 20–41.

Chen, Xiaomei. *Acting the Right Part: Political Theater and Popular Drama in Contemporary China*. Honolulu: U of Hawaii P, 2002, 17–72.

Chin, Frank. "Come All Ye Asian American Writers of the Real and the Fake." Chan 1–92.

Chin, Frank, and Jeffrey Paul Chan. "Racist Love." *Seeing Through Shuck*. Ed. Richard Kostelanetz. New York: Ballantine, 1972. 65–71.

Chu, Patricia E. *Race, Nationalism and the State in British and American Modernism*. New York: Cambridge UP, 2006.

Clifford, James. *Predicament of Culture: Twentieth-Century Ethnography, Literature, and Art*. Cambridge: Harvard UP, 1988.

———. *Routes: Travel and Translation in the Late Twentieth Century*. Cambridge: Harvard UP, 1997.

Coard, Robert L. "Edith Wharton's Influence on Sinclair Lewis." *Modern Fiction Studies* 31.3 (1985): 511–527.

Coats, Lauren, and Nihad Farooq. "Regionalism in the Era of the New Deal." Crow 74–91.

Cohen, Joshua, ed. *For Love of Country?* Boston: Beacon, 1996.

Cohen, Samuel. *After the End of History: American Fiction in the 1990s*. Iowa City: U of Iowa P, 2009.

Coles, Robert. *Doing Documentary Work*. New York: Oxford UP, 1997.

———. *Migrants, Sharecroppers, Mountaineers: Volume II of Children of Crisis*. 1967. Boston: Little, 1971.

Conkin, Paul K. *The New Deal*. 2nd ed. New York: Crowell, 1975.

Cotkin, George. *Existential America*. Baltimore: Johns Hopkins UP, 2003.

Cox, James. "Regionalism: A Diminished Thing," *Columbia Literary History of the United States*. Ed. Emory Elliott. New York: Columbia UP, 1988. 761–84.

Crampton, Jeremy, and Stuart Elden, eds. *Space, Knowledge, and Power: Foucault and Geography*. Burlington, VT: Ashgate, 2007.

Crow, Charles L., ed. *A Companion to the Regional Literatures of America*. Malden, MA: Blackwell, 2003.

Crump, G. B. *The Novels of Wright Morris: A Critical Interpretation*. Lincoln: U of Nebraska P, 1978.

Cuordileone, K. A. *Manhood and American Political Culture in the Cold War*. New York: Routledge, 2005.

Curtis, James. *Mind's Eye, Mind's Truth: FSA Photography Reconsidered*. Philadelphia: Temple UP, 1989.

Davidson, Michael. *Ghostlier Demarcations: Modern Poetry and the Material Word*. Berkeley: U of California P, 1997.

———. *Guys Like Us: Citing Masculinity in Cold War Poetics*. Chicago: U of Chicago P, 2004.

———. *The San Francisco Renaissance: Poetics and Community at Mid-Century*. Cambridge: Cambridge UP, 1989.

Debord, Guy. "Introduction to a Critique of Urban Geography." Trans. Ken Knabb. *Les Lèvres Nues* 6 (1955): N. pag. Web. 23 November 2011.

———. *The Society of the Spectacle*. Trans. Donald Nicholson-Smith. New York: Zone, 1994.

DeCurtis, Anthony. "'An Outsider in This Society': An Interview with Don DeLillo." *Introducing Don DeLillo*. Ed. Frank Lentricchia. Durham: Duke UP, 1991. 43–66.

Deleuze, Gilles, and Félix Guattari. *Kafka: Toward a Minor Literature*. Trans. Dana Polan. Minneapolis: U of Minnesota P, 1986.

———. *A Thousand Plateaus: Capitalism and Schizophrenia*. Trans. Brian Massumi. Minneapolis: U of Minnesota P, 1987.

Denning, Michael. *The Cultural Front*. New York: Verso, 1997.

Dewey, John. *The Later Works of John Dewey, 1925–1953: Volume 10, 1934, Art as Experience*. Ed. Jo Ann Boydston. Carbondale: U of Southern Illinois P, 2008.

Dickstein, Morris. *Leopards in the Temple: The Transformation of American Fiction 1945–1970*. Cambridge: Harvard UP, 1999.

Dirlik, Arif. "The Global in the Local." *Global/Local: Cultural Production and the Transnational Imaginary*. Ed. Rob Wilson and Wimal Dissanayake. Durham: Duke UP, 1996. 21–45.

Dos Passos, John. *U.S.A.* 1936. New York: Library of America, 1996.

Doss, Erika. *Benton, Pollock, and the Politics of Modernism: From Regionalism to Abstract Expressionism*. Chicago: U of Chicago P, 1991.

Douglas, Ann. Introduction. *The Dharma Bums*. By Jack Kerouac. 1958. New York: Penguin, 2007. vii–xxviii.

———. "Periodizing the American Century: Modernism, Postmodernism, and Postcolonialism in the Cold War Context." *Modernism/Modernity* 5.3 (1998): 71–98.

———. "'Telepathic Shock and Meaning Excitement': Kerouac's Poetics of Intimacy." *College Literature* 27.1 (2000): 8–21.

Du Bois, W. E. B. *The Negro*. New York: Holt, 1915.

———.*The Souls of Black Folk: Essays and Sketches*. Chicago: McClurg, 1903.

Eisinger, Chester E. *Fiction of the Forties*. Chicago: U of Chicago P, 1963.

Elie, Paul. *The Life You Save May Be Your Own: An American Pilgrimage*. New York: Farrar, 2003.

Ellison, Ralph. *Invisible Man*. 1952. New York: Vintage, 1990.

Entin, Joseph. "A New Deal for Thirties Literature." *Novel* 34.1 (2000): 136–142.

Faludi, Susan. *Stiffed: The Betrayal of the American Man*. New York: Perennial, 2000.

Farber, David. *The Age of Great Dreams: America in the 1960s*. New York: Hill and Wang, 1994.

Felski, Rita. Introduction. *New Literary History* 33.4 (2002): 607–622.

Ferlinghetti, Lawrence. "Thus Spake Ferlinghetti." *Exquisite Corpse* 8. Web. 23 November 2011.

Fetterley, Judith, and Marjory Pryse. *Writing Out of Place: Regionalism, Women, and American Literary Culture*. Urbana: U of Illinois P, 2003.

Fisher, Philip. "Democratic Social Space: Whitman, Melville, and the Promise of American Transparency." *Representations* 24 (1988): 60–101.

Foer, Jonathan Safran. *Everything Is Illuminated*. New York: Harper, 2002.

———. Interview by Robert Birnbaum. *identitytheory.com*. Identity Theory, 26 May 2003. Web. 10 May 2012.

Foley, Barbara. *Radical Representations: Politics and Form in U.S. Proletarian Fiction, 1929–1941*. Durham: Duke UP, 1993.

Foner, Eric. *The Reader's Companion to American History*. New York: Houghton, 1991.

Foote, Stephanie. *Regional Fictions: Culture and Identity in Nineteenth-Century American Literature*. Madison: U of Wisconsin P, 2001.

Foreman, Paul. "Sharecropper Novels." *Southern Exposure* 9.2 (1981): 107–110.

Frank, Robert. *The Americans*. 1959. New York: Grossman P, 1969.

Frank, Thomas. *What's the Matter with Kansas? How Conservatives Won the Heart of America*. New York: Holt, 2004.

Frank, Waldo. *Our America*. New York: Boni and Liveright, 1919.

Frankfurt, Harry G. *On Bullshit*. Princeton: Princeton UP, 2005.

Franzen, Jonathan. *The Corrections*. New York: Picador, 2001.

———. *Freedom*. New York: Farrar, 2010.

———. *How to Be Alone*. 2002. New York: Picador, 2003.

———. "I'll Be Doing More of the Same." *Review of Contemporary Fiction* 16.1 (1996): 34–38.

———. Interview by Stephen J. Burn. "The Art of Fiction No. 207." *Paris Review* 195 (Winter 2010): n. page. Web. 1 October 2011.

———. "Liking Is for Cowards. Go for What Hurts." *New York Times*, 28 May 2011. Web. 15 September 2011.

———. "Mainstream and Meaningful." *Atlantic Unbound*. Atlantic Monthly, 3 October 2001. Web. 7 December 2011.

———. "New York." *State by State: A Panoramic Portrait of America*. Ed. Matt Weiland and Sean Wilsey. New York: Harper, 2009. 320–338.

———. *The Twenty-Seventh City*. New York: Picador, 1988.

Giles, Paul. *The Global Remapping of American Literature*. Princeton: Princeton UP, 2011.

Ginsberg, Allen. *Howl and Other Poems*. San Francisco: City Lights, 1956.

Gitlin, Todd. *The Twilight of Common Dreams: Why America Is Wracked by Culture Wars*. New York: Metropolitan, 1995.

Glass, Loren. *Authors Inc.: Literary Celebrity in the Modern United States, 1880–1980*. New York: New York UP, 2004.

Glazener, Nancy. *Reading for Realism: The History of a U.S. Literary Institution, 1850- 1910*. Durham: Duke UP, 1997.

Gordon, Mary. Introduction. *Woman Warrior, China Men*. By Maxine Hong Kingston. New York: Knopf, 2005. ix–xvi.

Griffin, Paul Charles. "Sound and Fury, Signifying... What, Exactly?" *Common Review* 9.2 (2010/2011): n. pag. Web. 15 September 2011.

Guillory, John. *Cultural Capital: The Problem of Literary Canon Formation*. Chicago: U of Chicago P, 1993.

Halpern, Dan. "Lone Star: Kinky Friedman on the Campaign Trail." *New Yorker*. New Yorker, 22 August 2005. 26–32.

Hamalian, Linda. *A Life of Kenneth Rexroth*. New York: Norton, 1991.

———. "Regionalism Makes Good: The San Francisco Renaissance." *Reading the West: New Essays on the Literature of the American West*. Ed. Michael Kowalewski. New York: Cambridge UP, 1996. 213–230.

Hamblen, Abigail Ann. "Edith Wharton in New England." *New England Quarterly: A Historical Review of New England Life and Letters* 38.2 (1965): 239–244.

Haraway, Donna. *Simians, Cyborgs, and Women: The Reinvention of Nature*. New York: Routledge, 1991.

Harbach, Chad. "MFS vs. NYC" *n+1* 10 (2010): 1–12.

Harkin, James. "Get a (Second) Life." *ft.com*. Financial Times, 17 November 2006. Web. 23 November 2011.

Harris, Jonathan. *Federal Art and National Culture: The Politics of Identity in New Deal America*. Cambridge: Cambridge UP, 1995.

Hearle, Kevin. "These Are American People: The Spectre of Eugenics in *Their Blood Is Strong* and *The Grapes of Wrath*." *Beyond Boundaries: Rereading John Steinbeck*. Ed. Susan Shillinglaw and Kevin Hearle. Tuscaloosa: U of Alabama P, 2002. 243–254.

Hegeman, Susan. *Patterns for America: Modernism and the Concept of Culture.* Princeton: Princeton UP, 1999.

Heuvel, Katrina vanden. "Stand and Fight." *Nation*. Nation, 3 November 2004. Web. 13 March 2012.

Hicks, Granville. Introduction. *Wright Morris: A Reader*. By Wright Morris. New York: Harper, 1970. ix–xxxiii.

———. *Literary Horizons: A Quarter Century of American Fiction*. New York: New York UP, 1970.

———. *Small Town*. 1946. New York: Fordham UP, 2004.

Hilfer, Anthony Channell. *The Revolt from the Village, 1915–1930*. Chapel Hill: U of North Carolina P, 1969.

Hohenberg, John. *The Pulitzer Diaries: Inside America's Greatest Prize.* Syracuse: Syracuse UP, 1997.

Hollinger, David. *Postethnic America: Beyond Multiculturalism*. New York: Basic, 1995.

Holton, Robert. "Kerouac among the Fellahin: On the Road to the Postmodern." *Modern Fiction Studies* 41.2 (1995): 265–283.

Howe, Irving. "Mass Society and Post-Modern Fiction." *Partisan Review* 26 (1959): 420–436.

Hrebeniak, Michael. *Action Writing: Jack Kerouac's Wild Form*. Carbondale: Southern Illinois UP, 2006.

Huang, Yunte. *Transpacific Displacement: Ethnography, Translation, and Intertextual Travel in Twentieth-Century American Literature*. Berkeley: U of California P, 2002.

Huston, Nancy. "The Decline of Identity?" *Salmagundi* (1999): 10–22.

Hutner, Gordon. *What America Read: Taste, Class, and the Novel, 1920–1960*. Chapel Hill: U of North Carolina P, 2009.

Jacobs, Jane. *The Death and Life of Great American Cities*. 1961. New York: Modern Library, 1993.

Jameson, Fredric. *Postmodernism, or, The Cultural Logic of Late Capitalism*. Durham: Duke UP, 1991.

Jewett, Sarah Orne. *The Country of the Pointed Firs*. 1896. New York: Penguin, 1995.

Johnston, Allan. "Consumption, Addiction, Vision, Energy: Political Economies and Utopian Visions in the Writings of the Beat Generation." *College Literature* 32.2 (2005): 103–126.

Jones, Gavin. *American Hungers: The Problem of Poverty in U.S. Literature, 1840–1945*. Princeton: Princeton UP, 2008.

———. "Poverty and the Limits of Literary Criticism." *American Literary History* 15.4 (2003): 765–792.

Kazin, Alfred. *On Native Grounds: An Interpretation of Modern American Prose Literature*. 1942. Garden City: Doubleday, 1956.

Kerouac, Jack. *Big Sur*. 1962. New York: Penguin, 1992.

———. "Essentials of Spontaneous Prose." *Evergreen Review* 2.5 (1958): 72–73.

———. "From the Journals: 1949–1954." *Road Novels: 1957–1960*. Ed. Douglas Brinkley. New York: Library of America, 2007. 775–834.

———. *On the Road*. 1957. New York: Penguin, 2003.

———. *On the Road: The Original Scroll*. 1951. New York: Penguin, 2007.

———. "The Railroad Earth." *Road Novels: 1957–1960*. Ed. Douglas Brinkley. New York: Library of America, 2007. 658–694.

———. *The Town and the City*. 1950. New York: Harcourt, 1970.

———. *Visions of Cody*. New York: Penguin, 1972.

Kim, Elaine H. "Beyond Railroads and Internment: Comments on the Past, Present, and Future of Asian American Studies." *Privileging Positions: The Sites of Asian American Studies*. Ed. Gary Y. Okihiro, Marilyn Alquizola, Dorothy Fujita Rony, and K. Scott Wong. Pullman: Washington State UP, 1995. 11–19.

Kingston, Maxine Hong. *The Fifth Book of Peace*. New York: Vintage, 2003.

———. *Tripmaster Monkey: His Fake Book*. 1989. New York: Vintage, 1990.

———. *The Woman Warrior, China Men*. New York: Knopf, 2005.

Kirkpatrick, David D. "'Oprah' Gaffe by Franzen Draws Ire and Sales." *New York Times* 21 October 2001: E1.

Kirn, Walter. "*On the Road* Revisited: Entry 4." *Slate.com*. Slate.com, 7 September 2007. Web. 15 September 2011.

Kirsch, Adam. "The Importance of Being Earnest." *New Republic* 18 August 2011: 20–26.

Knapp, Steven, and Walter Benn Michaels. "Against Theory." *Against Theory: Literary Studies and the New Pragmatism*. Ed. W. J. T. Mitchell. Chicago: U of Chicago P, 1985. 11–30.

Kowalewski, Michael. "Contemporary Regionalism." Crow 7–24.

Kumar, Amitava. Introduction. *World Bank Literature*. Minneapolis: U of Minnesota P, 2003. xvii-xxxiii.

Laclau, Ernesto. *On Populist Reason*. New York: Verso, 2005.

———. "Universalism, Particularism, and the Question of Identity." *The Politics of Difference: Ethnic Premises in a World of Power*. Ed. Edwin Wilmsen and Patricia McAllister. Chicago: U of Chicago P, 1996. 45–58.

Laughlin, James. Editor's Note. *New Directions in Prose and Poetry, 1940*. New York: Kraus, 1967. 145–146.

———. Notes on Contributors. *New Directions in Prose and Poetry, 1940*. New York: Kraus, 1967. ix–xii.

Lears, T. J. Jackson. *No Place of Grace: Antimodernism and the Transformation of American Culture, 1880–1920*. New York: Pantheon, 1981.

Least Heat-Moon, William. *Blue Highways: A Journey into America*. Boston: Little, Brown, 1983.

Lee, James Kyung-Jin. "The City as Region." Crow 137–153.

Lee, Peggy. "Mañana." Capitol, 1947. CD.

Lee, Yoon Sun. "Kingston's China Men: Circumscribing the Romance of Deterritorialization." *Yale Journal of Criticism* 11.2 (Fall 1998): 465–484.

Lehan, Richard. *The City in Literature: An Intellectual and Cultural History*. Berkeley: U of California P, 1998.

Lerner, Richard, and Lewis MacAdams, dirs. *What Happened to Kerouac?* Ingram Home Entertainment, 1986. DVD.

Lewis, Sinclair. *Babbitt*. 1922. New York: Oxford UP, 2010.

Lhamon, W. T. *Deliberate Speed: The Origins of a Cultural Style in the American 1950s*. Washington, D.C.: Smithsonian Institution P, 1990.

Li, David Leiwei. "China Men: Maxine Hong Kingston and the American Canon." *American Literary History* 2.3 (1990): 482–502.

———. *Imagining the Nation: Asian American Literature and Cultural Consent*. Stanford: Stanford UP, 1998.

Lin, Patricia. "Clashing Constructs of Reality: Reading Maxine Hong Kingston's *Tripmaster Monkey: His Fake Book* as Indigenous Ethnography." *Reading the Literatures of Asian America*. Ed. Shirley Geok-lin Lim and Amy Ling. Philadelphia: Temple UP, 1992. 333–348.

Lisick, Beth. "San Francisco: The Tenderloin." *SFGate.com*. SFGate, May 2001. Web. 21 November 2011.

Locke, Edwin. "Adaptation of Reality in *The Grapes of Wrath*." *Films* 1.2 (1940): 49–55.

Lott, Eric. *The Disappearing Liberal Intellectual*. New York: Basic, 2006.

Lowe, John. "Monkey Kings and Mojo: Postmodern Ethnic Humor in Kingston, Reed, and Vizenor." *MELUS* 21:4 (1996): 103–126.

Lutz, Tom. "Cather and the Regional Imagination." *The Cambridge History of the American Novel*. Ed. Leonard Cassuto. New York: Cambridge UP, 2011. 437–451

———. *Cosmopolitan Vistas: American Regionalism and Literary Value*. Ithaca: Cornell UP, 2004.

Macdonald, Dwight. *Against the American Grain*. 1962. New York: De Capo, 1983.

Mackin, Jonna. "Split Infinities: The Comedy of Performative Identity in Maxine Hong Kingston's *Tripmaster Monkey*." *Contemporary Literature* 46.3 (2005): 511–534.

MacLeish, Archibald. "The Soundtrack-&-Picture Form: A New Direction."

New Directions in Prose and Poetry. Issue 3. Norfolk, CT: New Directions, 1938. 167–170.

Mailer, Norman. "The White Negro." *Dissent* (1957): n. pag. Web. 23 November 2011.

Maini, Irma. "Writing the Asian American Artist: Maxine Hong Kingston's *Tripmaster Monkey: His Fake Book.*" *MELUS* 25.3/4 (2000): 243–264.

Marcus, Ben. "Why Experimental Fiction Threatens to Destroy Publishing, Jonathan Franzen, and Life as We Know It: *A Correction.*" *Harper's Magazine* October 2005. 39–52.

McCann, Sean. *Gumshoe America: Hard-boiled Crime Fiction and the Rise and Fall of New Deal Liberalism.* Durham: Duke UP, 2000.

McClure, Michael. *Lighting the Corners: On Art, Nature, and the Visionary.* Albuquerque: U of New Mexico P, 1994.

McConnell, Michael. "Don't Neglect the Little Platoons." Joshua Cohen 78–84.

McGurl, Mark. "The Program Era: Pluralisms of Postwar American Fiction." *Critical Inquiry* 32.1 (2005): 102–129.

———. *The Program Era: Postwar Fiction and the Rise of Creative Writing.* Cambridge: Harvard UP, 2009.

———. "Understanding Iowa: Flannery O'Connor, B.A., M.F.A." *American Literary History* 19.2 (2007): 527–545.

Michaels, Walter Benn. *Our America: Nativism, Modernism, and Pluralism.* Durham: Duke UP, 1995.

———. *The Shape of the Signifier: 1967 to the End of History.* Princeton: Princeton UP, 2004.

———. *The Trouble with Diversity: How We Learned to Love Identity and Ignore Inequality.* New York: Metropolitan, 2006.

Mitchell, W. J. T. *Picture Theory.* Chicago: U of Chicago P, 1994.

———. "The Violence of Public Art: *Do the Right Thing.*" In *Spike Lee's "Do the Right Thing."* Ed. Mark Reid. New York: Cambridge UP, 1997.

Morris, Wright. "From *The Territory Ahead.*" *Wright Morris: A Reader.* New York: Harper, 1970. 636–648.

———. "Inhabitants." *New Directions in Prose and Poetry, 1940.* New York: Kraus Reprint, 1967. 147–179.

———. *The Man Who Was There.* Lincoln: Bison, 1977.

———. *The Territory Ahead.* New York: Harcourt, Brace, 1958.

———. The *Works of Love,* 1949. Lincoln: Bison, 1972.

Moy, James. *Marginal Cites: Staging the Chinese in America.* Iowa City: U of Iowa P, 1993.

Nguyen, Viet Thanh. "The Remasculinization of Chinese America: Race, Violence, and the Novel." *American Literary History* 12.1 (2000): 130–157.

Nichols, Bill. "Documentary Film and the Modernist Avant-Garde." *Critical Inquiry* 27.4 (2001): 580–610.

Niemi, Robert. *Russell Banks*. New York: Twayne, 1997.

Norris, Frank. *McTeague*. 1899. Ed. Donald Pizer. New York: Norton, 1977.

"A Novelist, a Talk-Show Host, and Literature High and Low." *Chronicle of Higher Education* 30 November 2001: B4.

Nussbaum, Martha. "Patriotism and Cosmopolitanism." Joshua Cohen 3–20.

Oates, Joyce Carol. *The Faith of a Writer: Life, Craft, Art*. New York: Harper, 2003.

———. Introduction. *The Oxford Book of American Short Stories*. New York: Oxford UP, 1992. 3–16.

O'Connor, Flannery. "The Teaching of Literature." *Mystery and Manners: Occasional Prose*. Ed. Sally Fitzgerald and Robert Fitzgerald. New York: Farrar, 1969. 121–134.

Ong, Aihwa. *Flexible Citizenship: The Cultural Logics of Transnationality*. Durham: Duke UP, 1999.

Perloff, Marjorie. "Modernism without the Modernists: A Response to Walter Benn Michaels." *Modernism/Modernity* 3.3 (1996): 99–105.

Pfeil, Fred. *Another Tale to Tell: Politics and Narrative in Postmodern Culture*. New York: Verso, 1990.

———. *White Guys: Studies in Postmodern Domination and Difference*. New York: Verso, 1997.

Phillips, John. "San Francisco (Be Sure to Wear Some Flowers in Your Hair)." Ode Records, 1967. CD.

Pinsky, Robert. "Eros Against Esperanto." Joshua Cohen 85–90.

———. *Thousands of Broadways: Dreams and Nightmares of the American Small Town*. Chicago: U of Chicago P, 2009.

Pinter, Jason. "Jodi Picoult and Jennifer Weiner Speak Out on Franzen Feud." *Huffington Post* 26 August 2010. Web. 1 October 2011.

Podhoretz, Norman. "The Know-Nothing Bohemians." *Partisan Review* (1958): 305–318.

Pollack, Oliver B. "Wright Morris and the Jews." *Shofar: An Interdisciplinary Journal of Jewish Studies* 20.4 (2002): 18–35.

Posnock, Ross. "The Dream of Deracination: The Uses of Cosmopolitanism." *American Literary History* 12.4 (2000): 802–818.

Pound, Ezra. "A Retrospect." *Toward the Open Field: Poets on the Art of Poetry 1800–1950*. Ed. Melissa Kwasny. Middleton: Wesleyan UP, 2004. 247–259.

Rabinowitz, Paula. "'Between the Outhouse and the Garbage Dump': Locating Collapse in Depression Literature." *American Literary History* 23.1 (2011): 32–55.

Rafferty, Terrence. "Coming of Age." *New Yorker* 19 December 1988. 101–106.

Rexroth, Kenneth. Afterword. *McTeague.* 1899. New York: Penguin, 1964. 340–348.

———. *Classics Revisited.* 1965. New York: New Directions, 1986.

———. "Disengagement: The Art of the Beat Generation." *New World Writing* 11 (1957): 28–41.

———. "San Francisco Letter." 1957. *San Francisco Stories: Great Writers on the City.* Ed. John Miller. San Francisco: Chronicle, 1990. 179–186.

Richardson, Mark. "Peasant Dreams: Reading *On the Road.*" *Texas Studies in Literature and Language* 43.2 (2001): 218–242.

Rilke, Rainer Maria. *The Notebooks of Malte Laurids Brigge.* 1910 Trans. Stephen Mitchell. New York: Vintage, 1990.

Robbins, Bruce. "Introduction Part I: Actually Existing Cosmopolitanism." *Cosmopolitics: Thinking and Feeling Beyond the Nation.* Ed. Bruce Robbins and Pheng Cheah. Minneapolis: U of Minnesota P, 1998. 1–19.

Robinson, Sally. *Marked Men: White Masculinity in Crisis.* New York: Columbia UP, 2000.

Rodriguez, Richard. "Late Victorians." *Days of Obligation: An Argument with My Mexican Father.* New York: Penguin, 1992. 26–47.

Rosenblum, Naomi. *A World History of Photography.* 3rd ed. New York: Abbeville, 1997.

Roth, Philip. "Writing American Fiction." *Reading Myself and Others.* 1975. New York: Penguin, 1985. 173–191.

Row, Jess. "Marcus vs. Franzen: The Latest Literary Wrangling in *Harper's* Leaves Everyone Confused." *Slate.com.* Slate.com, 20 October 2005. Web. 15 September 2011.

Royal, Derek Parker. "Literary Genre as Ethnic Resistance in Maxine Hong Kingston's *Tripmaster Monkey: His Fake Book.*" *MELUS* 29.2 (2004): 141–156.

Russo, Richard. *Empire Falls.* New York: Knopf, 2001.

Ryden, Kent C. "New England Literature and Regional Identity." Crow 195–212.

Savran, David. *Taking It Like a Man: White Masculinity, Masochism, and Contemporary American Culture.* Princeton: Princeton UP, 1998.

Scarry, Elaine. *The Body in Pain: The Making and Unmaking of the World.* New York: Oxford UP, 1985.

———. "The Difficulty of Imagining Other People." Joshua Cohen 98–110.

Schlesinger, Arthur M., Jr. *The Vital Center: The Politics of Freedom.* 1949. New Brunswick, NJ: Transaction P, 1998.

Sege, Irene. "Leading a Double Life." *Boston Globe.* Boston Globe, 25 October 2006. Web. 6 December 2011.

Shields, David. *Reality Hunger: A Manifesto.* New York: Knopf, 2010.

Shlaes, Amity. *The Forgotten Man: A New History of the Great Depression*. New York: Harper, 2007.

Siegel, Lee. "The Beat Generation and the Tea Party." *New York Times*. New York Times, 8 October 2010. Web. 1 November 2011.

Simon, Charlie May. *The Share-Cropper*. New York: Dutton, 1937.

Simpson, Aislinn. "Nobel Literature Prize Judge: American Authors 'Insular and Ignorant.'" *Telegraph*. Telegraph Media Group Limited, 2 October 2008. Web. 18 July 2012.

Skenazy, Paul. Introduction. *Conversations with Maxine Hong Kingston*. Ed. Paul Skenazy and Tera Martin. Jackson: UP of Mississippi, 1998. vii–xx.

———. "Kingston at the University." *Conversations with Maxine Hong Kingston*. Ed. Paul Skenazy and Tera Martin. Jackson: UP of Mississippi, 1998. 118–158.

Solomon, William. "Wound Culture and James Agee." *Arizona Quarterly* 58.4 (2002): 81–105.

Sontag, Susan. "Godard." *A Susan Sontag Reader*. New York: Vintage, 1982. 235.

———. *On Photography*. New York: Farrar, 1973.

Spencer, Thomas M. *The St. Louis Veiled Prophet Celebration: Power on Parade, 1877- 1995*. Columbia: U of Missouri P: 2000.

Spiegel, Alan. *James Agee and the Legend of Himself: A Critical Study*. Columbia: U of Missouri P, 1998.

Stein, Gertrude. *Everybody's Autobiography*. 1937. New York: Cooper Square, 1971.

Steinbeck, John. *The Grapes of Wrath*. 1939. New York: Penguain, 2002.

———. *The Harvest Gypsies*. 1936. Berkeley: Heyday Books, 1988.

Sterrit, David. *Mad to Be Saved: The Beats, the 50s, and Film*. Carbondale, IL: Southwestern UP, 1998.

Stott, William. *Documentary Expression and Thirties America*. New York: Oxford UP, 1973.

Szalay, Michael. *New Deal Modernism: American Literature and the Invention of the Welfare State*. Durham: Duke UP, 2000.

Tan, Amy. "In the Canon, for All the Wrong Reasons." *Harper's Magazine* December 1996: 27–31.

Tannen, Deborah. "Agonism in the Academy: Surviving Higher Learning's Argument Culture." *Chronicle of Higher Education* 31 March 2000: B7, B8.

Tagg, John. "Melancholy Realism: Walker Evans's Resistance to Meaning." *Narrative* 11.1 (2003): 3–77.

Thoreau, Henry David. *Walden*. 1854. New Haven: Yale UP, 2004.

Trachtenberg, Alan. Foreword. *You Have Seen Their Faces*. 1937. By Erskine Caldwell and Margaret Bourke-White. Athens: U of Georgia P, 1995. v–viii.

———. "Home Place." *Raritan* 26.1 (2006): 64–87.

———. *The Incorporation of America: Culture and Society in the Gilded Age.* New York: Hill and Wang, 1982.

Trilling, Lionel. *The Liberal Imagination: Essays on Literature and Society.* Garden City: Doubleday, 1950.

Tytell, John. *Naked Angels: The Lives and Literature of the Beat Generation.* New York: McGraw, 1976.

Vanderlan, Robert. *Intellectuals Incorporated: Politics, Art, and Ideas inside Henry Luce's Media Empire.* Philadelphia: U of Pennsylvania P, 2010.

Vollmann, William T. *Poor People.* New York: Harper, 2007.

Wakoski, Diane. "The Birth of the San Francisco Renaissance: Something Now Called the Whitman Tradition." *Literary Review* 32.1 (1988): 36–41.

Wald, Alan. *The New York Intellectuals: The Rise and Decline of the Anti-Stalinist Left from the 1930s to the 1980s.* Chapel Hill: U of North Carolina P, 1987.

Watson, Stephen. *The Birth of the Beat Generation: Visionaries, Rebels, and Hipsters, 1944–1960.* New York: Pantheon, 1995.

Weiland. Matt. Preface. *State by State: A Panoramic Portrait of America.* Ed. Matt Weiland and Sean Wilsey. New York: Harper, 2009. xi–xvii.

Weinreich, Regina. "The Beat Generation Is Now About Everything." *College Literature* 27.1 (2000): 263–268.

Wharton, Edith. *Ethan Frome.* 1911. New York: Scribner's, 1987.

Wheeler, Elizabeth. *Uncontained: Urban Fiction in Postwar America.* New Brunswick: Rutgers UP, 2001.

Whyte, William H., Jr. *The Organization Man.* Garden City: Anchor, 1956.

Williams, A. Noelle. "Parody and Pacifist Transformations in Maxine Hong Kingston's *Tripmaster Monkey: His Fake Book.*" *MELUS* 20.1 (1995): 83–100.

Williams, Raymond. *Keywords: A Vocabulary of Culture and Society.* 1976. New York: Oxford UP, 1983.

Wills, Garry. *Nixon Agonistes: The Crisis of the Self-Made Man.* New York: Signet, 1971.

Wilson, Edmund. *Boys in the Back Room: Notes on California Novelists.* San Francisco: Colt, 1941.

Wolfe, Tom. *The Electric Kool-Aid Acid Test.* 1968. New York: Bantam, 1999.

Wollenberg, Charles. Introduction. *The Harvest Gypsies.* By John Steinbeck. Berkeley: Heyday, 1988. v–xvii.

———. "John Steinbeck: On the Road to *The Grapes of Wrath.*" *The Human Tradition in California.* Ed. Clark Davis and David Igler. Wilmington: SR, 2002. 135–146.

Wrobel, David M. *The End of American Exceptionalism: Frontier Anxiety from the Old West to the New Deal.* Lawrence: UP of Kansas, 1993.

Wydeven, Joseph J. "Photography and Privacy: The Protests of Wright Morris and James Agee." *Midwest Quarterly: A Journal of Contemporary Thought* 23.1 (1981): 103–115.

Yeager, Patricia. "Introduction: Dreaming of Infrastructure." *PMLA* 122.1 (2007): 9–26.

Zagarell, Sandra A. "Crosscurrents: Registers of Nordicism, Community, and Culture in Jewett's *Country of the Pointed Firs*." *Yale Journal of Criticism* 10.2 (1997): 355–370.

Zinoman, Jason. "On the TV: Re-enacting Kerouac Interviews." *New York Times*. New York Times, 11 February 2006. Web. 7 December 2010.

INDEX

THE NEW AMERICAN CANON

Violet America:
Regional Cosmopolitanism in
U.S. Fiction since the Great Depression
by Jason Arthur

The Legacy of David Foster Wallace
edited by Samuel Cohen
and Lee Konstantinou